# SIXTH EDITION
# GRAMMAR 1
# IN CONTEXT

## TEACHER'S EDITION

## SANDRA N. ELBAUM

 NATIONAL GEOGRAPHIC LEARNING |  CENGAGE Learning·

Australia • Brazil • Mexico • Singapore • United Kingdom • United States

**Grammar in Context 1, Sixth Edition**

**Teacher's Edition**

**Sandra N. Elbaum**

Publisher: Sherrise Roehr

Executive Editor: Laura Le Dréan

Managing Editor: Jennifer Monaghan

Associate Development Editor:
  Jennifer Williams-Rapa

Executive Marketing Manager: Ben Rivera

Product Marketing Manager: Dalia Bravo

Senior Director, Production: Michael Burggren

Content Project Manager: Mark Rzeszutek

Manufacturing Planner: Mary Beth Hennebury

Interior Design: Brenda Carmichael

Compositor: SPi Global

Cover Design: Brenda Carmichael

ISBN 13: 978-1-305-07549-8

**National Geographic Learning**
20 Channel Center Street
Boston, Massachusetts 02210
USA

Cengage Learning is a leading provider of customized learning solutions with office locations around the globe, including Singapore, the United Kingdom, Australia, Mexico, Brazil, and Japan. Locate our local office at international.cengage.com/region

Cengage Learning products are represented in Canada by Nelson Education, Ltd.

Visit National Geographic Learning online at **ngl.cengage.com**
Visit our corporate website at **www.cengage.com**

Printed in the United States of America
Print Number: 01     Print Year: 2016

# CONTENTS

## *Grammar in Context 1, Sixth Edition*

# Welcome to *GRAMMAR IN CONTEXT,* Teacher's Edition!

*Grammar in Context, Sixth Edition,* contains a rich variety of material, making it easy to customize to any program's needs. This new *Teacher's Edition* will help you take full advantage of the National Geographic images and content in the *Student Book*. It includes extra resources to make planning your syllabus and preparing lessons easier than ever before. It also reinforces an active inductive approach to instruction that will encourage your students to discover answers and rules for themselves. Here's what the *Grammar in Context Teacher's Edition* offers you:

New suggestions for teaching a lesson (see page vi).

New Lesson Opener activities that include helpful background information for instructors on the opening thematic photos and quotations.

Ten easy solutions for customizing *Grammar in Context, Sixth Edition,* to meet your classroom needs (see page v).

Revised Presentation Ideas suggest alternative ways of presenting select grammar charts and checking students' understanding of the target grammar. They also provide suggestions for more detailed examination of select complex grammar points.

Updated Practice Ideas include ways to adapt grammar exercises to target specific skills: reading, writing, listening, and speaking.

Clearly identifiable "Fast Track" icons ⭐ highlight essential readings, charts, and exercises for courses that don't have the time to present and practice the full range of readings, grammar charts, and exercises available in *Grammar in Context, Sixth Edition.* Teaching these essential items gives students a basic understanding and practice of the most important grammar in each lesson.

Useful pacing guides for every activity provide a timing framework for lesson planning.

Supplemental activities provide students with additional practice, reinforcing their skills and building their confidence as language learners.

# Ten Tips for Customizing *GRAMMAR IN CONTEXT*, *Sixth Edition*, to fit your program

### 1. Work within your curriculum.

Let your curriculum guide you on what to cover from this rich, comprehensive series. For example, if your program doesn't expect students to learn about nonessential adjective clauses at this level, a teacher could skip the chart about nonessential adjective clauses. Also, it may be enough for your program to teach unreal conditions in the present without getting into unreal conditions in the past.

### 2. Do the Test/Review section at the start of each lesson.

One way to find out how much practice your students need is to give them the Test/Review section at the beginning of the lesson. If you find that most of your students can do this with relatively few errors, then you can skip the lesson altogether or focus only on the points that your students find difficult.

### 3. Assign the readings as homework.

All the readings are important in introducing the grammar in context and should not be skipped. To save class time, however, the readings can be done at home. The reading level is low enough that classroom instruction on how to read should not be necessary. The reading is not meant to challenge and improve students' reading skills; it is meant to illustrate the grammar in a stimulating context. Additionally, using the context notes, glossed words, and guided pre-reading activities in the *Teacher's Edition* can help ensure that students process the ideas and allow them to focus on relevant grammar functions.

### 4. Set time limits for each fill-in-the-blank exercise.

Set a maximum time limit for each exercise. Suggested times are given in this *Teacher's Edition*. Once the time limit has expired, ask students to put down their pens and move on to the next exercise. Students can complete the rest of the exercise at home.

### 5. Assign audio-based exercises for lab time.

Many exercises contain audio tracks (indicated with a listening icon 🎧). These exercises can take time to set up and run, so you may wish to assign these for lab credits or homework. You may also decide to do only one of these per class to add variety.

### 6. Use one of the "About You" exercises per class.

These exercises are fun to do; if you find your students' attention waning, you can insert one of these activities per lesson. If your students attend another class for speech and conversation, these exercises may be skipped.

### 7. Use Expansion Activities if there is time.

The Expansion Activities are fun, but time is limited. If you do have extra time, choose the activity that seems the most enjoyable. Students are likely to remember the lesson better if there is an element of fun.

### 8. Assign exercises for extra credit.

Students can go beyond the basic curriculum and do more of the exercises at home for extra credit.

### 9. Let students check answers at home.

Print the answer key for each lesson from the Cengage Learning website (NGL.Cengage.com/gic). You may wish to give the answer key to students at the start of each lesson so that they can check their answers at home. Set aside ten minutes every week to do a quick troubleshooting of particular grammar points.

### 10. Use this *Teacher's Edition*.

Each level of the student book has an accompanying *Teacher's Edition*, which offers comprehensive teaching suggestions on how to present and teach each grammar point.

# Suggestions for Teaching a Lesson of
## *GRAMMAR IN CONTEXT,* Sixth Edition

### 1. How to use the lesson opener photo and quote

Use the photo, caption, and quotation to interest students in the topic. Provide background information on the photo and person who is quoted. Have students look through the lesson to find out how the lesson opener photo and quote connect to photos and illustrations throughout. Have them identify reading topics and discuss what they know about them in pairs or small groups. Tell students the grammar functions they will practice in the lesson and elicit prior knowledge about them. Provide example sentences to model usage of the functions. Use Expansion Activities to stimulate interest, activate prior knowledge, and provide additional preparation.

### 2. How to approach the pre-reading activities

Use photos, captions, graphs, titles, and other special text features to guide students to predict main ideas in the reading. Set up a short discussion to activate students' knowledge of the reading topic. Have students discuss questions in pairs or small groups. Try to pair or group students of similar or different cultures together, depending on the questions. Ask for a few volunteers to share their answers with the class.

### 3. How to handle the reading

Have students first read the text silently. Tell them to pay special attention to the words and phrases in bold. Pre-teach essential terms students may not know. Play the audio and have students listen and read along silently. Encourage students to read for key ideas the first time and then to read or listen for details. In class, ask questions about the reading or the vocabulary to ensure that students read and understood the text. Ask *Additional Comprehension Questions* as follow up. Use *Context Notes* to clarify idiomatic language, provide bytes of culture background, and add interest. Before or after the reading, as appropriate, introduce materials for expansion, if desired.

### 4. How to teach the grammar charts

Use a variety of presentation approaches to hold students' interest. In addition to the suggestions included in this *Teacher's Edition*, you can use the Presentation Tool. When the material permits, guide students to discover rules and explanations for themselves. Clarify vocabulary students do not understand in the chart. Have students review examples, explanations, and Language, Pronunciation, and Punctuation Notes. Elicit example usages in complete sentences from students to check understanding, and provide models when needed. Use *Additional Practice* activities to concretize difficult target functions.

### 5. How to teach the exercises in general

Tell students what the exercise is about. Have students read the direction line. Direct students to the example. Elicit the grammar point being practiced. Complete the first item with the class. Have students complete the rest of the exercise individually. Remind them to review the grammar chart if necessary. Then have them check their answers in pairs or small groups, depending on the exercise. Monitor pair/group work. If necessary, check the answers as a class. Use *Additional Practice* ideas to help students further synthesize the material and practice language.

### 6. How to handle writing activities

Encourage students to prepare before writing. In opening lessons of your course, review brainstorming, mapping, and simple coherence and transition devices (e.g., *first, second, third, next, last*). Where appropriate, have students first discuss the topic with partners or a group. Periodically, model clear topic statements and conclusions. Collect assignments for assessment as desired.

# 1 STUDENT LIFE

## GRAMMAR CHARTS

## LESSON OPENER

Have students look at the photo and read the caption. Ask: *What is this place?* (a library) *Where is it?* (at the University of Chicago) *Who are the people in the photo, and what are they doing?* (students, studying) Have students read the quotation. Ask: *Do you agree with the quote? Why or why not?*

**Background:** To live and study in the United States at any age is a unique, fulfilling experience. Each year, thousands of international students come to study at American high schools and universities. According to the International Institute of Education, 886,052 international students enrolled in American schools in the 2013–2014 academic year. The United States has a long history of public and private education. Government-supported and free public school education was established after the American Revolution, and soon after states began to pass laws making schooling mandatory. By 1870 every state had free elementary schools. Now over 76.6 million students are enrolled in American schools from kindergarten through graduate school, but educational decisions and regulations are still controlled at the state and local level. Studying at community colleges and homeschooling are two educational systems uniquely popular in the United States. Community colleges are two-year public institutions of higher education that offer technical and high school degrees, among other

programs. Homeschooling has grown in popularity in the United States; today about 3.4 percent of Americans (around 2 million) are homeschooled. Some differences that stand out to international students about American universities are on-campus housing, college sports, and the hands-on experience in the classroom.

Nelson Mandela was a politician and philanthropist who was South Africa's first black chief executive as a party leader, and later president from 1994 to 1999. He was an influential figure involved in the fight against apartheid and racism in South Africa. He was awarded the Nobel Peace Prize in 1993 and left a legacy as an international hero after his death on December 5, 2013.

## CONTEXT

This unit is about student life in the United States. Students will read about Truman College, public school facts, and tests for college admission.

1. Give students a few minutes to look through the lesson. Have them look at the photos and titles. How do they relate to the context?
2. Elicit the topics that will be discussed.
3. Have students discuss what they know about student life in the United States in pairs or small groups.

## GRAMMAR

Students will learn about the present tense of the verb *be*, prepositions of place, and *this, that, these,* and *those*.

1. To activate students' prior knowledge, ask what students know about the present tense of the verb *be*.
2. Give several examples of prepositions of place and sentences using the verb *be* (e.g., *on, between, behind; The students are studying in the library.*).
3. Have volunteers identify verb tense in the example and give their own examples to write on the board.

## EXPANDING ON THE CONTEXT

The context for this lesson can be enhanced with the following items:

1. College catalogs and brochures
2. Your college yearbook or any college yearbook
3. Schedules for college activities and events, such as sports games and cultural fairs
4. College paraphernalia, such as apparel (sweaters, shirts) and accessories (pennants, key chains, foam fingers)

**READING**

# Truman College, page 4

## PRE-READING

Time: 5–10 min.

1. Have students look at the photo. Ask: *What is this building?*
2. Have students read the title and then skim the reading. Ask: *What is the reading about? How do you know?* Have students make predictions.
3. Pre-teach any vocabulary words your students may not know, such as *community*, *college credit*, and *nursing*.

## READING GLOSSARY

**community:** group of people who live in the same area
**college credit:** a unit that measures progress to earn a degree
**nursing:** job of taking care of people who are sick, injured, or old

## READING  CD 1 TR 2

Time: 10–15 min.
Go over the answers to the Comprehension Check on page 5: **1.** T; **2.** F; **3.** F.

## CONTEXT NOTE

As of 2014, there are 1,132 community colleges in the United States, and more than 7.7 million students are enrolled in degree programs at community colleges.

## ADDITIONAL COMPREHENSION QUESTIONS

*Where is Truman College located?* (Chicago, Illinois) *How many of the students at Truman College are Latino?* (about half) *Why is the college convenient?* (because it is near public transportation) *How much does it cost to take classes?* (Adult education classes are free)

## EXPANDING ON THE READING

The topic for this reading can be enhanced with the following items:

1. A map of U.S. community colleges by state
2. A map of Chicago, Illinois, and the area surrounding Truman College
3. The Chicago Transit Authority (CTA) public transit map
4. Class schedules at Truman College and other colleges in Chicago
5. Information and flyers for International Student Services at Truman College, such as the International Students Support Group

### PRACTICE IDEA: LISTENING

To provide listening practice, have students close their books and listen to the audio. Ask comprehension questions, such as: *Why do people like Truman College?* (Professors are friendly, classes are small, classes are interesting) *What is the oldest and most successful program at the college?* (nursing) Repeat the audio as needed.

### PRACTICE IDEA: SPEAKING

Have students work in small groups to look through the college catalogs and brochures you brought to class. Say: *Compare these programs with colleges and universities in your native countries. What's the same? What's different?* Have each group make two lists and share them with the whole class.

# 1.1 *Be*—Present Forms, page 5

🕐 Time: 10–15 min.

1. Have students close their books or cover grammar chart **1.1**. Write two columns on the board: *1) am, is, are; 2)* several subjects from the readings on the board in no particular order (e.g., *Truman College, Truman students, I, it, they, classes, professors, tuition*). Have students work in pairs to match the correct form of the verb *be* with each subject. Write students' ideas on the board.

2. Have students uncover and look at grammar chart **1.1** and check their answers. Have volunteers read aloud the example sentences in the chart.

3. Direct students' attention to the Language Notes. Point out that the subject will be a noun or a pronoun, and remind them that subjects begin sentences. Go over the examples. Have students provide additional examples.

## EXERCISE 1  pages 5–6
🕐 Time: 10–15 min.

**Answers: 1.** is; **2.** am; **3.** am; **4.** is; **5.** are; **6.** is; **7.** am; **8.** is; **9.** is; **10.** are; **11.** are; **12.** is; **13.** are; **14.** are; **15.** are; **16.** are; **17.** am; **18.** am; **19.** am; **20.** am; **21.** is

> ### PRACTICE IDEA: WRITING
>
> Write five mixed-up sentences from the reading on the board. Tell students they have 2 minutes to put the words in the correct order. Have them compare their answers in pairs, then elicit the rule for sentence order.

# 1.2 *Be*—Uses, page 6

🕐 Time: 10–15 min.

1. Write on the board:
   a. *description* of subject
   b. classification or *definition* of subject
   c. *location* of the subject
   d. *age* of the subject
   e. *weather*
   f. *time*

   Clarify the meaning of the words in the list on the board (e.g., *a description gives more information and details about something; a definition gives the meaning of a word; a location gives the place of something*).

2. Have students cover grammar chart **1.2**. Ask students to find example sentences from the readings for the six explanations in the list. Then have volunteers write sentences from the chart on the board.

3. Have students uncover and look at grammar chart **1.2** and compare their sentences with the example sentences in the chart. Review the example sentences in the grammar chart, including the examples for age, weather, and time.

4. Go around the room and ask students about their age, the weather, and the time.

## EXERCISE 2  page 6
🕐 Time: 5–10 min.

**Answers: 1.** is; **2.** am; **3.** is; **4.** are; **5.** is; **6.** are; **7.** are; **8.** are; **9.** is; **10.** is; **11.** is

## EXERCISE 3  page 7
🕐 Time: 5–10 min.

**Answers: 1.** d; **2.** a; **3.** j; **4.** c; **5.** b; **6.** e; **7.** i; **8.** h; **9.** g; **10.** f
**1.** Trains and buses are forms of transportation.; **2.** It is hot in Guatemala in the summer.; **3.** The University of Illinois is a state university.; **4.** Some adult education classes are free.; **5.** Truman College students are from many different countries.; **6.** Tuition is the cost of college courses.; **7.** I am an ESL student.; **8.** Truman College is a community college.; **9.** Rolando and Susana Lopez are from Guatemala.; **10.** Spanish is the language of Mexico.

> ### PRACTICE IDEA: WRITING
>
> 1. In pairs, have students change the word order of the subject and object and make new sentences based on the sentences in Exercise 3. Write on the board:
>    *Singular subject: An example of…*
>    *Plural subject: Examples of…*
> 2. Model numbers 1 and 2 on the board:
>    *1. Examples of forms of transportation are trains and buses.*
>    *2. An example of a state university is the University of Illinois.*
> 3. Monitor pair work. Give help as needed.

## EXERCISE 4 pages 7–8

⏱ Time: 5–10 min.

**Answers will vary.**

---

**PRACTICE IDEA: WRITING**

Have students write an e-mail to a friend about their English class. Tell them to use the relevant sentences in Exercise 4 as a guide. Say: *Make the information in the sentences true for you.* With students' help, write the start of an e-mail on the board as an example. When students are finished, have them exchange e-mails with a partner and read each other's. Encourage them to help each other with any corrections.

---

## 1.3 Subject Pronouns and Nouns, page 8

⏱ Time: 10–15 min.

1. Ask students to underline every subject in the first two paragraphs in the reading on page 4. Instruct students to work in pairs to categorize these subjects into two groups: nouns and pronouns. Have them make lists of the two groups on a sheet of paper and check their answers with another pair of students. Review lists as a class.

2. Now have students return to the reading on page 4 and circle all the subjects that are plural. Elicit the plural subjects from students and write them on the board.

3. Have students look at grammar chart **1.3**. Review the example sentences and explanations, directing students' attention to the subject pronouns and plural subjects.

4. Explain that *you* is both singular and plural. Provide additional examples. Say: *You are all my students.* Indicate this with a sweeping gesture that includes the whole class. Then point to one student in particular and say: *[Student name], you are my student.*

5. Direct students' attention to the Language Note and discuss the difference between informal conversational English and formal written English. Provide additional examples as necessary.

---

## EXERCISE 5 pages 8–9

⏱ Time: 5–10 min.

**Answers: 1.** They; **2.** We; **3.** It; **4.** It; **5.** They; **6.** I; **7.** It; **8.** They; **9.** It; **10.** You; **11.** She; **12.** We

## EXERCISE 6 page 9

⏱ Time: 5–10 min.

**Answers: 1.** My college is a 2-year college.; **2.** I am a student.; **3.** My parents are in Guatemala.; **4.** Tuition at a 4-year college is high.; **5.** My college is convenient for me.; **6.** My teacher is 40 years old.; **7.** My teacher is from New York.; **8.** The summer semester is 8 weeks long.; **9.** Rolando is married.; **10.** It is cold in the winter.

---

**PRACTICE IDEA: WRITING**

Divide the class into two teams. Give each team ten mixed-up sentences (with subject + *be* + complement) on small pieces of paper. Say: *You must put the words in the correct order and write the sentences on the board. The first team to finish is the winner.*

---

## 1.4 Contractions with *Be*, page 10

⏱ Time: 10–15 min.

1. Have students cover grammar chart **1.4**. Write on the board:
   a. *I am in Minneapolis.* =
   b. *You are a student.* =
   c. *She is a young teacher.* =
   d. *We are busy.* =
   e. *Rolando is from Guatemala.* =
   f. *Here is a class schedule.* =
   g. *My class is big.* =
   h. *Textbooks are expensive.* =

   Ask: *What are the subjects of these sentences?* Underline the subjects as students say them. Ask: *Which subjects are nouns, and which subjects are pronouns?* Put an asterisk next to the subject pronouns. Ask: *Which subjects are plural?* Circle the plural subjects as students say them (*we, textbooks*).

2. Have students work in pairs to make a contraction with the subject and verb of each example sentence. Have volunteers explain each contraction. Ask: *How did you make the contraction she's?* (*she is* = take out the first letter of *is* and add an apostrophe)

3. Have students uncover and look at grammar chart **1.4** and check their answers. Have students read aloud the additional example sentences in the grammar chart. Review the explanations for each example.

4. Demonstrate what American speech would sound like if there were no contractions. To illustrate, enunciate each word and exaggerate the difference. Have students practice with example sentences on board.

### EXERCISE 7 page 10

🕐 Time: 10–15 min.

**Answers: 1.** 'm; **2.** 's; **3.** 'm; **4.** 's; **5.** 's; **6.** 's; **7.** 's; **8.** 's; **9.** 's; **10.** 'm; **11.** 's; **12.** 're; **13.** 's; **14.** 're

---

**PRACTICE IDEA: SPEAKING**

Have students read the conversation aloud in pairs. Have them share how they would feel if they were in a similar situation as Speaker A.

---

### EXERCISE 8 page 11

🕐 Time: 5–10 min.

**Answers: 1.** 's; **2.** 're; **3.** 's; **4.** is; **5.** 'm; **6.** 's; **7.** 's; **8.** is; **9.** is; **10.** 's; **11.** is

---

**PRACTICE IDEA: SPEAKING**

In groups, have students take turns reading parts of the paragraph aloud—first without contractions, then with contractions. Circulate to observe group work. Give help as needed.

---

### EXERCISE 9 page 11

🕐 Time: 10–15 min.

**Answers: 1.** 'm; **2.** 'm; **3.** 's; **4.** 's; **5.** is; **6.** 's; **7.** is; **8.** are; **9.** 're; **10.** are; **11.** 's; **12.** 's; **13.** are; **14.** 're; **15.** is

---

**PRACTICE IDEA: LISTENING**

To provide practice with listening skills, have students close their books and listen to the audio. Repeat the audio as needed. Ask comprehension questions such as: *What is the student's teacher's name?* (Charles Madison) *How many students come from Asia?* (five) Then have students open their books and complete Exercise 9.

---

**PRACTICE IDEA: WRITING**

Have students write a paragraph about their English class. Tell students to use Exercise 9 as a model. Instruct students not to use contractions. Then have students exchange paragraphs with a partner. The partner should correct the paragraph, inserting contractions where they should be used.

---

## 1.5 *Be* with Descriptions, page 12

🕐 Time: 10–15 min.

1. Have students cover grammar chart **1.5**. Ask volunteers to describe the school, the classroom they're in, and their classmates. As they talk, write adjectives they use on the board. If they need help, prompt: *Is the classroom big or small? Is the school expensive? Are your classmates married?* Ask students if they know what the words you've written on the board are called. (adjectives) Remind students that in English, adjectives are not plural.

2. Have students uncover and look at grammar chart **1.5**. Review the example sentences and explanations in the grammar chart. Explain that the word *very* strengthens the meaning of the adjectives and shows emphasis. Say the example sentences with and without *very*, exaggerating the stress on *very* to demonstrate difference in meaning.

3. Direct students' attention to the Language Note. Point out that adjectives can have many different kinds of endings.

---

**PRACTICE IDEA: WRITING**

Have students work in pairs to brainstorm as many different adjectives as they know. Tell them to circle the adjectives that are physical or mental conditions. Have them write a sentence about themselves or somebody they know for each of the adjectives they circled.

---

## EXERCISE 10 page 12

⏱ Time: 5–10 min.

**Answers will vary.**

## EXERCISE 11 pages 12–13

⏱ Time: 5–10 min.

**Answers will vary.**

---

**PRACTICE IDEA: WRITING**

Have students get in pairs. Have one student make a list of adjectives, and have the other student make a list of subjects. Then, have students get together and match the subjects with the adjectives. Tell students to write five sentences based on their matches.

---

**PRACTICE IDEA: SPEAKING**

In pairs, have students compare classrooms and schools in the United States with classrooms and schools in another country. Have them use the sentences in Exercise 11 as models.

---

# 1.6 *Be* with Definitions and Classifications, page 13

⏱ Time: 10–15 min.

1. Have students cover grammar chart **1.6**. Point to yourself and say: *I am* … Elicit the answer from the students, (a teacher) Now say: *You all are* …. Elicit the response from the students. (students) Write both sentences on the board, pointing out the different between the singular and plural subjects. Again, point to yourself and say: *I am an American*. Point to another student (preferably one from another country) and say: *You are*….

2. Have students uncover and look at grammar chart **1.6**. Review the example sentences in the chart.

3. Direct students' attention to the Language Notes. Remind students to use *an* before a vowel sound. Also, tell students that saying *an* is like saying *one,* so plural nouns do not use *a/an*.

## EXERCISE 12 page 13

⏱ Time: 5–10 min.

**Answers: 1.** are; **2.** is a; **3.** is an; **4.** is an; **5.** are; **6.** are a; **7.** am an; **8.** are; **9.** is a

## EXERCISE 13 page 14

⏱ Time: 5–10 min.

**Answers will vary.**

---

**PRACTICE IDEA: SPEAKING**

Have students stand in two concentric circles, with half the students standing in an outer ring around the classroom and the other half standing in an inner ring, facing each other. Every minute or so, say *turn* and call out a new subject for students to define or classify in pairs. Students in the inner ring should move one space clockwise. The pairs should come up with at least one or two definitions or classifications each turn. For example: Teacher: *English!* Students: *English is a language. English is an interesting subject to study.* Teacher: *Fast food!* Students: *Fast food is a cheap food. Having fast food is an unhealthy way to eat.* Make sure students look at each other when they're speaking.

---

# 1.7 Negative Statements with *Be,* page 14

⏱ Time: 10–15 min.

1. Have students cover grammar chart **1.7**. If appropriate, ask a few students: *Are you married?* If the students say yes, write on the board: *(student's name) is married*. If the student says no, write on the board: *(student's name) is not married*.

2. Write on the board:

   *married*

   *American*

   *hungry*

   *busy*

   Have students point to themselves and make a negative statement with the subject pronoun *I* and the adjectives on the board. Have them point directly to another classmate and make a negative statement with the subject pronoun *you* and the adjectives on the board. Repeat for other subject pronouns. Model sentences if necessary (e.g., *I am American. I am not hungry. He is busy*.). Elicit additional adjectives from students. Add them to the list on the board and repeat activity.

3. Have students uncover and look at grammar chart **1.7**. Carefully review the example sentences and additional contractions in the chart. Explain to students that

there are two ways to make contractions. Review how to make both contractions with the students. *You're not*—remove the first letter in the verb *be* and replace with an apostrophe. *You aren't*—remove the *o* from *not* and replace with an apostrophe. Say: *You can use both contractions. Both are common.*

4. Direct students' attention to the Language Notes. Point out that there is only one way to contract *I am not*—*I'm not*. Emphasize that we can make contractions with most nouns, but there are certain words we cannot. Review example and provide additional examples.

### EXERCISE 14 page 15

🕑 Time: 5–10 min.

**Answers: 1.** It isn't dirty. It's not small.; **2.** We aren't in the library. We're not in the cafeteria.; **3.** It isn't Saturday. It's not Sunday.; **4.** I'm not a teacher.; **5.** They aren't lazy. They're not tired.; **6.** You aren't early. You're not late.; **7.** We aren't in the cafeteria. We're not in the library.

### EXERCISE 15 pages 15-16

🕑 Time: 5–10 min.

**Answers will vary.**

---

**PRACTICE IDEA: SPEAKING AND WRITING**

In pairs, have students create surveys to collect information about the students in the class. Each pair should write five questions (e.g., *Where are you from? What is your first language? Are you married? What is your favorite food?*). Have students mingle and ask each other the questions. Then have students write a short paragraph about what they learned. Have volunteers report their results to the class.

---

`READING`
# Public School FAQs, page 17

## PRE-READING

🕑 Time: 5–10 min.

1. Have students look at the photo. Ask: *Who are the people in the photo?* (students) *What are they doing?* (studying)

2. Have students read the title and then skim the reading. Ask: *What is the reading about? How do you know?* Have students make predictions.

3. Pre-teach any vocabulary words your students may not know, such as *frequently, public,* and *rules.*

## READING GLOSSARY
**frequently:** happening often
**public:** paid for by government
**rules:** what is and is not allowed

## READING  CD 1 TR 4
🕑 Time: 10–15 min.

Go over the answers to the Comprehension Check on page 18: **1.** F; **2.** F; **3.** T.

## CONTEXT NOTE
Education is free in the United States from kindergarten through high school. Some school districts also offer free preschool for 3- and 4-year-olds, but that isn't very common. College and university programs can be very expensive. State-run universities charge lower fees to state residents, but even state institutions can be expensive. Expensive private colleges can cost as much as $50,000 a year.

## ADDITIONAL COMPREHENSION QUESTIONS

*Is education in the United States free?* (It is free in public schools) *What percent of children are in public schools?* (88 percent) *How many months a year are children in school?* (10 months) *How do you define a* freshman, sophomore, junior, *and* senior? (first, second, third, and fourth year of high school or college) *How many years are students in school?* (12 years)

---

**EXPANDING ON THE READING**
The topic for this reading can be enhanced with the following items:

1. Visual aids (infographics, charts, or graphs) showing information about location, student population, graduation rates, and cost of public versus private high schools
2. Rankings of the best public schools in the United States
3. Academic calendars showing holidays and breaks from public schools
4. Example class schedules from public elementary and high schools
5. Public high school yearbooks

---

## 1.8 *Yes/No* Questions and Short Answers with *Be*,
### page 18

🕐 Time: 10–15 min.

1. Have students cover grammar chart **1.8**. Ask students to find *Yes/No* questions in the reading on page 17. Write examples on the board. (*Is education in the United States free?*)

2. Have students uncover and look at grammar chart **1.8**. Review the example sentences in the grammar chart.

3. Explain to students that in a question you put the verb—*am, is, are*—before the subject.

4. Point out that *Yes/No* questions are usually answered with a short answer, such as *Yes, it is.* Or *No, it isn't.* Affirmative short answers are not contracted. (*Yes, it is.*) Negative short answers are usually contracted. (*No, it isn't; No it's not.*)

5. Direct students' attention to the Pronunciation Note. Demonstrate the rising intonation of *Yes/No* questions. Lead students in a choral practice of the intonation. Write one or two questions on the board with arrows to show the rising intonation.

### EXERCISE 16  pages 18-19
🕐 Time: 10–15 min.

**Answers: 1.** 's; **2.** 'm; **3.** 's; **4.** Are you; **5.** I'm not; **6.** Are you; **7.** I am; **8.** Are we; **9.** we are; **10.** Is; **11.** she isn't/she's not; **12.** Is it; **13.** is; **14.** It's

### EXERCISE 17  page 19
🕐 Time: 5–10 min.
**Answers will vary.**

## 1.9 *Wh-* Questions with *Be*,
### page 19

🕐 Time: 10–15 min.

1. Have students cover grammar chart **1.9**. Activate students' prior knowledge. Say: *What are* Wh- *words?* Write students' ideas on the board. Then ask students to find *Wh-* questions in the reading on page 17. Write examples on the board (e.g., *How many months a year are students in school? What's a freshman?*).

2. Have students uncover and look at grammar chart **1.9**. Review the examples of statements and questions in the chart. Explain that *Wh-* questions ask for information. In contrast, *Yes/No* questions ask only for a *yes* or *no* response.

3. Direct students' attention to the Language Notes. Write the contractions for *Wh-* words and *is* on the board. Explain that there is no contraction for *which is* and that there is no written contraction for *Wh-* words and *are*, but that it's acceptable in informal speech. Then ask students to find contractions with *Wh-* words in the reading on page 17. Write the examples on the board. Review the rules about the word *how*, providing additional examples if necessary.

### ADDITIONAL PRACTICE

1. Model the pronunciation of *Wh-* questions in the chart. Be sure to exaggerate a falling intonation. Lead the class in a choral practice of the *Wh-* question intonation. Write one or two questions on the board with arrows to show the falling intonation. Have students practice with the *Wh-* questions in grammar chart **1.9**.

## PRACTICE IDEA: SPEAKING

Have students take turns asking and answering the *Wh-* questions in the reading on page 17 in pairs (e.g., Student A: *How many months a year are students in school?* Student B: *They're in school for 10 months a year.*). Encourage students not to look at the reading when answering the questions.

## PRACTICE IDEA: WRITING AND SPEAKING

Write on the board:

  Student A: *When are you very _____?*
  Student B: *I am very _____ when…*

Have students write ten questions with the verb *be* and physical or mental conditions. They can use the adjectives in grammar chart **1.5** and think of three more on their own. Then, have students do a mingle activity and ask their classmates the questions. Have them follow the dialog example on the board.

### EXERCISE 18  page 20
⏱ Time: 5–10 min.

**Answers: 1.** What's; **2.** Who's; **3.** When's; **4.** What; **5.** Where are; **6.** Where's; **7.** What's; **8.** Why isn't he; **9.** is his daughter/is she

### EXERCISE 19  page 21
⏱ Time: 10–15 min.

**Answers: 1.** are you; **2.** Are you; **3.** I am; **4.** What time is it; **5.** aren't you; **6.** How's; **7.** Is it; **8.** it is; **9.** They're; **10.** How old is he; **11.** Where's he; **12.** Where are Mom and Dad; **13.** They're; **14.** are they; **15.** It's; **16.** What's; **17.** I'm

## PRACTICE IDEA: WRITING

Have students work individually to write an example phone conversation they would have with a friend or family member back home using Exercise 19 as a model. Monitor student work and answer questions as necessary. Have volunteers share their conversations.

### EXERCISE 20  page 22
⏱ Time: 5–10 min.
**Answers: 1.** Bosnia, Where are you from?; **2.** *Answers will vary.,* What's your name?; **3.** *Answers will vary.,* Where are you from?; **4.** *Answers will vary.,* Who's the

president/prime minister of your country?; **5.** *Answers will vary.,* What color is the flag from your country?; **6.** *Answers will vary.,* Where's your country?; **7.** *Answers will vary.,* How tall are you?; **8.** *Answers will vary.,* When's your birthday?; **9.** *Answers will vary.,* What's your favorite subject (in school)?; **10.** *Answers will vary.,* What time is it in your hometown?

## PRACTICE IDEA: SPEAKING

Have students practice asking and answering the questions from Exercise 20 with a partner. Say: *Answer the questions with your own information.*

### EXERCISE 21  page 23
⏱ Time: 5–10 min.
**Answers: 1.** are you; **2.** Is today; **3.** is; **4.** aren't you; **5.** long is; **6.** 's your English class; **7.** are they; **8.** Is; **9.** is; **10.** What time is it; **11.** Are you; **12.** are you

## PRACTICE IDEA: SPEAKING

Have students stand in two concentric circles, with half the students standing in an outer ring around the classroom and the other half standing in an inner ring, facing each other. Instruct students to ask and answer the questions from Exercise 20 and/or Exercise 21. Call out *turn* every minute or so. Students in the inner ring should move one space clockwise. Students now ask and answer *Wh-* questions with their new partners. Make sure students look at each other when they're speaking.

## 1.10 Prepositions of Place,
 pages 24–25
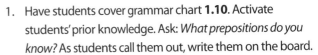

⏱ Time: 10–15 min.

1. Have students cover grammar chart **1.10**. Activate students' prior knowledge. Ask: *What prepositions do you know?* As students call them out, write them on the board.

2. Then ask students to demonstrate the prepositions. First model an example. (Point to the book on the desk.) Say: *on; My book is on the desk.*

3. Have students uncover and look at grammar chart **1.10**. Review the examples in the grammar chart. Point out the illustrations that show the meanings of the prepositions. As you go down the chart, demonstrate the prepositions yourself or have volunteers demonstrate them.

4. Direct students' attention to the Language Notes. Review the difference between *at* and *in*, and point out the alternative word order for prepositions.

**EXERCISE 22**  page 25

🕐 Time: 5–10 min.

**Answers will vary.**

---

**PRACTICE IDEA: SPEAKING**

In pairs, have students point to different objects around the classroom and describe their location and origin using prepositions. Have volunteers share their answers in front of the class.

---

**PRACTICE IDEA: WRITING AND READING**

1. Have students work in pairs. At the front of the room, create an interesting still life with fruit and other objects. Say: *Write one paragraph to describe this still life using prepositions.* Circulate and observe groups work. Have a volunteer from each group read the description. Then have pairs compare paragraphs.

2. Divide students into groups. Line up a number of interesting objects on a table in the front. Ask the groups to design a still life using prepositions. Say: *Don't draw a picture. Just describe it using prepositions.* Have groups exchange descriptions and take turns trying to build the other groups' still life. The group that builds the most accurate still life wins.

---

`READING`

# Test for College Admission, page 26

## PRE-READING

🕐 Time: 5–10 min.

1. Have students look at the photo. Ask: *Who are the people in the photo?* (students) *What are they doing?* (taking a test)

2. Have students read the title and then skim the reading. Ask: *What is the reading about? How do you know?* Have students make predictions.

3. Pre-teach any vocabulary words your students may not know, such as *application, practice, multiple-choice,* and *subject.*

---

## READING GLOSSARY

**application:** formal written request for admission
**practice:** to do something again and again to get better
**multiple-choice:** several answers from which one is chosen
**subject:** area of knowledge studied in school

## READING

🕐 Time: 10–15 min.

Go over the answers to the Comprehension Check on page 27: **1.** T; **2.** F; **3.** F.

## ADDITIONAL COMPREHENSION QUESTIONS

*What is the SAT?* (a test for college admission) *How many times a year is the test?* (a few times a year) *What kinds of questions are there?* (multiple-choice and essay) *What subjects are on the test?* (reading, math, and writing)

---

**EXPANDING ON THE READING**

The topic for this reading can be enhanced with the following items:

1. SAT fact sheets
2. SAT preparation tip videos
3. Sample SAT questions and answers

---

**PRACTICE IDEA: LISTENING**

To provide listening practice, have students close their books and listen to the audio. Have them count how many times they hear the words *this, that, these* or *those* (eleven). Repeat the audio as needed.

---

## 1.11 *This, That, These, Those,*
page 27
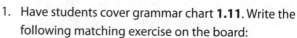

🕐 Time: 10–15 min.

1. Have students cover grammar chart **1.11**. Write the following matching exercise on the board:

   A. *this/that*
   B. *these/those*
   1. *professor*
   2. *dates*
   3. *prices*
   4. *application*

Say: *Match each noun with either* A *or* B. Have students complete the exercise in pairs. (**Answers: 1.** A; **2.** B; **3.** B; **4.** A)

2. Have students uncover and look at grammar chart **1.11** and check their answers. Review the explanations and additional examples. Demonstrate the adjectives again—exaggerating distances. Point out that once you identify a noun, you can use a pronoun in the second sentence.

3. Direct students to the Language Notes. Explain that *that is* can be contracted to *that's*. Point out the difference between *that* and *those* questions and answers.

**EXERCISE 23** page 27
🕐 Time: 10–15 min.
**Answers: 1.** this; **2.** It's; **3.** those; **4.** They're; **5.** This; **6.** Those; **7.** They're; **8.** are; **9.** That's; **10.** that; **11.** Is it; **12.** That's; **13.** It's; **14.** they're; **15.** it's; **16.** This is

---

**PRACTICE IDEA: SPEAKING**

In pairs, have students take turns asking and answering questions about objects in the room using *this/that* and *these/those* (e.g. Student A: *What is that?* Student B: *That is the clock.*). Be sure students are exaggerating the distance of the objects as they point.

---

## SUMMARY OF LESSON 1

🕐 Time: 20–30 min.

## PART A  FORMS OF *BE: AM, IS, ARE*
Have students write two additional sentences for each of the statements and questions in the chart. If necessary, have students review:

**1.1**  *Be*—Present Forms (page 5)

## PART B  USES OF *BE*
In pairs, have students go to the reading on page 4 and find a sentence for each use of *be*. If necessary, have students review:

**1.2**  *Be*—Uses (page 6)
**1.5**  *Be* with Descriptions (page 12)
**1.6**  *Be* with Definitions and Classifications (page 13)

## PART C  SUBJECT PRONOUNS
Have students close their books. Instruct students to write a sentence for each subject pronoun. If necessary, have students review:

**1.3**  Subject Pronouns and Nouns (page 8)

## PART D  CONTRACTIONS WITH *BE*
Have students write eight negative sentences with the verb *be* with different pronouns using both forms of negative contractions. Then, have students write one question for each *Wh-* question word. If necessary, have students review:

**1.4**  Contractions with *Be* (page 10)
**1.7**  Negative Statements with *Be* (page 14)
**1.8**  *Yes/No* Questions and Short Answers with *Be* (page 18)
**1.9**  *Wh-* Questions with *Be* (page 19)

## PART E  ARTICLES *A/AN*
Play a chain game. Have students sit in a circle. The first person says his or her name and some other information (e.g., *I'm John. I'm a mechanic.*). The second person repeats the first person's information and adds his or her own (e.g., *He's John. He's a mechanic. I'm Marta; I'm a…*). If necessary, have students review:

**1.6**  *Be* with Definitions and Classifications (page 13)

## PART F  *THIS/THAT/THESE/THOSE*
Have students practice *this, that, these,* and *those* in pairs. Say: *Your partner is a new student in this classroom. Show him or her around the classroom.* If necessary, have students review:

**1.10**  Prepositions of Place (pages 24–25)
**1.11**  *This, That, These, Those* (page 27)

## TEST/REVIEW

🕐 Time: 15 min.
Have students do the exercise on page 29. For additional practice, use the Assessment CD-ROM with Exam*View*® and the Online Workbook.
**Answers: 1.** It's; **2.** I'm; **3.** are you; **4.** is/'s; **5.** Is she; **6.** she is; **7.** from; **8.** She's/She is; **9.** Who's your teacher; **10.** a very good teacher; **11.** I'm not; **12.** aren't you; **13.** on; **14.** next to; **15.** How big is your class; **16.** That's; **17.** class isn't; **18.** in; **19.** are; **20.** are the; students from; **21.** That's; **22.** 're/are; **23.** Is Mr. Sanchez American; **24.** he's not/he isn't; **25.** English isn't; **26.** that's not/that isn't; **27.** is; **28.** Ms. Lee is; **29.** old is Mr. Sanchez; **30.** He's a young man

# WRITING

## PART 1  EDITING ADVICE

🕐 Time: 10–15 min.

1. Have students close their books. Write the first few sentences without editing marks or corrections on the board. For example:
   *My father he lives in Australia.*
   *Is small Cuba.*

2. Ask students to correct each sentence and provide a rule or an explanation for each correction. This activity can be done individually, in pairs, or as a class.

3. After students have corrected each sentence, tell them to turn to page 30. Say: *Now compare your work with the Editing Advice in the book.* Have students read through all the advice.

## PART 2  EDITING PRACTICE

🕐 Time: 10–15 min.

1. Tell students they are going to put the Editing Advice into practice. Ask: *Do all the shaded words and phrases have mistakes?* (no) Go over the examples with the class. Then do #1 together.

2. Have students complete the practice individually. Then have them compare answers with a partner before checking answers as a class.

3. For the items students had difficulties with, have them go back and find the relevant grammar chart and review it. Monitor and give help as necessary.

**Answers: 1.** C; **2.** I'm; **3.** C; **4.** C; **5.** are you; **6.** I'm; **7.** is Rwanda; **8.** It's; **9.** a very small country; **10.** Is Latvia a city or a country; **11.** C; **12.** It's in/It is in; **13.** C; **14.** French is; **15.** What's; **16.** Russian is; **17.** Are you; **18.** I am; **19.** isn't; **20.** C; **21.** C; **22.** I'm not; **23.** C; **24.** How old is your sister; **25.** C; **26.** Is your sister in high school; **27.** C; **28.** These are; **29.** twins; **30.** Jimmy is; **31.** Lance is; **32.** teacher is; **33.** It's

## PART 3  WRITE ABOUT IT

◑ Time: 20–30 min..

Review the example with the students. Have them rewrite the paragraph with affirmative and negative statements. Encourage students to add more information.

## PART 4  EDIT YOUR WRITING

🕐 Time: 10–15 min.

Have students edit their writing by reviewing the Lesson Summary on page 28 and the Editing Advice on page 30. Collect for assessment and/or have students share their paragraphs in small groups.

## EXPANSION ACTIVITIES

1. Have students complete descriptions of themselves individually. Then collect them and read them aloud and have students guess who is being described.

2. Instruct students to choose a famous person that the class would know. Have students complete the descriptions with a partner. Monitor pair work. Give help as needed. Have pairs read their descriptions to the class for other students to guess who the famous person is.

3. Ask: *How much do you know about your native country?* Have students work in pairs. If possible, put students from the same country together. Have pairs complete the chart with information about their country. Have volunteers report interesting information to the class (e.g., *Disneyland is a popular tourist attraction in the United States.*).

4. Have students interview a native speaker of English (a neighbor, a co-worker, another student, or a teacher at this college). Write the following questions on the board for students to copy:
   a. *What city are you from?*
   b. *Are your parents or grandparents from another country? Where are they from?*
   c. *Is most of your family in this city?*
   d. *Are you happy with this city? Why or why not?*
   e. *What are your favorite places in this city?*

   Tell students to ask these questions and then report back to the class.

5. Tell students to use the Internet to find the Web site of a college they are interested in. Ask them to identify what information is on the home page. What links are on the home page?

# 2 PLACES TO VISIT

## GRAMMAR CHARTS

## LESSON OPENER

Have students look at the photo and read the caption. Ask: *What is this place?* (the Grand Canyon) *Where is it?* (Arizona) Have students read the quotation. Ask: *Do you agree with the quote? Why or why not?*

**Background:** With millions of international and domestic tourists every year, the United States receives more visitors than any other country in the world. In all major American cities, tourism is a booming industry. With Hollywood, Times Square, Broadway, and the nation's capital, respectively, the cities of Los Angeles, New York City, and Washington, DC, have the most visited tourist attractions in the United States. It is estimated that Times Square in Manhattan, New York, attracts around 35 million visitors every year. According to the Institute for Museum and Library Services, the United States also has over 35,000 museums and galleries, the majority focused on history and art. But perhaps one of the most valuable recreation and vacation tourist attractions in the country is the National Park System, a collection of parks, monuments, recreation areas, trails, and other protected scenic areas. The system, created in 1916 by the U.S. Congress, is home to such treasures as the Grand Canyon and Yosemite National Park. Many parks charge low entrance fees, allowing American and international visitors to learn more about the United States by engaging in activities such as camping, hiking, hunting, fishing, and long-distance scenic drives. Other popular places in the United States to visit include amusement parks, such as Disneyland and Walt Disney World; festivals; and many famous hotels.

Lao Tzu was a philosopher and poet of ancient China in the sixth century B.C. He is known as the father of Taoism, a system of beliefs, attitudes, and practices that advocates simplicity, honesty, and living in harmony with nature rather than a strict, regulated life and society. Because of this, his teachings are often associated with anti-authoritarian movements.

## CONTEXT

This unit is about places to visit in the United States. Students will read about Washington, DC, the Great Smoky Mountain National Park, and Times Square.

1.  Give students a few minutes to look through the lesson. Have them look at the photos and titles. How do they relate to the context?

2.  Elicit the topics that will be discussed.

3.  Have students discuss what they know about places to visit in the United States in pairs or small groups.

## GRAMMAR

Students will learn about the simple present verb tense.

1.  To activate students' prior knowledge, ask what students know about the simple present verb tense.

2.  Give several examples of the simple present verb tense (e.g., *The president lives in the White House. The class studies English every day.*).

3.  Have volunteers give examples and write them on the board.

## EXPANDING ON THE CONTEXT

The context for this lesson can be enhanced with the following items:

1. Tourist paraphernalia including postcards, key chains, T-shirts, and pennants from different states and attractions
2. National Park Service digital image archives and historic photograph collections
3. Local maps and tourist guides

## READING

# Washington, DC, page 34

## PRE-READING

🕐 Time: 5–10 min.

1. Have students look at the photo. Ask: *What is this building?* (the Washington Monument) *Where is it located?* (in Washington, DC)
2. Have students read the title and then skim the reading. Ask: *What is the reading about? How do you know?* Have students make predictions.
3. Pre-teach any vocabulary words your students may not know, such as *capital, district, factory, subway,* and *law.*
4. Ask: *What is the capital city of your country? Have you been there? Has anyone visited the Capitol in the United States?* Have volunteers share their knowledge and personal experiences.

## READING GLOSSARY

**capital:** the official city where a state, provincial, or national government is located
**district:** an area officially marked for a purpose
**factory:** a building or group of buildings where goods are produced
**law:** a rule made by a government body that must be followed by the people in a nation, state, etc.
**subway:** a public transportation system with trains that run underground

## READING 🎧 CD 1 TR 6 ⭐

🕐 Time: 10–15 min.

Go over the answers to the Comprehension Check on page 35: **1.** F; **2.** F; **3.** T.

## CONTEXT NOTE

New York City was the capital of the United States from 1785 to 1790. Philadelphia temporarily served as the U.S. capital from 1790 to 1800, when the capital was permanently moved to Washington, DC. George Washington, the first U.S. president, never resided in the White House in Washington, DC, although he did oversee its construction. John Adams, the second U.S. president, was the first resident of the White House. The White House is the only private residence of a head of state to be open to the public free of charge. This practice has been in place since Thomas Jefferson's presidency.

## ADDITIONAL COMPREHENSION QUESTIONS

*Is Washington, DC, a state?* (no) *Are there tall buildings in Washington, DC?* (no) *Who works in the Capitol?* (state senators and representatives)

## EXPANDING ON THE READING

The topic for this reading can be enhanced with the following items:

1. Images from the top tourist attractions in Washington, DC
2. Brochures/books about the White House
3. Interactive street map of Washington, DC

## PRACTICE IDEA: LISTENING

Have students first listen to the audio alone. Ask a few comprehension questions, such as: *How many people live in Washington, DC?* (more than a half million) *What are the main businesses of Washington?* (government and tourism) *What are the two states where most people who work in Washington, DC, live?* (Virginia and Maryland) *What does Congress do?* (They make the country's laws) Repeat the audio if necessary. Then have students open their books and read along as they listen to the audio.

# 2.1 The Simple Present— Affirmative Statements, page 35

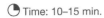

🕐 Time: 10–15 min.

1. Have students close their books. Write the verb *live* at the top of the board. Then write the subject pronouns on the board in the same order they are in the book. Ask: *How do you form the simple present tense?* (use *live* or *lives*) Write students' responses on the board.

2. Have students look at grammar chart **2.1**. Explain that the simple present tense has two forms: the base form and the *-s* form, and the subject determines which form we use. Ask: *When do we use the base form?* (when subject is *I, you, we, they,* or a plural noun) *When do we use the –s form?* (when the subject is *he, she, it,* or a singular subject). Point out that *family* is a singular subject. Read the example sentences.

3. Explain that *have* is an irregular verb. Go over the example sentences.

---

### PRACTICE IDEA: READING

Have students go back to the reading on page 34. Ask students to underline the regular -*s* form verbs and circle the irregular -*s* form of *have*.

---

### PRACTICE IDEA: WRITING

Write the following on the board:

    a. *I / businessperson*
    b. *he / know / French*
    c. *you / wrong*
    d. *we / need / the phone number*
    e. *she / relaxed*
    f. *he / work / hard*

Tell students to write affirmative sentences using the words on the board. Have volunteers write them on the board.

---

**EXERCISE 1** pages 35–36  CD 1 TR 7

🕐 Time: 10–15 min.

**Answers: 1.** plan; **2.** has; **3.** want; **4.** has; **5.** needs; **6.** is; **7.** has; **8.** need; **9.** want; **10.** have; **11.** visit; **12.** shows; **13.** plan; **14.** has; **15.** loves; **16.** have; **17.** hope

---

### PRACTICE IDEA: WRITING

Have students write three to five sentences about a place they plan to visit in the near future. Students can use Exercise 1 as a guide. Have students share their sentences in pairs.

---

# 2.2 The Simple Present— Use, page 36

🕐 Time: 10–15 min.

1. Have students close their books. Elicit sample sentences using the simple present tense from the students. Write a few sentences on the board. Ask: *When do we use the simple present tense?* Have students discuss in pairs and then share ideas. Write students' ideas on the board.

2. Have students look at grammar chart **2.2**. Review the explanations and have volunteers read the example sentences aloud. Give additional examples and have students make similar sentences (e.g., general truth: *Ms. Grant teaches English*; custom: *Americans shake hands when they greet each other*; repeated action: *We have English class twice a week*; place of origin: *I come from Colombia*).

---

**EXERCISE 2** page 36

🕐 Time: 5–10 min.

**Answers: 1.** like; **2.** lives; **3.** work; **4.** has; **5.** visit; **6.** connects; **7.** need; **8.** means; **9.** want

---

**EXERCISE 3** page 37

🕐 Time: 5–10 min.

**Answers will vary.**

---

### PRACTICE IDEA: LISTENING

Play a guessing game. Read (or have a volunteer read) a student's answers to Exercise 3. Then have the class guess who the student is (and the student's native country and city).

---

## 2.3 Spelling of the -s Form, page 37

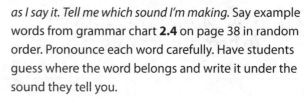

🕐 Time: 10–15 min.

1. Copy the base forms of the verbs from grammar chart **2.3** on the board. Elicit from students the -s forms. Write their suggestions on the board, correcting as necessary.

2. Have students cover grammar chart **2.3**. Say: *There are four rules for adding an -s to verbs. Do you know what they are?* If students have difficulty, give them hints. Say: *Look at the endings of these four verbs* (miss, wash, catch, mix). *What do you add along with the s?* (e) *So what's the rule for these verbs?* (When the base form ends in *ss, sh, ch,* or *x* add *es*…, etc.) Continue with the other verbs.

3. Have students uncover and look at grammar chart **2.3**. Say: *Compare our rules with the rules in the book.* Review the rules in the grammar chart.

---

**PRACTICE IDEA: WRITING**

Have students write about their friends and family members using some of the verbs in grammar chart **2.3**. Remind students to use *he/she/my family* as the subject, and suggest the verbs *hopes, misses, worries, enjoys, goes, does,* and *has.* Have students share their sentences in pairs.

---

**EXERCISE 4** page 38

🕐 Time: 10–15 min.

**Answers: 1.** eats; **2.** studies; **3.** watches; **4.** tries; **5.** plays; **6.** has; **7.** goes; **8.** worries; **9.** wants; **10.** does; **11.** pushes; **12.** enjoys; **13.** thinks; **14.** says; **15.** changes; **16.** brushes; **17.** likes; **18.** reaches; **19.** fixes; **20.** raises; **21.** charges; **22.** sees

## 2.4 Pronunciation of the -s Form, page 38

🕐 Time: 10–15 min.

1. Have students close their books. Say: *There are three ways to pronounce the -s form.* List them across the board: *1. /s/, 2. /z/, 3. /z/.*
   Pronounce each sound. Give an example from each list. Remind students that this is about pronunciation, not spelling or writing. Then say: *Listen to each word*

*as I say it. Tell me which sound I'm making.* Say example words from grammar chart **2.4** on page 38 in random order. Pronounce each word carefully. Have students guess where the word belongs and write it under the sound they tell you.

2. Have students look at grammar chart **2.4**. Say: *Compare our lists with the lists in the book.* Go over any errors.

3. Direct students to the Pronunciation Notes. Pronounce *do/does* and *say/says* for the students. Tell them that these verbs end in a vowel sound and have a change in the vowel sound when the -s is added.

### ADDITIONAL PRACTICE

1. Have students close their books. Read the verbs in the first list in grammar chart 2.4 (*hopes, eats, picks, laughs*). Ask students to repeat what they think the /s/ sound is for that group of words. Then read the verbs from the second list and ask the students to repeat what they think the /s/ sound is for that group of words, and so on. After the last group of verbs, ask students to look at the chart.

2. Have students make flash cards with the base form of the verbs in grammar chart **2.4**. (or other verbs). In pairs, they show a flash card and have their partner pronounce the -s form.

3. Have a Spelling and Pronunciation Bee. Make a list of about forty verbs. Divide the class into Team A and Team B. Give one member from Team A a verb and ask him or her to spell the -s form on the board. Do the same with Team B. Then give another member from Team A another verb and ask him or her to pronounce the -s form, and so on. Make sure that team members take turns. To make the exercise more challenging, give extra points if the team can say (or act out) what the word means.

**EXERCISE 5** page 39

🕐 Time: 10–15 min.

**Answers: 1.** eats /s/; **2.** studies /əz/; **3.** watches /əz/; **4.** tries /z/; **5.** plays /z/; **6.** has /z/; **7.** goes /z/; **8.** worries /z/; **9.** wants /s/; **10.** does /z/; **11.** pushes /əz/; **12.** enjoys /z/; **13.** thinks /s/; **14.** says /z/; **15.** changes /əz/; **16.** brushes /əz/; **17.** likes /s/; **18.** reaches /əz/; **19.** fixes /əz/; **20.** raises /əz/; **21.** charges /əz/

## PRACTICE IDEA: SPEAKING

Have students get in groups of three with classmates from different nationalities and/or cultural backgrounds. Have them share cultural customs, traditions, and rituals with each other. Make sure students are using the simple present tense. Have volunteers share new information they learned about other cultures with the class.

**EXERCISE 6** page 39

🕐 Time: 5–10 min.

**Answers: 1.** likes; **2.** want; **3.** enjoys; **4.** prefer; **5.** wants; **6.** get up; **7.** takes

## PRACTICE IDEA: SPEAKING

Have students read the sentences in Exercise 6 aloud in pairs. For each number, have one student read the first sentence (*I like to visit big cities*), and the other student read the second (*My wife likes to sit by a pool and read*). Tell students to exaggerate the difference in pronunciation.

**EXERCISE 7** page 39

🕐 Time: 5–10 min.

**Answers will vary.**

## PRACTICE IDEA: WRITING

Have students write three statements about themselves using verbs in the simple present tense: two of the statements should be general truths, and one statement should be a lie. Write three model sentences on the board as students write. When students finish, read your sentences aloud and have the class guess which is a lie. Then have students read their statements to a partner. Have the partner guess which statement is a lie. Have volunteers share new information or funny stories about their partners with the class.

# 2.5 The Simple Present— Negative Statements,

page 39

🕐 Time: 10–15 min.

1. Have students close their books. Ask a student: *Do you study English?* Write the affirmative statement on the board (e.g., *Abdullah studies English*.). Then ask: *Do you study Italian?* If the student says no, elicit the complete sentence and write it on the board (e.g., *Abdullah does not study Italian*.). If the student says yes, ask another question to solicit a negative statement.

2. Have students discuss in pairs the differences between the affirmative and negative statement. Have volunteers share their ideas and make notes of the differences on the board.

3. Have students look at grammar chart **2.5**. Review the examples and explanations. Show how to form the contraction (*don't* + base form; *doesn't* + base form). Say: *The contraction is more common in conversation.*

4. Direct students' attention to the Language Note. Give several additional examples comparing the negative form with *be* and other simple present verbs.

## ADDITIONAL PRACTICE

Write the following on the board:

   a. *I / not / from Washington*
   b. *I / not / work for the government*
   c. *The museums / not / open on Christmas Day*
   d. *They / not / have tours on Christmas Day*
   e. *Washington, DC / not / a very big city*
   f. *It / not / have tall buildings*

Tell students to write negative statements using the words on the board. Remind them to use the simple present tense of the verb *be*. Then have volunteers write them on the board.

## PRACTICE IDEA: READING AND WRITING

Ask students to find examples of negative statements in the reading on page 34. (*Washington doesn't have factories. Some people who work in Washington don't live there.*) Have them work in pairs to make the negative statements into affirmative statements.

## EXERCISE 8 page 40

Time: 5–10 min.

**Answers: 1.** don't need; **2.** doesn't have; **3.** doesn't run; **4.** don't need; **5.** doesn't have; **6.** doesn't live; **7.** don't like; **8.** doesn't live; **9.** doesn't serve; **10.** don't have; **11.** doesn't make

---

**PRACTICE IDEA: WRITING AND SPEAKING**

Tell students to make items 3, 4, 5, 8, 9, and 10 true for their native country by writing either affirmative or negative statements. Then have students compare information in pairs. If possible, put students together from different countries.

---

## EXERCISE 9 pages 40–41

Time: 5–10 min.
**Answers will vary.**

---

**PRACTICE IDEA: WRITING**

Have students do the same exercise with another student in the class. Say: *For each statement, change* I *to he or she. First, guess your partner's answer; then, check with your partner. If your partner's answer is negative, write the sentence.* Write a model sentence on the board (e.g., *His hometown doesn't have a zoo.*). For an extra challenge, have students write an alternative answer. Write a model sentence on the board (e.g., *His hometown doesn't have a zoo, but it has a museum.*). Provide vocabulary as necessary.

---

## EXERCISE 10 page 41

Time: 10–15 min.

**Answers: 1.** is; **2.** lives; **3.** works; **4.** doesn't live; **5.** has; **6.** doesn't use; **7.** takes; **8.** doesn't work; **9.** is; **10.** leads; **11.** don't need; **12.** need; **13.** has; **14.** work; **15.** are; **16.** don't have

---

**PRACTICE IDEA: SPEAKING**

Have students read Exercise 10 aloud in pairs to practice pronunciation of the negative statements and contractions.

---

# The Smokies, page 42

## PRE-READING

Time: 5–10 min.

1. Have students look at the photo. Ask: *What do you see in the photo?* (There are mountains, trees, and the sun) *Where do you think this place is?* (somewhere in the west/south of the United States, a park)

2. Have students read the title and then skim the reading. Ask: *What is the reading about? How do you know?* Have students make predictions.

3. Pre-teach any vocabulary words your students may not know, such as *national park, visitor, beauty,* and *cost.*

4. Ask: *Have you ever been to a national park in the United States? What was that experience like?* Have students share their knowledge and personal experiences.

## READING GLOSSARY

**national park:** area of land protected by government because of its importance
**visitor:** someone who visits a person or a place
**beauty:** the good or appealing part of something
**cost:** the price of something

## READING

Time: 10–15 min.

Go over the answers to the Comprehension Check on page 43: **1.** F; **2.** T; **3.** F.

## ADDITIONAL COMPREHENSION QUESTIONS

*How many visitors go to the park each year?* (9 million) *How many different species of trees are in the park?* (one hundred) *How many species of birds?* (200) *Where do most visitors in the park stay?* (in the lodge)

## EXPANDING ON THE READING

The topic for this reading can be enhanced with the following items:

1. Short videos from the Great Smoky Mountains Association
2. Photos and multimedia about the Great Smoky Mountains from the National Park Service Web site
3. Excerpts from the historic video about Great Smoky Mountains National Park, filmed by the United States Division of Motion Pictures in 1936
4. Trail map of the Great Smokies area

### PRACTICE IDEA: LISTENING

Have students first listen to the audio alone. Ask a few comprehension questions, such as: *What are some activities that people do in the park?* (drive to see natural beauty, hike) *Are there bears in the park?* (yes, about 1,500) *How much does it cost to enter the park?* (It's free)

Repeat the audio if necessary. Then have students open their books and read along as they listen to the audio.

## 2.6 The Simple Present—*Yes/No* Questions and Short Answers, page 43

Time: 10–15 min.

1. Have students close their books. Ask students if they remember any *Yes/No* questions with the verb *be* from Lesson 1, and have volunteers write them on the board (e.g., *Are you a state university student? Is it vacation time?*). Ask: *Is the* be *verb before the subject?* (Yes.)
2. Write on the board: *My cousin speaks English. This class studies every week. I have two children.* Have students work in pairs to make the affirmative statements into *Yes/No* questions. (**Answers:** Does your cousin speak English? Does this class study every week? Do you have two children?) Ask: *What is the verb in each sentence?* Circle *speaks, studies*, and *have.* Ask: *Is the verb before the subject?* (No, it's after the subject) *What*

*comes before the subject?* (Do)

3. Have students look at grammar chart **2.6**. Have students read the table aloud in pairs.
4. Direct students' attention to the Language Notes. Review the word order in questions and short answers. Provide additional examples to compare *be* with other simple present verbs.

### PRACTICE IDEA: WRITING

Write the following on the board:

   a. *they / lost?*
   b. *you / need help?*
   c. *we / late?*
   d. *I / have / the directions?*
   e. *he / from Haiti?*
   f. *she / speak Chinese?*

Tell students to write *Yes/No* questions using the words on the board. Have volunteers write the questions on the board.

### PRACTICE IDEA: SPEAKING

Have students go back and read aloud the reading on page 42 in pairs. Ask them to underline *Yes/No* questions with *Do* and circle *Yes/No* questions with *Does,* paying special attention to the subject that comes after the verb. Monitor pair work and clarify the difference between *Yes/No* and *Wh-* questions if necessary.

**EXERCISE 11** pages 43-44
Time: 5–10 min.
**Answers: 1.** Yes, she does.; **2.** No, she doesn't.; **3.** No, she doesn't.; **4.** Yes, she does.; **5.** No, she doesn't.; **6.** Yes, they do.; **7.** No, they don't.; **8.** No, they don't.

**EXERCISE 12** pages 44-45
Time: 10–15 min.
**Answers: 1.** Does the United States have; **2.** does; **3.** It has; **4.** Is Grand Canyon National Park; **5.** isn't; **6.** Do a lot of people visit; **7.** Do I need; **8.** don't; **9.** Is it; **10.** is; **11.** Do we need; **12.** don't; **13.** Does this park charge; **14.** does; **15.** Do buses go; **16.** do; **17.** Do people go; **18.** Does the helicopter go; **19.** does; **20.** Is it; **21.** is

## PRACTICE IDEA: SPEAKING

Have students read the conversation in Exercise 12 aloud in pairs. Have volunteers read the conversation in front of the class.

## PRESENTATION IDEA

In small groups, have students describe and/or show photos, if possible, of a tourist attraction they are knowledgeable about. As one student shows the photos, have the other students ask *Yes/No* questions in the simple present tense. Tell students to use the questions in Exercise 12 as models. Students may also use the *be* verb (e.g., *Do I have to pay to enter the park? Is the stadium open all year?*). After 15–20 minutes, have each group make a pamphlet or poster describing one of their group's tourist attractions.

## EXERCISE 13 pages 45-46

◷ Time: 5–10 min.

**Answers: 1.** Is Grand Canyon National Park in California? No, it isn't.; **2.** Does Yosemite National park get about 5 million visitors a year? No, it doesn't.; **3.** Does Yosemite National Park have black bears? Yes, it does.; **4.** Do giant sequoia trees grow in Grand Canyon National Park? No, they don't.; **5.** Does Yosemite National Park have waterfalls? Yes, it does.; **6.** Is the entrance fee for Grand Canyon National Park $30 per car? No, it isn't.; **7.** Does Grand Canyon National Park have bicycle trails? No, it doesn't.; **8.** Is Grand Canyon National Park part of the National Park Service? Yes, it is.

## PRACTICE IDEA: SPEAKING

When students have completed Exercise 13, have them take turns quizzing each other on the information in pairs. Student A asks the questions while Student B tries to remember the short answer. Student B should not look at the book.

## EXERCISE 14 pages 46-47

◷ Time: 5–10 min.

**Answers: 1. a.** Does Washington have, **b.** doesn't; **2. a.** Do they run, **b.** don't; **3. a.** Do all passengers pay, **b.** don't; **4. a.** Do you need, **b.** do; **5. a.** Does it have,

**b.** does; **6. a.** Does he work, **b.** doesn't; **7. a.** Does the president make, **b.** doesn't; **8. a.** Does the vice president live, **b.** doesn't; **9. a.** Is Washington State, **b.** isn't; **10. a.** Is the zoo free?, **b.** is

# 2.7 The Simple Present—*Wh-* Questions, page 47

◷ Time: 10–15 min.

1. Have students close their books. Have them turn back to the reading on page 42 and find *Wh-* questions. Have volunteers write them on the board as students say them aloud.

2. Write on the board:
   *Does the museum have exhibits?*
   *What does the museum have?*
   (Make sure *does* lines up in each sentence)
   Have students discuss the differences between *Yes/No* and *Wh-* questions in pairs. Take notes on the board as students share ideas.

3. Have students look at grammar chart **2.7**. Ask the *Wh-* questions in the chart, one by one, and have volunteers answer them following the example statements.

4. Direct students' attention to the Language Notes. Review the word order for affirmative and negative *Wh-* questions. Review preposition use at the end of *Wh-* questions and provide additional examples.

## PRACTICE IDEA: WRITING

Write the following on the board:
   a. *who / she?*
   b. *where / she / live?*
   c. *how / you?*
   d. *how / you / feel?*
   e. *where / I?*
   f. *what / I / need?*
Tell students to write *Wh-* questions using the words above. Say: *Write the missing verbs.* Have volunteers write them on the board.

## EXERCISE 15 page 48  CD 1 TR 9

◷ Time: 5–10 min.

**Answers: 1.** Where do you plan; **2.** What do you want; **3.** do they have; **4.** have; **5.** What do they show; **6.** How big is it; **7.** How long does it take; **8.** How much does it cost; **9.** Why don't they charge; **10.** pay

## EXERCISE 16  page 49

⏱ Time: 5–10 min.

**Answers: 1.** do you plan; **2.** do you want; **3.** does it/
Yosemite National Park get; **4.** does she/your wife have;
**5.** doesn't she/your wife like; **6.** do you like

---

**PRACTICE IDEA: WRITING AND SPEAKING**

In pairs, have students write a short conversation
about their weekend or holiday plans using the
verbs and sentences in Exercise 16 as a model.
Have students practice the conversation. Have
volunteers perform their conversation in front of
the class.

---

## EXERCISE 17  pages 49-50

⏱ Time: 5–10 min.

**Answers: 1.** How many floors does it have?; **2.** Why don't
we pay to go to the museum?; **3.** What kind of programs
does it/the museum have?; **4.** What time does it/the
museum close?; **5.** How many visitors does it/the Grand
Canyon get?; **6.** Where is Grand Canyon National Park?;
**7.** How much money does it/Yosemite National Park
charge?; **8.** How many national parks does it/the United
States have?

## EXERCISE 18  page 50

⏱ Time: 5–10 min.

**Answers: 1.** do you want; **2.** don't you like; **3.** do you
want; **4.** don't you like; **5.** does it/the museum have;
**6.** does it/the museum close

## EXERCISE 19  page 51

⏱ Time: 5–10 min.

**Answers will vary.**

---

**PRACTICE IDEA: WRITING AND SPEAKING**

Have students write a numbered list of three to
five more things they like or like to do (e.g., *1.
like to dance; 2. like to eat chicken and rice; 3. like
video games; 4. like classical piano music; 5. like
amusement parks*). Have students mingle and talk
to several classmates asking *Yes/No* and follow-up
*Wh-* questions based on their list.

---

## 2.8 Questions About Meaning, Spelling, Cost, and Time,
page 51

⏱ Time: 10–15 min.

1. Have students close their books. Create a matching
   exercise on the board:

   *1. _____ does DC <u>mean</u>?*

   *2. _____ do you <u>spell</u> government?*

   *3. _____ do you <u>say</u> government in your language?*

   *4. _____ does it <u>cost</u> to enter the park?*

   *5. _____ does it <u>take</u> to see the museum?*

   a. *how*

   b. *how*

   c. *how long*

   d. *how much*

   e. *what*

   Have them complete the matching exercise in pairs
   (**Answers: 1.** e; **2.** b/c; **3.** b/c; **4.** d; **5.** c). Then have
   them look at grammar chart **2.8** and compare their
   answers. Clarify any confusion about the *Wh-* words.

2. Have students come up with more *Wh-* questions
   using the verbs *mean, spell, say, cost,* and *take.* Have
   volunteers write sentences on the board.

## EXERCISE 20  pages 51-52

⏱ Time: 5–10 min.

**Answers: 1.** does it cost; **2.** does it take; **3.** do you spell;
**4.** does "DC" mean / does DC mean; **5.** does it cost; **6.** do
you say

## EXERCISE 21  page 52

⏱ Time: 5–10 min.

**Answers: 1.** are they; **2.** Does he work; **3.** does "IRS" mean
/ does IRS mean; **4.** does it take; **5.** does she live; **6.** do you
spell; **7.** does she work; **8.** do you say

---

**PRACTICE IDEA: SPEAKING**

Have students bring in photos or pull up photos of
friends and family on their phone, tablet, or laptop.
Using Exercise 21 as a model, have students have
a conversation in pairs or small groups. As one
student shows the photos, the other student(s) ask
*Wh-* questions using the verbs *mean, spell, say, cost,*
and *take.* Students can ask other *Yes/No* or *Wh-*
questions as well.

---

# Times Square, page 53

## PRE-READING

🕐 Time: 5–10 min.

1. Have students look at the photo. Ask: *What is happening in the photo?* (people are walking around, it's cold, there are a lot of advertisements) *Where is this place?* (Times Square in New York City, a large city)

2. Have students read the title and then skim the reading. Ask: *What is the reading about? How do you know?* Have students make predictions.

3. Pre-teach any vocabulary words your students may not know, such as *busy, midnight, temperature,* and *theater.*

4. Ask: *Have you ever been to Times Square in New York City? What was your experience like?* Have volunteers share their knowledge and personal experiences.

## READING GLOSSARY

**busy:** actively doing something
**midnight:** the middle of the night; 12 o'clock
**temperature:** how hot or cold something is
**theater:** where plays and shows are performed on a stage

## READING   CD 1 TR 10

🕐 Time: 10–15 min.

Go over the answers to the Comprehension Check on page 54: **1.** F; **2.** F; **3.** T.

## ADDITIONAL COMPREHENSION QUESTIONS

*How many pedestrians pass through Times Square every day?* (more than 300,000) *What do over a million people do on New Year's Eve at midnight?* (watch the Waterford Crystal ball drop) *What is expensive in Times Square?* (parking, theater tickets) *What is the temperature like in New York for New Year's Eve?* (very cold)

## EXPANDING ON THE READING

The topic for this reading can be enhanced with the following items:

1. Video clips and excerpts from Broadway shows or music
2. A 360-degree virtual tour of Times Square
3. Images of the real-life superheroes of Times Square
4. Photos and short biographies of the trending celebrity wax sculptures on Madame Tussaud's website
5. *Ripley's Believe It or Not!* free episodes and short videos

### PRACTICE IDEA: LISTENING

Have students first listen to the audio alone. Ask a few comprehension questions, such as: *What do tourists do in Times Square?* (go to hotels, restaurants, theaters, go shopping) *What is an especially wonderful time of year in Times Square?* (New Year's Eve) *Is it a cheap or expensive tourist attraction?* (expensive) Repeat the audio if necessary. Then have students open their books and read along as they listen to the audio.

# 2.9 Frequency Words and Expressions with the Simple Present, page 54

🕐 Time: 10–15 min.

1. Have students close their books. Copy the vertical frequency arrow from grammar chart **2.9** on the board, with *100 percent* at the top and *0 percent* at the bottom. In random order, write the ten frequency words and expressions from the chart on the board. Have students work in pairs to put the words and expressions in the list in order. If necessary, write *always* at the top and *never* at the bottom and have students guess the order of the rest.

2. Have students look at grammar chart **2.9** and compare their answers. Have volunteers read the example sentences aloud.

3. Direct students' attention to the Language Notes. Provide example sentences for the formal and informal frequency words.

## EXERCISE 22 page 54
🕐 Time: 5–10 min.
**Answers will vary.**

---

**PRACTICE IDEA: WRITING AND SPEAKING**

Have students write six more statements about themselves using different frequency words or expressions. Three of the statements should be true, and three should be false. Have them read the statements aloud in pairs, and have each partner guess which statements are true and which are false.

---

# 2.10 Position of Frequency Words and Expressions,
page 55

🕐 Time: 10–15 min.
Have students close their books. Create a matching exercise on the board:

1. *Times Square is busy.*
2. *I drive to Times Square.*
3. *It's cold on New Year's Eve.*
4. *People visit Times Square.*

a. *sometimes*
b. *every night*
c. *never*
d. *always*

Have students match the frequency word or expression with the sentence it best describes. (**Answers: 1.** d; **2.** c; **3.** a; **4.** b) Review the answers with the students. Then have students rewrite sentences 1 through 4 including the frequency word or expression.
Have students look at grammar chart **2.10** and compare their answers. Review additional examples and explanations.
Direct students' attention to the Language Notes and emphasize that we can't put *always*, *hardly ever*, or *never* before the subject. Provide additional examples.

## EXERCISE 23 pages 55–56
🕐 Time: 5–10 min.

---

**Answers: 1.** I often travel with my family.; **2.** Every year my family and I take a vacation in the summer.; **3.** We are always interested in seeing something new.; **4.** We often visit major cities, like New York and San Francisco.; **5.** We sometimes visit relatives in other cities.; **6.** We usually travel by car.; **7.** We hardly ever fly.; **8.** We always take a lot of pictures.; **9.** We are never bored.

---

**PRACTICE IDEA: SPEAKING**

Have students read through the answers in Exercise 23 and share in pairs if the answer is true for them. If it's not, have them rewrite the sentence in the negative. Then, do a class survey. In groups, have students compare their answers. Have students report their results to the class. Record the information on the board for selected categories (e.g., *All the students in the class travel with their family.*).

---

**PRACTICE IDEA: SPEAKING**

Have students share information about their favorite holidays in pairs. Remind them to use frequency words in their descriptions (e.g., *My favorite holiday is Eid. We never eat or drink until sundown. At night, we always have traditional dishes. Sometimes we listen to music.*).

---

# 2.11 Questions and Short Answers with *Ever,*
page 56

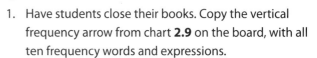

🕐 Time: 10–15 min.

1. Have students close their books. Copy the vertical frequency arrow from chart **2.9** on the board, with all ten frequency words and expressions.

2. Write on the board and ask: *Do you _ever_ study English?* After students say *yes*, point to the frequency arrow and ask: *Sometimes? Always? Hardly ever?* Write students' answers next to the question on the board (e.g., *Yes, I always study English.*). Write on the board and ask: *Are you _ever_ angry?* Point to the frequency arrow and ask: *Sometimes? Always? Hardly ever?* Write students' answers next to the question on the board (e.g., *No, I'm hardly ever angry.*).

3. Circle the words *Do* and *Are* in the questions on the board. Have students look at grammar chart **2.11** and read the example questions and short answers aloud in pairs. Clarify that *do/does* is an auxiliary verb.

4. Direct students' attention to the Language Notes. Review the word order in short answers and the rules with the frequency word *never*. Provide additional examples if necessary.

**EXERCISE 24** page 56

🕐 Time: 5–10 min.

**Answers will vary.**

## 2.12 Questions and Answers with *How Often*, page 57

🕐 Time: 10–15 min.

1. Have students close their books. Write on the board and ask again: *Do you ever study English?* After students say *yes*, write on the board and ask: *How often do you study English? Once a week? Twice a week? Every day?* Write students' answers on the board. Repeat with a couple more *How often* questions.

2. Circle the word *Do* in the questions on the board. Have students look at grammar chart **2.12**. Review the examples and explanations. Model the pronunciation of the frequency words and expressions, and have students practice them in pairs.

3. Direct students' attention to the Language Notes. Point out the flexibility of the word order, but highlight the use of the comma when the frequency expression is at the beginning of the sentence.

---

**PRACTICE IDEA: WRITING**

Have students follow up on their oral holiday descriptions by writing a short paragraph about their favorite holiday using frequency words or expressions. Have volunteers share their descriptions with the class, and have other students ask follow-up questions using *ever* and *how often*.

---

**EXERCISE 25** page 57

🕐 Time: 5–10 min.

**Answers will vary.**

---

**PRACTICE IDEA: SPEAKING**

Have students stand in two concentric circles, with half the students standing in an outer ring around the classroom and the other half standing in an inner ring, facing each other. Instruct students to ask and answer the questions from Exercise 25. Call out *turn* every minute or so. Students in the inner ring should move one space clockwise. Students now ask and answer with their new partners. Have students ask questions in random order. Make sure students look at each other when they're speaking.

---

**EXERCISE 26** pages 57–58

🕐 Time: 10–15 min.

**Answers: 1.** you ever; **2.** rarely; **3.** Once; **4.** How; **5.** Once in a while; **6.** never; **7.** It's sometimes; **8.** ever; **9.** never; **10.** always says; **11.** ever go; **12.** do; **13.** It's always; **14.** often get together

---

**PRACTICE IDEA: SPEAKING**

Have students role-play the conversation from Exercise 26 in pairs. Have volunteers perform in front of the class.

---

## 2.13 Prepositions of Time, page 58

🕐 Time: 10–15 min.

1. Have students close their books. Create a matching exercise:

   1. *I eat breakfast _____.*
   2. *My favorite time to travel is _____.*
   3. *My birthday is _____.*
   4. *Our class starts _____.*
   5. *Summer break is _____.*
   a. *at 9 o'clock*
   b. *in the morning*
   c. *in the spring*
   d. *from July until August*
   e. *on November 27*

   Have students match each prepositional phrase of time with the best sentence. (**Answers: 1.** b; **2.** c; **3.** e; **4.** a; **5.** d) Review the answers with students.

2. Say: *When do we use* in, on, at, *and* from… to/until? Have students discuss possible rules in pairs. Write their ideas on the board.

3. Have students look at grammar chart **2.13**. Review examples and explanations, and have students compare their ideas with the rules in the chart.

4. Direct students' attention to the Language Note. Provide several additional examples of the information use of *from…until*, reading them aloud to model pronunciation. Have students create their own examples and practice the pronunciation of *till*.

### EXERCISE 27 page 59

🕐 Time: 5–10 min.

**Answers: 1.** on; **2.** in; **3.** in; **4.** on; **5.** at; **6.** on; **7.** on

---

**PRACTICE IDEA: SPEAKING**

Have students do a timed mingle activity with the questions in Exercise 27. Tell students to ask and answer the questions with five different classmates. Each new pair should talk for no more than 3 minutes. After the activity, have volunteers share any new information and similarities they learned about their classmates.

---

### EXERCISE 28 page 59

🕐 Time: 5–10 min.

**Answers will vary.**

## SUMMARY OF LESSON 2

◑ Time: 20–30 min.

### PART A THE SIMPLE PRESENT—FORMS

Have students write *Yes/No* and *Wh-* questions using all the subject pronouns. Have students read their sentences aloud in pairs. The partner should respond with a short answer (*Yes/No* questions) or additional information (*Wh-* questions). If necessary, review:

**2.3** Spelling of the *-s* Form (page 37)

**2.4** Pronunciation of the *-s* Form (page 38)

**2.6** The Simple Present—*Yes/No* Questions and Short Answers (page 43)

**2.7** The Simple Present—*Wh-* Questions (page 47)

### PART B THE SIMPLE PRESENT—USE

Have students make affirmative and negative sentences for each use. If necessary, review:

**2.1** The Simple Present—Affirmative Statements (page 35)

**2.2** The Simple Present—Use (page 36)

**2.3** Spelling of the *-s* Form (page 37)

**2.5** The Simple Present—Negative Statements (page 39)

### PART C FREQUENCY WORDS AND EXPRESSIONS

Have students write *True/False* statements about themselves using frequency words or expressions. Have them read the statements aloud in pairs. The partner should guess if the statement is true or false. If necessary, review:

**2.1** The Simple Present—Affirmative Statements (page 35)

**2.5** The Simple Present—Negative Statements (page 39)

**2.9** Frequency Words and Expressions with the Simple Present (page 54)

**2.10** Position of Frequency Words and Expressions (page 55)

### PART D QUESTIONS AND ANSWERS WITH FREQUENCY WORDS

Have students write five to ten questions with *ever*. Have them conduct interviews in pairs, asking and answering the questions with *ever* and following up each answer with a question using *how often*. When the interview is completed, have the pairs report what they learned about their partner in small groups to practice using different subject pronouns.

**2.10** Position of Frequency Words and Expressions (page 55)

**2.11** Questions and Short Answers with *Ever* (page 56)

**2.12** Questions and Answers with *How Often* (page 57)

### PART E PREPOSITIONS OF TIME

Have students write at least one sentence for every use of the prepositions of time. Have them share their sentences in pairs and give peer feedback.

**2.13** Prepositions of Time (page 58)

## TEST/REVIEW

🕐 Time: 20 min.

Have students do the exercise on page 61. For additional practice, use the Assessment CD-ROM with Exam*View*® and the Online Workbook.

**Answers:**

**Part A** **1.** lives; **2.** loves; **3.** does she do; **4.** goes; **5.** does she do; **6.** has; **7.** like; **8.** does "MOMA" mean / does MOMA mean; **9.** means; **10.** does it cost; **11.** costs; **12.** pays; **13.** gets; **14.** Does your sister have; **15.** uses;

**Part B** **1.** you ever; **2.** sometimes do; **3.** in; **4.** ever; **5.** on; **6.** do; **7.** don't you; **8.** like; **9.** We always; **10.** often; **11.** come; **12.** usually comes; **13.** in; **14.** I'm always; **15.** has; **16.** cost; **17.** doesn't cost; **18.** has; **19.** does she do; **20.** She works; **21.** on

# WRITING

## PART 1 EDITING ADVICE

🕐 Time: 10–15 min.

1. Have students close their books. Write a few sentences without editing marks or corrections on the board. For example:

    a.  *He need more money.*

    b.  *This school have a big library.*

    c.  *My father doesn't has a car.*

    d.  *Does your mother speaks English well?*

2. Ask students to correct each sentence and provide a rule or an explanation for each correction. This activity can be done individually, in pairs, or as a class.

3. After students have corrected each sentence, tell them to turn to page 62. Say: *Now compare your work with the Editing Advice in the book.* Have students read through all the advice.

## PART 2 EDITING PRACTICE

🕐 Time: 10–15 min.

1. Tell students they are going to put the Editing Advice into practice. Ask: *Do all the shaded words and phrases have mistakes?* (no) Go over the examples with the class. Then do #1 together.

2. Have students complete the practice individually. Then have them compare answers with a partner before checking answers as a class.

3. For the items students had difficulties with, have them go back and find the relevant grammar chart and review it. Monitor and give help as necessary.

**Answers: 1.** I; **2.** C; **3.** visits; **4.** C; **5.** C; **6.** C; **7.** I; **8.** like; **9.** always want; **10.** C; **11.** doesn't like; **12.** cries; **13.** go; **14.** C; **15.** don't you; **16.** C; **17.** C; **18.** C; **19.** do the tickets cost; **20.** don't; **21.** C; **22.** C; **23.** C; **24.** don't like; **25.** C; **26.** comes

## PART 3 WRITE ABOUT IT

🕐 Time: 30–40 min.

1. Review the topic with students and have them brainstorm, either with a mind map or writing a list, all the interesting places they have been to in their current city and/or another city. If necessary, do a sample brainstorm on the board (e.g., *New York City; exciting; tall buildings; wonderful stores and restaurants.*). Write students' ideas on the board. Remind them to include any useful and relevant vocabulary from this lesson on places to visit and to double-check the simple perfect verb tense. If necessary, write model topic sentences on the board first (e.g., *I love New York City. It's very exciting. It has tall buildings. It has wonderful stores and restaurants.*). Collect for assessment and/or have students present their paragraphs to the class.

2. Review the topic with students. Have students write all the words or phrases they associate with their past celebrations of New Year's Eve. Have them share these ideas with a partner. Encourage them to organize the ideas into a series of events before they write their sentences or paragraphs. If necessary, write model topic sentences on the board first.

## PART 4 EDIT YOUR WRITING

🕐 Time: 15–20 min.

Have students edit their writing by reviewing the Lesson Summary on page 60 and the Editing Advice on page 62. Collect for assessment and/or have students share their writings in small groups.

## EXPANSION ACTIVITIES

1. Have students interview somebody outside of the class about his or her favorite tourist attraction in the United States. Suggest these starter questions: *Why do you like this place? How often do you go? What activities does this place have?* Make sure students take notes during the interview. Then have students report back to the class.

2. Have students use the Internet to find information about one of the following places: Disneyland, the White House, the Holocaust Museum, Ellis Island, Mount Rushmore, the Alamo, or any other American tourist attraction that interests them. Have them answer these questions: *What is it? Where is it? What does it cost to enter? What does it have? Have you ever been there?*

3. Have students use the Internet to find information about a museum or place of special interest in their current city. Have them answer these questions: *What is it? What neighborhood is it in? What does it cost to enter? What does it have? How often do you go?*

4. Have students create a schedule of their daily routines using frequency words or expressions and prepositions of time. As a follow-up activity, volunteers can act out and present their daily routine in front of the class. The audience could receive a blank schedule and have to fill in the activities and times as they listen. If they miss some information, they have to ask follow-up questions (e.g., *Wait, what do you always do in the morning? Can you repeat what you usually do at 8:00 A.M.?*).

# 3 HOUSING

## GRAMMAR CHARTS

## LESSON OPENER

Have students look at the photo and read the caption. Ask: *What do you see in this photo?* (houses, trees, streets, water) *Where is it?* (a city on the ocean, Miami Beach, Florida) Have students read the quotation. Ask: *Do you agree with the quote? Where do you call "home"?*

**Background:** There are several types of housing configurations in the United States. The two most traditional types of living are owning or renting a house or apartment. As of 2014, about 63 percent of living units in the United States are owner-occupied while about 35 percent are rented. Older generations of Americans are more likely to own, but younger generations tend to rent or participate in shared living situations. Other common housing configurations in the United States are mobile homes, housing cooperatives, senior living communities, and public housing. As of 2014, over 5 million Americans rent and live in mobile homes or trailers, making up 5 percent of the U.S. housing sector (according to the U.S. Census). These people are either traveling or living in a mobile home park with other trailer renters. Housing cooperatives, or co-ops, are a growing form of residential arrangement. Co-ops are membership-based, with membership granted by a financial contribution to the living space. The members screen and select who lives in the cooperative, unlike other forms of home ownership. Senior living communities, or retirement communities, are designed for seniors 55 years and over and often have convenient services, senior-friendly surroundings, and increased social opportunities. The average number of seniors living in these communities is around 245,000. Finally, public housing, funded by the U.S. Department of Housing and Urban Development, provides affordable housing to low-income individuals. As of 2014, more than 1.2 million households live in public housing of some type.

Laura Ingalls Wilder was an American teacher and author, best known for a series of children's novels called *Little House on the Prairie*. The series was based on Wilder's childhood growing up in a family of settlers who migrated around the United States in the late 1800s in an attempt to establish a permanent residence. The series was later turned into a popular American western drama TV series, making Wilder a household name. She passed away at the age of 90 in 1957.

## CONTEXT

This unit is about housing in the United States. Students will read about the high cost of housing, finding an apartment, and tiny houses.

1. Give students a few minutes to look through the lesson. Have them look at the photos and titles. How do they relate to the context?

2. Elicit the topics that will be discussed.

3. Have students discuss what they know about housing in the United States in pairs or small groups.

## GRAMMAR

Students will learn about singular and plural nouns, *there is/there are*, and articles.

1. To activate students' prior knowledge, ask what students know about singular and plural nouns, *there is/there are*, and articles.

2. Give several examples of singular and plural nouns, *there is/there are*, and articles (e.g., *teacher/teachers*; *child/children*; *a/an/the*).

3. Have volunteers give examples and write them on the board.

## EXPANDING ON THE CONTEXT

The context for this lesson can be enhanced with the following items:

1. Interior and exterior photos of your house or apartment
2. Photos of houses and apartments from magazines
3. Photos of different kinds of living spaces and floor designs: big houses, tiny houses, apartments, co-op housing, dorm rooms
4. Photos of residential arrangements from around the world

## READING

# The High Cost of Housing, page 66

## PRE-READING

⏲ Time: 5–10 min.

1. Have students look at the photo and read the sign, "For Sale By Owner." Ask: *What does this sign mean?* (somebody is selling their own house) *Where is this sign?* (in front of a house on the front lawn)
2. Have students read the title and then skim the reading. Ask: *What is the reading about? How do you know?* Have students make predictions.
3. Pre-teach any essential vocabulary words your students may not know, such as *paycheck, bills, income,* and *expense.*
4. Ask: *Who did you live with before living in the United States? Is it expensive to own a house in your home community or city? Who do you live with here? Is it expensive to live in the United States?* Have volunteers share their knowledge and personal experiences.

## READING GLOSSARY

**paycheck:** the money you earn for work
**bills:** documents that say how much money is owed for something bought or used
**income:** money that is earned from work
**expense:** the amount of money needed to pay for or buy something

## READING

⏲ Time: 10–15 min.

Go over the answers to the Comprehension Check on page 67: **1.** T; **2.** T; **3.** F.

## ADDITIONAL COMPREHENSION QUESTIONS

*How many months of expenses do financial planners tell people to keep for emergencies?* (3 to 6 months) *Who are millennials?* (people born between 1980 and 2000) *What cities have the most expensive rent in the United States?* (New York City, Los Angeles, San Francisco, and Oakland) *What percent of young Americans live with their parents?* (56 percent)

## EXPANDING ON THE READING

The topic for this reading can be enhanced with the following items:

1. Real estate advertisements for houses, apartments, and condos in the area
2. Web sites and apps that list housing prices
3. Charts or graphs that show statistics of how many Americans own versus rent, considering variables like age, job, location, etc.

---

### PRACTICE IDEA: LISTENING

Have students first listen to the audio alone. Ask a few comprehension questions, such as: *How many Americans are middle-class?* (about one-third) *Why do some Americans not want to own a house?* (They prefer to rent an apartment because they don't want debt) *Is renting cheap or expensive?* (expensive) Repeat the audio if necessary. Then have students open their books and read along as they listen to the audio.

---

### PRACTICE IDEA: READING AND SPEAKING

Have students research similar statistics about housing from their native country. If possible, put students of the same nationality in the same group. Have group members compare information. Finally, have groups present their information to the class.

# 3.1 Singular and Plural Nouns,

page 67

⏱ Time: 10–15 min.

1. Have students close their books. Write a brief list of singular nouns on the board (e.g., *kid, beach, American, man*). Ask: *Are these nouns singular or plural?* (singular) *What does singular mean?* (one) *How do we say more than one?* (plural)

2. Have students work in pairs to write the plural of each word on the board (*kids, beaches, Americans, men*). Write students' ideas on the board.

3. Review the examples and explanations in grammar chart **3.1**. Explain that the plural usually ends in *-s* or *-es*, although some plural forms are irregular (e.g., *men*).

4. Direct students' attention to the Language Notes. Read the examples aloud and provide additional examples as necessary.

> ### PRACTICE IDEA: READING
>
> Have students go back to the reading on page 66 and make a list of ten different nouns: five singular and five plural. Have them change the nouns in the singular list to plural, and the nouns in the plural list to singular.

# 3.2 Regular Plural Nouns— Spelling, page 67

⏱ Time: 10–15 min.

1. Copy the lists of nouns (the singular and plural form columns) from grammar chart **3.2** on the board. Keep nouns in the same groups and in the same order.

2. Have students close their books. First, point to different letters in the words on the board and have students say if that letter is a vowel or a consonant. Repeat this until all students understand the difference. Leave a list of the vowels on the board.

3. Then, have students work in pairs or small groups to analyze the spelling changes between the two lists and guess what the rules for adding *-s* are. If they have difficulty, give them hints. Say: *Look at the endings of the four nouns in row 3 (ss, sh, ch, and x). What do you add?* (es) *So what's the rule?* (When the noun ends in *ss, sh, ch,* or *x,* add *es.*)

4. Have students look at grammar chart **3.2** and compare their rules with the rules in the book. Carefully read through the rules and exceptions.

## EXERCISE 1 page 68

⏱ Time: 10–15 min.

**Answers: 1.** questions; **2.** things; **3.** decisions; **4.** Condos; **5.** rules; **6.** associations; **7.** dogs; **8.** Homeowners; **9.** responsibilities; **10.** activities; **11.** jobs; **12.** kids; **13.** bicycles; **14.** toys

> ### PRACTICE IDEA: LISTENING
>
> Have students first listen to the audio alone. Have them count how many questions they hear (five). Then have students open their books and complete Exercise 1 as they listen to the audio again.

> ### PRACTICE IDEA: SPEAKING
>
> Have students take turns asking and answering the questions in Exercise 1 in small groups. Then have them discuss their preferences for owning a home or renting an apartment or condo. Have volunteers share their group's preferences with the class.

## EXERCISE 2 pages 68–69

⏱ Time: 10–15 min.

**Answers: 1.** loaves; **2.** toys; **3.** brushes; **4.** countries; **5.** halves; **6.** books; **7.** valleys; **8.** lives; **9.** stories; **10.** sofas; **11.** keys; **12.** ages; **13.** kisses; **14.** potatoes; **15.** rents; **16.** watches; **17.** photos; **18.** lips; **19.** taxes; **20.** videos; **21.** moths; **22.** studios; **23.** adults; **24.** illnesses

## EXERCISE 3 page 69

⏱ Time: 5–10 min.

**Answers: 1.** Houses; **2. a.** kids, **b.** grandparents; **3. a.** adults, **b.** parents; **4.** families; **5. a.** families, **b.** life; **6.** emergencies

## 3.3 Plural Nouns— Pronunciation, page 69

⏱ Time: 10–15 min.

1. Have students close their books. Write three headings across the board:

    1. /s/
    2. /z/
    3. /z/

    Say: *There are three ways to pronounce the endings of plural nouns.* Pronounce each sound. Say words from grammar chart **3.3** in random order, exaggerating the pronunciation of the plural endings. Have students guess where the word belongs and write it under the sound they tell you.

2. Have students look at grammar chart **3.3** and compare the board with the chart in the book. Go over any errors. Have students pronounce the pairs of words with a partner.

**EXERCISE 4** page 69

⏱ Time: 10–15 min.

**Answers: 1.** /z/; **2.** /z/; **3.** /əz/; **4.** /z/; **5.** /z/; **6.** /s/; **7.** /z/; **8.** /z/; **9.** /z/; **10.** /z/; **11.** /z/; **12.** /əz/; **13.** /əz/; **14.** /z/; **15.** /s/; **16.** /əz/; **17.** /z/; **18.** /s/; **19.** /əz/; **20.** /z/; **21.** /s/; **22.** /z/; **23.** /s/; **24.** /əz/

## 3.4 Irregular Plural Nouns, page 70

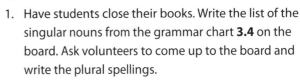

⏱ Time: 10–15 min.

1. Have students close their books. Write the list of the singular nouns from the grammar chart **3.4** on the board. Ask volunteers to come up to the board and write the plural spellings.

2. Have students look at grammar chart **3.4** and compare the list on the board with the plural column in the chart. Review the explanations and remind students that there are no rules for spelling changes with these nouns; they need to be memorized.

3. Direct students' attention to the Language and Pronunciation Notes. Give additional examples of the more common use of *people*. Demonstrate the pronunciation differences between *woman* and *women* several times and have students guess if you're saying the singular or plural. Have students repeat the short activity in pairs.

**EXERCISE 5** page 70

⏱ Time: 5–10 min.

**Answers: 1.** men; **2.** feet; **3.** women; **4.** policemen; **5.** children; **6.** fish; **7.** mice; **8.** sheep; **9.** teeth; **10.** people / persons

**EXERCISE 6** page 70

⏱ Time: 5–10 min.

**Answers: 1.** houses; **2.** people; **3.** times; **4. a.** men, **b.** women, **c.** parents; **5.** Homes, **b.** cities; **6. a.** countries, **b.** children; **7.** feet; **8.** mice

**READING**

## Finding an Apartment, page 71

### PRE-READING

⏱ Time: 5–10 min.

1. Have students look at the photo. Ask: *What do you see in the photo?* (the outside of an apartment, a building) *Where do you think it is?* (a large city, New York City)

2. Have students look at the title of the reading. Ask: *What is the reading about? How do you know?* Have students make predictions.

3. Pre-teach any vocabulary words your students may not know, such as *owner, manager, appointment,* and *janitor.*

4. Activate students' prior knowledge. Ask: *Have you ever lived in an apartment? Are houses or apartments more common where you grew up?* Have students discuss the questions in pairs.

## READING GLOSSARY

**owner:** a person who owns something

**manager:** a person who is in charge of something

**appointment:** an agreement to meet with somebody at a particular time, place, and date

**janitor:** the person who cleans and fixes things in a building

## READING
CD 1
TR 13

🕑 Time: 10–15 min.

Go over the answers to the Comprehension Check on page 72: **1.** F; **2.** F; **3.** T.

## ADDITIONAL COMPREHENSION QUESTIONS

*Name two ways to look for an apartment.* (online, ads in a newspaper, "For Rent" signs in front of buildings) *What are some questions you should ask when you call about the apartment?* (How much is the rent? How many bedrooms are there?) *What are some questions you should ask when you see the apartment?* (Is there a lease? Are there smoke detectors?)

## CONTEXT NOTE

In 1995, Craig Newmark began an online social event calendar in the San Francisco Bay Area. His desire for sharing information grew rapidly, and he soon founded the leading online classified service of any medium, the Web site Craigslist. Today, the site has over 20 billion page views per month and is among the top ten most accessed Web sites in the United States and abroad. It now has sections focused on jobs, housing, personals, for sale, and discussion forums, among others, covering over seventy countries.

## EXPANDING ON THE READING

The topic for this reading can be enhanced with the following items:

1. Online listings of apartments on Web sites or phone apps

2. Real estate brochures or newspaper ads of apartment listings with full descriptions

3. Floor plans of apartments

4. Applications to rent an apartment

---

**PRACTICE IDEA: LISTENING**

Have students first listen to the audio alone. Write on the board: *there is/there are* and *is there/are there.* Say the phrases aloud and tell students to count how many times they hear these phrases in the audio (eighteen). Repeat the audio if necessary. Then have students open their books and read along as they listen to the audio.

---

## 3.5 *There Is/There Are,* page 72

🕑 Time: 10–15 min.

1. Have students look at the reading on page 71. Ask students to find examples of *there is* and *there are* in the reading (e.g., *There is usually a number on the sign. There are also ads for houses for rent and houses for sale.*). Write students' responses on the board. Now have students identify the nouns that follow *there is* and *there are* (*a map, ads*). Ask: *Which ones are plural and which ones are singular?*

2. Have students look at grammar chart **3.5**. Have a volunteer read aloud the examples in each category. Have students pay attention to the negative categories. Point out the contractions *isn't and aren't.* Explain that there are two forms of contraction for the negative: *there isn't* and *there aren't.*

3. Go through the Language Notes carefully. Provide additional examples as necessary.

**PRACTICE IDEA: SPEAKING**

Have students walk around the classroom in pairs and say singular and plural affirmative and negative statements to describe the space. Write examples on the board: *There is a clock on the wall. There are desks in the classroom, but there aren't any desktop computers.*

**EXERCISE 7** page 73

🕐 Time: 5–10 min.

**Answers will vary.** (Note: *There's* and *There is* are both acceptable.)

**EXERCISE 8** page 74

🕐 Time: 5–10 min.

**Answers will vary.** (Note: *There's* and *There is* are both acceptable.)

**PRACTICE IDEA: SPEAKING**

Have students mingle and compare information about their house, apartment, or dorm with their classmates. Write a short example conversation on the board: *A: There's carpet in the living room. B: There's no carpet in my living room.* Clarify vocabulary as needed.

**PRACTICE IDEA: PRESENTATION IDEA**

Have students draw their dream house and present it in pairs. Do a model on the board first and describe it to the class (e.g., *Here, there are three large sofas in the living room. There is a back door, which opens up to a huge garden. There isn't a microwave oven in the kitchen, but there is a large stove to cook on.*). Have volunteers share their dream houses with the class.

# 3.6 Questions and Short Answers with *There,* page 75

🕐 Time: 10–15 min.

1. Have students close their books. Write on the board:
   a. *There is a laundry room in the building.*
   b. *There are some children in my building.*
   c. *There are ten apartments in my building.*

Have students work in pairs to turn the statements into questions.

2. Have students look at grammar chart **3.6** and compare their answers. Review the examples and clarify questions about word order.

3. Direct students' attention to the Language Notes. Explain that *any* is often used in questions and negatives with plural nouns. *Any*, which means *some*, is not used in affirmative statements.

4. Review short answers. There are two contractions for short negative answers in the singular: *No, there isn't* and *No, there's not*. In the plural, *Yes, there are* is not contracted. The contraction for the negative is *No, there aren't*.

## ADDITIONAL PRACTICE

Have students ask and answer questions about the classroom or school using *there is/there are*. Model an example: *Is there a library at this school? Yes, there is.* Display images of different houses and apartments and have students ask and answer questions about the photo using *there is/there are*.

**EXERCISE 9** page 75

🕐 Time: 5–10 min.

**Answers will vary.** (Note: *There's* and *There is* are both acceptable. Usually *any* is optional.)

**PRACTICE IDEA: SPEAKING**

Have students get in pairs. Give both students very different photos. Have students ask and answer questions about their partner's photo.

**PRACTICE IDEA: SPEAKING**

Have students get in pairs. Give both students similar images with only a few different details. Have students ask and answer questions about their partner's image until they discover all the differences.

**EXERCISE 10** page 76

🕐 Time: 10–15 min.

**Answers: 1.** There's; **2.** Is there; **3.** are (there); **4.** There are; **5.** Are there (any); **6.** There are; **7.** many; **8.** are (there); **9.** There are; **10.** there aren't; **11.** there are; **12.** Is there; **13.** There are; **14.** There are

## 3.7 *There, They,* and Other Pronouns, page 76

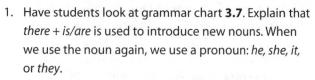

○ Time: 10–15 min.

1. Have students look at grammar chart **3.7**. Explain that *there + is/are* is used to introduce new nouns. When we use the noun again, we use a pronoun: *he, she, it,* or *they.*

2. Review the examples in the chart. Have volunteers make sentences using *there is/are* and pronouns with *be.* For example: *There is a big chalkboard in the room. It is at the front of the room.*

3. Direct students' attention to the Spelling Note. Point out that people often get confused with *there* and *they're*—especially since their pronunciations are exactly the same. Demonstrate their pronunciations. Have students practice the pronunciation in pairs.

### EXERCISE 11 page 77

○ Time: 5–10 min.

**Answers: 1. a.** There's, **b.** It's; **2. a.** There's, **b.** She's; **3. a.** There are, **b.** They're; **4. a.** There is, **b.** He's; **5. a.** There's, **b.** Is she; **6. a.** Is there, **b.** is he; **7. a.** are (there), **b.** Are they; **8. a.** Is there, **b.** Is it; **9. a.** There's, **b.** He's

### EXERCISE 12 page 77

○ Time: 5–10 min.

**Answers:** [Note: Contractions or full forms are correct except for items 2, 6, and 9 (full form only).] **1.** Is there; **2.** there is; **3.** It's; **4.** There's / There is; **5.** are there; **6.** There are; **7.** They're; **8.** Is there; **9.** there is; **10.** He's / She's

**READING**

# Tiny Houses, page 78

## PRE-READING

○ Time: 5–10 min.

1. Have students look at the photo and read the caption. Ask: *What do you see in this photo?* (a man, rugs, chairs, pillows, dishes, a ladder, a stove) *Where is this man?* (in his tiny house) *Where is his tiny house?* (Pasadena, Maryland)

2. Have students read the title and caption of the reading. Ask: *What is the reading about? How do you know?* Have students make predictions.

3. Pre-teach any vocabulary words your students may not know, such as *square feet, salary, interest,* and *insurance.*

4. Activate students' prior knowledge. Ask: *Would you prefer to live in a large house, or a tiny house?* Have students discuss the questions in pairs.

## READING GLOSSARY

**square feet:** a measurement of area used primarily in the United States

**salary:** amount of money an employee is paid each year

**interest:** extra money paid by a borrower for use of borrowed money

**insurance:** financial help if something in the house is damaged, lost, or destroyed

# READING

🕐 Time: 10–15 min.

Go over the answers to the Comprehension Check on page 79: **1.** F; **2.** F; **3.** T.

## ADDITIONAL COMPREHENSION QUESTIONS

*How many square feet is the typical American home?* (2,600 square feet) *How much of their salary do Americans spend on housing costs?* (one-third to one-half) *How big are tiny houses?* (usually between 100 and 400 square feet) *How much does an average tiny house cost?* ($23,000)

## CONTEXT NOTE

The traditional American home is around 2,600 square feet. For many Americans, the economic burden of large homes takes up almost half their income and perpetuates a cycle of debt. The tiny house movement, also known as the small house movement, is a social movement aimed to decrease the economic, social, and environmental burden of the typical American home. Tiny houses come in a variety of designs, but the goal is the same: simpler living in a more efficient space.

### EXPANDING ON THE READING

The topic for this reading can be enhanced with the following items:

1. Web sites showing photos of tiny houses and their owners
2. Tiny house floor plans with dimensions
3. The Tiny Life's Tiny House Building Checklist
4. Short videos such as "The Tiny Life––Tiny Houses, Simple Living" or "How to Start Designing a Tiny House"
5. Charts and graphs showing the cost of buying traditional houses over a lifetime

### PRACTICE IDEA: LISTENING

Have students first listen to the audio alone. Tell them to listen for the articles *a* and *the* and write any words they hear come after it. Write an example on the board: *a dream*. Repeat the audio if necessary. Then have students open their books and read along as they listen to the audio.

## 3.8 Definite and Indefinite Articles, page 79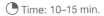

🕐 Time: 10–15 min.

1. Have students go to the reading on page 78. Ask them to:
   a. underline articles *a/an* + noun
   b. double underline definite articles
   c. circle *the* + noun
   d. circle nouns without articles

2. Have students discuss in pairs why a noun in the reading has *a/an* and not *the*, and why some of the nouns don't have an article. Have volunteers share ideas.

3. Have students look at grammar chart **3.8.** Have volunteers read the examples aloud. Review the explanations.

4. Direct students' attention to the Language Notes. Explain that *the* is also used if this noun is the only one or if the speaker and listener share the same experience. Provide additional examples. For example, when students refer to you, they may say *the teacher* because they share the same experience (same classroom, same teacher).

5. Review the expressions and certain familiar places of people that require the definite article *the*. Provide additional examples as necessary.

**EXERCISE 13** pages 79–80

🕐 Time: 10–15 min.

**Answers: 1.** a; **2.** the; **3.** The; **4.** a; **5.** the; **6.** the; **7.** the; **8.** a; **9.** a; **10.** The; **11.** a; **12.** the; **13.** the; **14.** a; **15.** a; **16.** an

**EXERCISE 14** pages 80–81

🕐 Time: 10–15 min.

**Answers: 1.** the; **2.** the; **3.** the; **4.** an; **5.** a; **6.** a; **7.** a; **8.** any; **9.** the; **10.** the; **11.** a; **12.** a; **13.** the; **14.** The; **15.** the; **16.** some; **17.** a; **18.** any; **19.** a; **20.** any; **21.** a; **22.** the; **23.** a; **24.** the; **25.** the; **26.** the; **27.** the; **28.** any; **29.** the

### PRACTICE IDEA: SPEAKING

Have students practice the conversations in Exercise 13 and 14 in pairs. Give help as needed. Have volunteers role-play the conversation in front of the class.

# 3.9 Making Generalizations,
### page 81

🕐 Time: 10–15 min.

1. Explain the word *generalization* and give an example. Say: *Students are noisy. That means that all students, everywhere, are noisy. Is this true?* (no) Point out that generalizations can be true or false.

2. Have students look at grammar chart **3.9**. Review examples and explanations.

## ADDITIONAL PRACTICE

Write the following words on the board:

1. *parents*
2. *cats*
3. *sharks*
4. *doctors*
5. *buses*
6. *taxes*

Ask students to write a generalization about each topic. Have them compare their generalizations in small groups. Have volunteers write their sentences on the board.

**EXERCISE 15** pages 81–82

🕐 Time: 5–10 min.

**Answers:**

1. Homeowners have a lot of expenses.
2. Houses in San Francisco are expensive.
3. Condo associations have a lot of rules.
4. Building managers take care of buildings.
5. Renters pay rent every month.
6. Yards are good for small children.

**EXERCISE 16** page 82

🕐 Time: 5–10 min.

**Answers will vary.**

**EXERCISE 17** page 82

🕐 Time: 5–10 min.

**Answers will vary.**

**EXERCISE 18** page 83

🕐 Time: 10–15 min.

**Answers: 1.** any; **2.** any / Ø; **3.** the; **4.** a; **5.** The; **6.** Ø; **7.** a; **8.** Ø; **9.** some / Ø; **10.** the; **11.** the; **12.** a; **13.** an; **14.** a

## SUMMARY OF LESSON 3

🕐 Time: 20–30 min.

### PART A  SINGULAR AND PLURAL NOUNS

Review the rules for forming the plural of nouns. Have students review and pronounce the examples in the book. If necessary, have students review:

**3.1**  Singular and Plural Nouns (page 67)

**3.2**  Regular Plural Nouns—Spelling (page 67)

**3.3**  Plural Nouns—Pronunciation (page 69)

**3.4**  Irregular Plural Nouns (page 70)

### PART B  *THERE IS/THERE ARE*

Have students close their books. On the board, write:
  *affirmative*
  *negative*
  yes/no *question with short answer*
  *how many*

Instruct students to write two affirmative sentences (singular and plural); two negative sentences (singular and plural); two *Yes/No* questions with short answers (singular and plural); and one question using *How many*.

Say: *You can write the questions about this classroom or about where you live.* If necessary, have students review:

**3.5** *There Is/There Are* (page 72)

**3.6** Questions and Short Answers with *There* (page 75)

**3.7** *There, They,* and Other Pronouns (page 76)

## PART C ARTICLES AND *SOME/ANY*

Have students read the examples and write sentences of their own. Then put students in pairs to compare work. Circulate to observe and give help as needed. If necessary, have students review:

**3.8** Definite and Indefinite Articles (page 79)

**3.9** Making Generalizations (page 81)

## TEST/REVIEW

Time: 15 min.

Have students do the exercise on page 85. For additional practice, use the Assessment CD-ROM with Exam*View*® and the Online Workbook.

**Answers: 1.** a; **2.** bedrooms; **3.** feet; **4.** There are; **5.** apartments; **6.** the; **7.** an; **8.** It's; **9.** some; **10.** There's; **11.** a; **12.** the; **13.** days; **14.** kids; **15.** There are; **16.** families; **17.** children; **18.** the; **19.** women; **20.** the; **21.** any; **22.** guests; **23.** The; **24.** owners; **25.** people; **26.** the; **27.** The; **28.** Are there; **29.** there are; **30.** Pets are; **31.** There's; **32.** condos; **33.** Ø; **34.** the rules

## WRITING

## PART 1 EDITING ADVICE

Time: 10–15 min.

1. Have students close their books. Write a few sentences without editing marks or corrections on the board. For example:
   *People in my country is very poor.*
   *The dogs are friendly animals.*

2. Ask students to correct each sentence and provide a rule or an explanation for each correction. This activity can be done individually, in pairs, or as a class.

3. After students have corrected each sentence, tell them to turn to page 86. Say: *Now compare your work with the Editing Advice in the book.* Have students read through all the advice.

## PART 2 EDITING PRACTICE

Time: 10–15 min.

1. Tell students they are going to put the Editing Advice into practice. Ask: *Do all the shaded words and phrases have mistakes?* (no) Go over the examples with the class. Then do #1 together.

2. Have students complete the practice individually. Then have them compare answers with a partner before checking answers as a class.

3. For the items students had difficulties with, have them go back and find the relevant grammar chart and review it. Monitor and give help as necessary.

**Answers: 1.** C; **2.** a; **3.** C; **4.** There; **5.** There's (OR: Each bedroom has a large closet.); **6.** There's; **7.** the; **8.** Ø; **9.** C; **10.** think; **11.** microwaves; **12.** C; **13.** C; **14.** neighbors; **15.** They're (They are); **16.** C; **17.** woman

## PART 3 WRITE ABOUT IT

Time: 30–40 min.

1. Read the direction line aloud and tell students they can write about either their current neighborhood or a past neighborhood. Give students time to brainstorm words and phrases about their neighborhood. Do an example brainstorm on the board (e.g., *small, friends and family, market, deli, coffee shop, wide streets, children playing*) and encourage students to draw a map of their neighborhood if that helps. Before they begin writing, have students describe their neighborhood aloud in pairs. Then have them write their compositions individually. Remind students to use relevant vocabulary from the lesson on housing and use *there is/there are* in some of their sentences. Write model sentences on the board (e.g., *My neighborhood is small. There is a market and a deli. There are many children playing in the wide streets.*).

2. Repeat the procedure for the second topic. Provide examples of a brainstorm and of model sentences on the board (e.g., *my house: three bedrooms, two bathrooms, wood floors, front and back yard, one dog, big windows / In my house, there are three bedrooms. There is a front and back yard where one dog plays.*).

## PART 4 EDIT YOUR WRITING

Time: 15–20 min.

Have students edit their writing by reviewing the Lesson Summary on page 84 and the Editing Advice on page 86. Collect for assessment and/or have students share their paragraphs in pairs or small groups.

## EXPANSION ACTIVITIES

1. Have students bring in the classified section of a newspaper. Put students in groups to compare apartments. Monitor group work. Give help as needed. Have groups report "good apartment deals" to the class (e.g., *There's a really nice apartment by the park. It's only $600 a month.*).

2. Ask students to take pictures of their current homes or apartments. Ask volunteers to display the photos and describe their homes to a group or to the class. Have the audience ask follow-up questions (e.g., *Is there an elevator? Is there a garage?*).

3. Write on the board: *Renting an apartment.* Ask students what questions they have about this topic and write them on the board (e.g., *How do you find an apartment to rent in this city? Is it easy to rent an apartment? Is it very expensive?*). Then have students discuss the questions in pairs or small groups.

4. Tell students to use the Internet to look for apartments for rent and houses for sale in this city (or nearby suburbs). Tell them to find out what parts of the city or the suburbs have the highest rent and housing prices. Have them report back with their findings. As a follow-up activity, have students share their research and collaborate to make a class map illustrating their findings.

# 4 FAMILIES AND NAMES

## GRAMMAR CHARTS

## LESSON OPENER

Have students look at the photo and read the caption. Ask: *What do you see in the photo?* (trees, road sign, a highway) *Where do you think this photo was taken?* (a highway, a road in the United States) Have students read the quotation. Ask: *Are names important? Why or why not? Do you think a person's name influences the person they become? How?*

**Background:** Americans have long valued individuality as a strong American quality, and nowhere is this characteristic more salient than in naming customs. Aside from a few restrictions, Americans have the freedom to choose whatever name they like for their children and for themselves. Upon marriage, a woman traditionally adopted the family name of her spouse, but now many women either keep their birth name or hyphenate their surname with their spouse's. Cultural and religious diversity in the United States also fuel a variety of naming customs and norms. For example, African Americans typically view names as a symbol of solidarity within their communities. Latinos tend to practice customs similar to those in Spain with two given names in addition to a paternal and maternal last name. Religious names rooted in the Bible, such as Jacob, Noah, John, and Elizabeth are popular, but names from other religions, such as Mohammed, also rank very high. Over the years, other naming trends have popped up. Names that were once considered last names are now being used as first names, like Parker, Cooper, and Riley, and many parents are choosing more androgynous names, such as Casey or Taylor for their children. Other modern names have become popular through their usage in movies and TV.

William Shakespeare is widely regarded as the greatest writer in the English language. His creative contributions shaped many words and expressions used in modern-day English. He was a poet, playwright, and actor, who wrote 38 plays and 154 sonnets. He produced most of this work between 1589 and 1613, and passed away in April, 1616 at the age of 52.

## CONTEXT

This unit is about families and names. Students will read about unusual names, naming customs, and how names are assigned to hurricanes.

1.  Give students a few minutes to look through the lesson. Have them look at the photos and titles. How do they relate to the context?

2.  Elicit the topics that will be discussed.

3.  Have students discuss what they know about families and naming traditions in the United States in pairs or small groups.

4.  Ask: *What does your name mean? Is your last name your father's, mother's, spouse's, etc.? What are some naming traditions in your country or culture?* Have students share their knowledge and personal experiences.

## GRAMMAR

Students will learn about possession, object pronouns, and questions about the subject.

1.  To activate students' prior knowledge, ask what students know about possession, object pronouns, and questions about the subject.

2.  Give several examples of possessives and object pronouns (e.g., *father's, children's; me, you, him, her, us, it, them*).

3.  Have volunteers give examples and write them on the board.

## Unusual Names, page 90

### PRE-READING

🕐 Time: 5–10 min.

1. Have students look at the photo. Ask: *Who is the woman in the photo?* (Moon Unit Zappa) *What is special about her?* (she has an unusual name)

2. Have students read the title and then skim the reading. Ask: *What is the reading about? How do you know?* Have students make predictions.

3. Pre-teach any vocabulary words your students may not know, such as *popular, common, out of fashion,* and *cool.*

4. Activate students' prior knowledge about unusual names. Ask: *Do you prefer a common or an unusual name? What is the most unusual name you have ever heard? How can you describe the person with the unusual name?* Have students discuss the questions in pairs. Have a few pairs share their answers with the class.

### READING GLOSSARY

**popular:** liked or enjoyed by many people
**common:** shared by two or more people or groups
**out of fashion:** not popular or considered unattractive at the time in question
**cool:** very fashionable or appealing

### READING  🎧 CD 1 TR 16

🕐 Time: 10–15 min.

Go over the answers to the Comprehension Check on page 91: **1.** T; **2.** F; **3.** F.

---

### ADDITIONAL COMPREHENSION QUESTIONS

*What is one example of a popular boy name today in the United States?* (Noah, Liam, Mason) *What is one example of a popular girl name today?* (Sophia, Emma, Olivia) *What is one example of a name that was once out of fashion but is now popular?* (Helen, Rose, Henry, Max)

**PRACTICE IDEA: LISTENING**

Have students first listen to the audio alone. Ask a few comprehension questions, such as: *What is one example of a name that could be a girl's or boy's name?* (Arizona or Dakota) *What is one example of an unusual name?* (Zowie Bowie, Moon Unit Zappa, or Sparrow James Midnight) Repeat the audio if necessary. Then have students open their books and read along as they listen to the audio.

## 4.1 Possessive Form of Nouns, page 91

🕐 Time: 10–15 min.

1. Have students close their books. Copy grammar chart **4.1** on the board. Keep the "rule" column empty. Have volunteers read the examples aloud and confirm students' understanding of the possessive.

2. Have students study the chart in pairs and guess the rules for the endings. Have volunteers write students' ideas on the board.

3. Then ask students to look at grammar chart **4.1** and compare their answers. Review rules for understanding and point out that possession by

inanimate objects is expressed in the following way: the ___ of ___. Provide more examples as necessary.

4. Direct students' attention to the Language Notes. Provide several more examples.

## EXERCISE 1  page 91  CD 1 TR 17

🕐 Time: 10–15 min.

**Answers: 1.** My; **2.** My; **3.** My wife's; **4.** Her; **5.** Her; **6.** her grandmother's; **7.** Grandma's; **8.** their husband's; **9.** her; **10.** my; **11.** Our son's; **12.** His; **13.** Charles's; **14.** their; **15.** our; **16.** your

> ### PRACTICE IDEA: SPEAKING
> Have students get in pairs and share nicknames, if applicable. Ask them to explain the stories behind how they got the nicknames. Have volunteers share stories with the class.

## EXERCISE 2  page 92

🕐 Time: 5–10 min.

**Answers: 1.** parents' names; **2.** sisters' names; **3.** brother's name; **4.** Luis's son; **5.** grandparents' names; **6.** men's names; **7.** women's names; **8.** brother's wife

> ### PRACTICE IDEA: WRITING AND SPEAKING
> Have students write questions from the statements in Exercise 2. Then have pairs ask and answer the questions.

## EXERCISE 3  page 92

🕐 Time: 5–10 min.
**Answers will vary.**

> ### PRACTICE IDEA: SPEAKING
> Play a chain game. Have students sit in a circle. The first person says his or her name and a relative's name (e.g., *My name is Maria, and my aunt's name is Sophia.*). The person sitting next to her repeats her information and then adds his or her own information (e.g., *Her name is Maria, and her aunt's name is Sophia. My name is Oscar, and my father's name is Juan.*). The last person in the circle tries to repeat everyone's information.

## EXERCISE 4  pages 92–93

🕐 Time: 5–10 min.
**Answers:**

**1.** The teacher knows the students' names.; **2.** NC; **3.** NC; **4.** What are you parents' names?; **5.** Do you use your father's last name?; **6.** What is your dog's name?; **7.** My sisters' names are Julie and Jessica.; **8.** NC

# 4.2 Possessive Adjectives,
page 93

🕐 Time: 10–15 min.

1. Have students close their books. Copy the entire first row of grammar chart **4.2** on the board, but leave the examples and the possessive adjectives columns blank. Ask: *What is my name?* When students say your name (e.g. *Christina*), write on the board: *I am Christina. Christina is my name,* underlining the subject pronoun *I* and the possessive adjective *my*. Say the two example sentences aloud and point to *I* and *my* as you say them. Write *Christina is my name.* in the example column, and *my* in the possessive adjective column.

2. Have student work in pairs to guess the other possessive adjectives and come up with examples. Have volunteers write students' ideas on the board.

3. Have students look at grammar chart **4.2** and compare their answers. Have volunteers read additional examples aloud. Review the last two rows and solicit additional examples from the class.

4. Direct students' attention to the Language Notes. Point out the difference between *its* (the possessive adjective) and *it's* (the contraction for *it is*).

## EXERCISE 5  pages 93–94

🕐 Time: 5–10 min.

**Answers: 1.** my; **2.** his; **3.** her; **4.** its; **5.** their; **6.** your; **7.** my; **8.** our

> ### PRACTICE IDEA: WRITING AND SPEAKING
> Have students write five sentences about what they like or love. Remind them to use possessive adjectives (e.g., *I love my cell phone. I like my cousin's dog.*). Have them get in small groups and share their sentences aloud. Then have students go around, one by one, and say one thing each person likes or loves (e.g., *You love your cell phone. You like your cousin's dog.*). Finally, have a volunteer from each group share the information with the class (e.g. *She loves her cell phone. He likes his cousin's dog.*).

## 4.3 Questions with *Whose*,
### page 94

🕐 Time: 5–10 min.

1. Have students look at grammar chart **4.3**. Review the word order pattern for questions with *whose*.

2. Have student read aloud the questions and answers in pairs. Then, have them write three more questions and answers of their own.

---

**PRACTICE IDEA: SPEAKING**

Have students get in a circle and write on the board: *Whose ___ is this?* Have students select something of their own and secretly collect their objects in a bag. Go around the circle with the bag, and have students pick an object from the bag, one by one. Student A takes out an object and asks Student B to the left: *Whose <u>comb</u> is this?* If Student B guesses wrong (e.g., *It's Luisa's comb.*), Student A asks the next student to the left: *Whose <u>comb</u> is this?* Student A keeps asking until somebody gets the answer correct. Then, Student B picks an object from the bag and repeats the activity.

---

### EXERCISE 6  pages 94–95

🕐 Time: 5–10 min.

**Answers:**

1. Whose kids are they?
2. Whose book is it?
3. Whose last name do your children use?
4. Whose class do you have for math?
5. Whose cat is it/that?
6. Whose name do you like?

---

**PRACTICE IDEA: SPEAKING**

Have students read the conversations from Exercise 6 aloud in pairs. Have volunteers role-play them in front of the class.

---

## 4.4 Possessive Pronouns,
### page 95

🕐 Time: 5–10 min.

1. Have students close their books. Copy the first row of grammar chart **4.4** on the board, but leave the examples and the possessive pronouns columns

blank. Ask: *What is my name?* When students say your name (e.g. *Christina*), write on the board: *Christina is my name,* underlining the possessive adjective *my*. Say: *Some names are hard for Americans to pronounce. Mine is easy.* Write *Mine is easy.* in the example column, and *mine* in the possessive pronoun column. Underline the possessive pronoun *Mine.* Say the two example sentences aloud and point to *my* and *mine* as you say them.

2. Have students work in pairs to guess the other possessive pronouns and come up with examples. Have volunteers write students' ideas on the board.

3. Have students look at grammar chart **4.4** and compare their answers. Have volunteers read additional examples aloud. Review the last row and provide several examples.

### EXERCISE 7  page 96

🕐 Time: 5–10 min.

**Answers: 1.** Mine; **2.** it; **3.** yours; **4.** his; **5.** Hers; **6.** Theirs; **7.** Ours

---

**PRACTICE IDEA: SPEAKING**

Have students make comparisons using possessive pronouns. Write on the board: *Your ____ is ____, but mine is ____.* Model a couple of comparisons (e.g., *Your hair is long, but mine is short. Your backpack is black, but my purse is dark green.*). Have students mingle and compare themselves and their objects.

---

### EXERCISE 8  page 96

🕐 Time: 5–10 min.

**Answers: 1.** your; **2.** yours; **3.** Mine; **4.** my; **5.** Your; **6.** his; **7.** our; **8.** our; **9.** their; **10.** my; **11.** theirs

---

**PRACTICE IDEA: SPEAKING**

Have students write their own conversation in pairs and read it aloud. Have volunteers role-play the conversation for the class.

---

## READING

# Naming Customs, page 97

## PRE-READING

🕐 Time: 5–10 min.

1. Have students look at the photo and read the caption. Ask: *Who are the people in the photo?* (a man and his baby; a dad and his son)

2. Have students read the title and then skim the reading. Ask: *What is the reading about? How do you know?* Have students make predictions.

3. Pre-teach any vocabulary words your students may not know, such as *nickname*.

4. Activate students' prior knowledge about naming customs and traditions. Ask: *What are some common naming customs in your country? Do you have a nickname?* Have students share their experiences in pairs. Have a few volunteers share their answers with the class.

## READING GLOSSARY

**nickname:** an informal name given to a person, in addition to a legal one

## READING

🕐 Time: 10–15 min.

Go over the answers to the Comprehension Check on page 97: **1.** T; **2.** F; **3.** F.

## ADDITIONAL COMPREHENSION QUESTIONS

*How many names does William have?* (four) *Why do William's friends call him Bill?* (It's a common nickname for William) *Why does William include "Junior" when he signs his name?* (because he has the same name as his father) *What is his wife's nickname?* (Annie) *Why does his wife have two last names?* (One is hers, and one is her husband's)

### EXPANDING ON THE READING

The topic for this reading can be enhanced with the following items:

1. Lists of baby-naming traditions from around the world

2. Family trees

3. Videos about naming traditions in various religions and cultures, such as Jewish, Sikh, and Navajo traditions

### PRACTICE IDEA: LISTENING

Have students first listen to the audio alone. Write the object pronouns on the board (*me, you, him, her, us, it, them*). Have them count how many object pronouns they hear (thirteen). Then have students open their books and read along as they listen to the audio.

# 4.5 The Subject and the Object, page 98

🕐 Time: 5–10 min.

1. Write on the board:
   *1. I teach.*
   *2. I teach three classes.*
   *3. I teach about the English language.*

   Ask: *What are the subjects of the sentences? What are the verbs? What are the objects?* Have students discuss in pairs, then share ideas with the class. Write *S, V,* and *O* above examples. Explain that objects can be a person or a thing that give essential or additional information.

2. Have students look at grammar chart **4.5** (the first chart). Read through the examples and explanations. Have students provide additional examples of sentences with objects to check for comprehension.

3. Review the second chart. Have volunteers read the examples aloud. Encourage them to emphasize subject and object pronouns as they read.

4. Direct students' attention to the Language Notes. Provide several additional examples.

### EXERCISE 9  pages 98–99

🕐 Time: 5–10 min.

**Answers: 1.** me; **2.** it; **3.** them; **4.** you; **5.** her; **6.** him; **7.** us

### EXERCISE 10  page 99

🕐 Time: 5–10 min.

**Answers: 1.** us; **2.** you; **3.** her; **4.** him; **5.** me; **6.** them; **7.** her; **8.** it; **9.** her; **10.** me; **11.** them

**EXERCISE 11** page 99

Time: 5–10 min.

**Answers: 1.** I'm; **2.** I'm; **3.** I; **4.** My; **5.** Mine; **6.** me

**EXERCISE 12** page 100

Time: 5–10 min.

**Answers: 1.** You're; **2.** You; **3.** you; **4.** Yours; **5.** You're; **6.** Your

**EXERCISE 13** page 100

Time: 5–10 min.

**Answers: 1.** His; **2.** He's; **3.** He; **4.** his; **5.** him; **6.** His

**EXERCISE 14** page 100

Time: 5–10 min.

**Answers: 1.** Her; **2.** She's; **3.** her; **4.** She; **5.** Hers; **6.** Her

**EXERCISE 15** page 101

Time: 5–10 min.

**Answers: 1.** it; **2.** It's; **3.** it; **4.** It's; **5.** It; **6.** Its

**EXERCISE 16** page 101

Time: 5–10 min.

**Answers: 1.** We're; **2.** We; **3.** We're; **4.** Our; **5.** us; **6.** Ours

**EXERCISE 17** page 101

Time: 5–10 min.

**Answers: 1.** They; **2.** They're; **3.** They; **4.** Their; **5.** Theirs; **6.** them

## READING

# Who Names Hurricanes?

pages 102–103

## PRE-READING

Time: 5–10 min.

1. Have students look at the photo. Ask: *What is in the photo?* (Hurricane Earl) *Where is it heading?* (toward the United States)

2. Have students read the title and then skim the reading. Ask: *What is the reading about? How do you know?* Have students make predictions.

3. Pre-teach any vocabulary words your students may not know, such as *tropical, storm, Atlantic,* and *Pacific.*

4. Activate students' prior knowledge about hurricanes. Ask: *Have you ever been in a hurricane or known anybody who has been in a hurricane? What was the experience like?* Have students discuss the questions in pairs. Have a few pairs share their answers with the class.

## READING GLOSSARY

**tropical:** near the equator where the weather is very warm

**storm:** bad weather with a lot of rain, snow, and wind

**Atlantic:** area separating North and South America from Europe and Africa

**Pacific:** area separating North and South America from Asia and Australia

## READING CD 1 TR 19

Time: 10–15 min.

Go over the answers to the Comprehension Check on page 103: **1.** F; **2.** T; **3.** T.

## ADDITIONAL COMPREHENSION QUESTIONS

*What is one thing the World Meteorological Organization (WMO) does?* (names hurricanes and topical storms) *A storm gets a name when it reaches how many miles per hour?* (39) *Does the WMO use men's or women's names?* (both) *How many lists of names are there?* (six)

### EXPANDING ON THE READING

The topic for this reading can be enhanced with the following items:

1. Photos and news articles of the famous hurricanes of the twentieth and twenty-first centuries
2. Clips from videos from the World Meteorological Organization
3. Maps of regions most affected by hurricanes and tropical storms

### PRACTICE IDEA: LISTENING

Have students first listen to the audio alone. Have them write all the *Wh-* words they hear (*Who, When, What, Why*). Then have students open their books and read along as they listen to the audio.

### PRACTICE IDEA: SPEAKING

Have students look at the chart of 2017 Hurricane Names in pairs. Have them choose their top three favorite names and explain why to their partner.

## 4.6 Subject Questions and Nonsubject Questions, pages 103–104

🕐 Time: 10–15 min.

1. Have students analyze the reading on page 102. Have them underline the questions with *do* or *does* and circle the questions with a verb in the *-s* form.
2. Have students look at grammar chart **4.6**. Read the examples with volunteers answering your questions. Read through the explanations carefully.
3. Have students match the questions in the reading with the explanations in the chart.

---

4. Direct students' attention to the Language Notes. Emphasize that *who* is more common in informal English. Provide additional examples of *who* versus *whom*, and the use of *Who knows?*

### EXERCISE 18 pages 104–105

🕐 Time: 5–10 min.

**Answers:**

**1. a.** has, **b.** does, **c.** calls, **d.** do, **e.** do you call; **2. a.** has, **b.** do, **c.** don't you like calling; **3. a.** has, **b.** does, **c.** does it have, **d.** do you spell, **e.** does it come from, **f.** does it mean; **4. a.** Do you like, **b.** replaces, **c.** does, **d.** has, **e.** does

### PRACTICE IDEA: SPEAKING

Write questions from Exercise 18 on the board: *Who has an uncommon name in your family? Who in your family has a nickname? How many letters are in your name? Where does your name come from? What does your name mean? Do you like your name?* Have students stand in two concentric circles, with half the students standing in an outer ring around the classroom and the other half standing in an inner ring, facing each other. Have students ask and answer the questions from Exercise 18. Call out *turn* every minute or so. Students in the inner ring should move one space clockwise. Now have students ask and answer with their new partners. Have students ask questions in random order. Make sure students look at each other when they're speaking.

## 4.7 Who, Whom, Whose, Who's, page 105

🕐 Time: 5–10 min.

1. Have students close their books. Write on the board:

   | | |
   |---|---|
   | 1. who | a. who is |
   | 2. whose | b. object |
   | 3. who's | c. possession (ownership) |
   | 4. who(m) | d. subject |

   Then ask students to match the columns. (**Answers: 1.** d; **2.** c; **3.** a; **4.** b)

2. Have students look at grammar chart **4.7**. Have volunteers read examples aloud and review the explanations. Remind students that *whom* is now considered very formal, and it is more common to hear *who* as the object.

## EXERCISE 19 page 106

🕐 Time: 5–10 min.

**Answers: 1.** Whose; **2.** Who(m); **3.** Who's; **4.** Who; **5.** Whose; **6.** Who

---

**PRACTICE IDEA: SPEAKING**

Have students practice the conversation from Exercise 19 in pairs. Ask volunteers to role-play all or part of the conversation in front of the class.

---

## EXERCISE 20 pages 106–107

🕐 Time: 5–10 min.

**Answers: 1.** Whose; **2.** Mine; **3.** Who; **4.** decides; **5.** happens

## EXERCISE 21 page 107

🕐 Time: 10–15 min.

**Answers: 1.** your; **2.** it's; **3.** parent's; **4.** His; **5.** He's; **6.** his; **7.** girl's; **8.** His; **9.** I; **10.** sister's; **11.** her; **12.** she's; **13.** Who's; **14.** She's; **15.** has; **16.** Its; **17.** Whose coat is that; **18.** yours; **19.** mine; **20.** yours; **21.** mine; **22.** Whose; **23.** him

---

**PRACTICE IDEA: WRITING AND SPEAKING**

Have pairs write a conversation using subject pronouns, object pronouns, possessive pronouns, possessive nouns, and possessive adjectives. Ask volunteers to role-play their conversations in front of the class.

---

## SUMMARY OF LESSON 4

🕐 Time: 20–30 min.

## PART A POSSESSIVE NOUNS—FORMS

Review the example sentences. Then have students talk about things in the classroom using possessive pronouns (e.g., *Maria's notebook is blue and white.*). If necessary, have students review:

**4.1** Possessive Nouns—Form (page 91)

## PART B PRONOUNS AND POSSESSIVE FORMS

Have students close their books. Write the chart headings across the top of the board. Write the subject pronouns in the first column. Have students come up to the board to fill in the chart with pronouns and possessive forms. Then have volunteers write sentences and questions with the pronouns and possessive forms. Have students open their books and compare their charts with the charts in the book. Go over the example sentences in the book. If necessary, have students review:

**4.2** Possessive Adjectives (page 93)

**4.3** Questions with *Whose* (page 94)

**4.4** Possessive Pronouns (page 95)

**4.5** The Subject and the Object (page 98)

**4.6** Subject Questions and Nonsubject Questions (pages 103–104)

**4.7** *Who, Whom, Whose, Who's* (page 105)

---

## TEST/REVIEW

🕐 Time: 15 min.

Have students do the exercise on page 109. For additional practice, use the Assessment CD-ROM with Exam*View*® and the Online Workbook.

**Answers: 1.** Who's; **2.** My; **3.** yours; **4.** Charles's; **5.** His; **6.** hers; **7.** her; **8.** husband's; **9.** Whose; **10.** They; **11.** your; **12.** her; **13.** our; **14.** her; **15.** ours; **16.** his; **17.** him; **18.** he's; **19.** it's; **20.** It's; **21.** She; **22.** them; **23.** their; **24.** mine; **25.** we're

---

## WRITING

## PART 1 EDITING ADVICE

🕐 Time: 10–15 min.

1. Have students close their books. Write the first few sentences without editing marks or corrections on the board. For example:

   *Your a good person.*

   *Where's you're book?*

2. Ask students to correct each sentence and provide a rule or an explanation for each correction. This activity can be done individually, in pairs, or as a class.

3. After students have corrected each sentence, tell them to turn to page 110. Say: *Now compare your work with the Editing Advice in the book.* Have students read through all the advice.

## PART 2 EDITING PRACTICE
🕐 Time: 10–15 min.

1. Tell students they are going to put the Editing Advice into practice. Ask: *Do all the shaded words and phrases have mistakes?* (no) Go over the examples with the class. Then do #1 together.

2. Have students complete the practice individually. Then have them compare answers with a partner before checking answers as a class.

3. For the items students had difficulties with, have them go back and find the relevant grammar chart and review it. Monitor and give help as necessary.

**Answers: 1.** My; **2.** C; **3.** names; **4.** parents'; **5.** C; **6.** C; **7.** her; **8.** her; **9.** husband's; **10.** C; **11.** Her; **12.** Their; **13.** C; **14.** My sister and I; **15.** our; **16.** you're; **17.** C; **18.** They're; **19.** It's; **20.** C

## PART 3 WRITE ABOUT IT
🕐 Time: 30–40 min.

1. Review the topic with students. Do a class brainstorm of traditional and unusual names. Write students' ideas on the board. Have students answer the question in pairs, explaining their point of view to their partner. Encourage students to organize their thoughts and make notes before they begin to write. Remind them to include any useful and relevant vocabulary from this lesson on families and names and to be careful with their use of possessive forms. If necessary, write model topic sentences on the board first.

2. Have students brainstorm naming customs in their cultures. Provide guidance and clarification with vocabulary and ideas. Then have them write their compositions individually. Encourage students to add more information about their name and their families' names. Collect for assessment and/or have students share their compositions with the group.

## PART 4 EDIT YOUR WRITING
🕐 Time: 15–20 min.

Have students edit their writing by reviewing the Lesson Summary on page 108 and the Editing Advice on page 110. Collect for assessment and/or have students share their essays in small groups.

## EXPANSION ACTIVITIES

1. Have students learn and remember each other's name. Have students stand in a circle. Write on the board: *What's your name? What do you like?* The student introduces him or herself using this format: *My name is x, and I like x.* The thing students like should start with the same sound as their name. Give your own example to the class (e.g., *My name is Christina, and I like coffee.*) Every student uses the same format. Start the activity by asking a student in the circle. The person who asked the question has to introduce his or her classmate using the answers they provide, and then the student who answered asks the questions to someone else. Repeat until all students have introduced themselves.

2. Have students interview three people from different cultures about their names. Brainstorm questions students can ask. Write them on the board (e.g., *Your name is interesting—tell me about it. Do you have your father's name? Is your last name your father's name or your mother's name?*). Tell students to ask these questions and then report back to the class. Compare what cultures have similar naming customs.

3. Have students browse different baby name directories and lists on the Internet. Have them make a list of their top five favorite names. Then, have students share the names on their lists with a partner and explain why they like them.

4. Have students make acrostic name poems (write the letters of their name to spell it out in a vertical line). For each line, students should write an adjective or phrase for each letter of the name that describes their own qualities or characteristics (e.g., CHAO would be Comfortable, Happy, Always on time, Organized). Help students with adjectives as necessary. Have students share in pairs and post the name poems around the room.

# 5 PLANET IN DANGER

## GRAMMAR CHARTS

## LESSON OPENER

Have students look at the photo and read the caption. Ask: *What is happening in the photo?* (An underwater pipe exploded; there is fire in the ocean) *Where was this photo taken?* (the Gulf of Mexico) Have students read the quotation. Ask: *Do you agree with the quote? Why or why not?*

**Background:** Since the nineteenth century, the people of the United States have had a passion for nature and a commitment to preservation. The early conservation movement began, thanks to the work of key figures such as John Muir. Federal legislation was written to protect the National Park System and its natural resources and wildlife. In 1948, the Federal Water Pollution Act was passed, and the Air Pollution Control Act followed in 1955. Since then, the United States has attempted to keep up with global efforts aimed at reducing global warming and fighting climate change. In the 2015 Global Summit, a global team negotiated an agreement to reduce greenhouse gas emissions to limit the global temperature increase. The United States plays an important role in this agreement as it is a top emitter of greenhouse gases, second only to China. Some activities that contribute to these high emissions are logging, mining, and other digging, and development practices such as hydraulic fracturing, also known as fracking.

Throughout his life, Mahatma Gandhi, born Mohandas Karamchand Gandhi, was an advocate for civil rights and a proponent of peaceful forms of civil disobedience. At home, he led the struggle for India's independence from British rule, but his influence was worldwide. At age 78, he was shot and killed on his way to a prayer meeting.

## CONTEXT

This unit is about our planet in danger. Students will read about saving lemurs, disappearing birds, and climate change.

1. Give students a few minutes to look through the lesson. Have them look at the photos and titles. How do they relate to the context?

2. Elicit the topics that will be discussed.

3. Have students discuss what they know about why our planet is in danger in pairs or small groups.

## GRAMMAR

Students will learn about the present continuous verb tense.

1. To activate students' prior knowledge, ask what students know about the present continuous verb tense.

2. Give several examples of the present continuous verb tense (e.g., *I am walking. We are studying.*).

3. Have volunteers give examples and write them on the board.

### EXPANDING ON THE CONTEXT

The context for this lesson can be enhanced with the following items:

1. Clips from climate change documentaries such as *Chasing Ice* or *An Inconvenient Truth*

2. Diagrams illustrating climate change, global warming, and weather patterns

3. Animal encyclopedias

## READING

# Saving Lemurs, page 114–115

## PRE-READING

⏱ Time: 5–10 min.

1. Have students look at the photo and read the caption. Ask: *What is this animal?* (a lemur) *Where does it live?* (Madagascar)

2. Have students read the title and then skim the reading. Ask: *What is the reading about? How do you know?* Have students make predictions.

3. Pre-teach any vocabulary words your students may not know, such as *to raise, to try, to disappear,* and *population.*

4. Ask: *Have you ever seen a lemur? What are some animals native to your home country and region?* Have volunteers share their knowledge and personal experiences.

## READING GLOSSARY

**to raise:** to take care of and teach
**to try:** to make an effort to do something
**to disappear:** to stop existing
**population:** the number of people who live in a place

## READING  CD 1 TR 20

⏱ Time: 10–15 min.

Go over the answers to the Comprehension Check on page 115: **1.** T; **2.** T; **3.** F.

## CONTEXT NOTE

According to scientists in 2015, ten of the animal species most likely to go extinct in the near future are:

1. Northern White Rhino
2. Ivory-billed Woodpecker
3. Amur Leopard
4. South China Tiger
5. Little Dodo Bird
6. Mountain Gorilla
7. Saola
8. Vaquita
9. Hawaiian Crow
10. Javan Rhino

---

### PRESENTATION IDEA

Display photos of the animal species most likely to go extinct. Have students describe the animals in pairs using possessive nouns, pronouns, and adjectives to review material from Lesson 4. Have volunteers share descriptions in front of the class.

## ADDITIONAL COMPREHENSION QUESTIONS

*About how many lemurs are scientists raising at Duke University?* (250) *How many species of lemurs are there?* (about one hundred) *How much does it costs per year to take care of a lemur?* (over $7,000)

### EXPANDING ON THE READING

The topic for this reading can be enhanced with the following items:

1. Photos of different lemur species
2. Educational videos from the Duke Lemur Center
3. Live cam of lemurs at the Reid Park Zoo
4. Clips from the animated movie *Madagascar*
5. Maps of Madagascar and its protected areas
6. Excerpts from video interviews with Earthwatch scientist Dr. Luke Dollar about Madagascar's protected areas

### PRACTICE IDEA: LISTENING

Have students first listen to the audio alone. Ask a few comprehension questions, such as: *What is the lemur's native country?* (Madagascar) *Where are scientists breeding lemurs?* (at Duke University in North Carolina) *How do you know if a baby lemur is healthy?* (if it is gaining weight) Repeat the audio if necessary. Then have students open their books and read along as they listen to the audio.

## 5.1 The Present Continuous—Forms, pages 115–116

⏱ Time: 10–15 min.

1. Have students analyze the bold-faced phrases in the reading on page 114. Ask: *What do these bold-faced phrases have in common?* Have them work in pairs to notice patterns and guess the rule for forming the present continuous verb tense. Write students' ideas on the board.

2. Have students look at grammar chart **5.1** and compare their ideas. Read the examples aloud and explain that the present continuous is used to describe an action in progress at this moment.

3. Direct students' attention to the Language Notes. Explain that contractions are made with the pronoun and the verb *be*. Also point out that most nouns can form a contraction with *is*. Give several more examples of adverbs used with the present continuous.

### EXERCISE 1  pages 116–117   CD 1 TR 21

⏱ Time: 5–10 min.

**Answers: 1.** 'm watching; **2.** 'm not doing; **3.** are living; **4.** is studying; **5.** are trying; **6.** are cutting down; **7.** are losing; **8.** 're looking; **9.** are dying; **10.** is working; **11.** 's trying

---

**PRACTICE IDEA: SPEAKING**

Have students compare their answers in pairs and read the conversation aloud. Have volunteers read the conversation aloud in front of the class.

---

**PRACTICE IDEA: SPEAKING**

Put students in groups and play charades. Say: *One student acts out an activity, and the other students in the group guess what it is.* If necessary, write activities on slips of paper and have students choose an activity. Model the activity first and remind students to use the present continuous tense to describe the activity (e.g., *Pedro's watching TV.*).

---

## 5.2 Spelling of the *-ing* Form, page 117

⏱ Time: 10–15 min.

1. Have students close their books. Copy the example lists of verbs (base form and *-ing* form) from grammar chart **5.2** on the board. Make sure you separate the seven sets of verbs. For example:

| | |
|---|---|
| eat | eating |
| plan | planning |
| show | showing |
| refer | referring |
| open | opening |
| write | writing |
| lie | lying |

2. First, elicit the vowels in English and write them on the board. Then, review the number of syllables in the base verbs on the board. Clap the syllables out as students guess how many syllables each base verb has. Write the number of syllables by the base verbs and underline the syllable that is stressed.

3. With this information, have students work in pairs to analyze the spelling changes and come up with the seven spelling rules to form the *-ing* form. Remind them to focus on consonants, vowels, syllables, and stress. Write students' ideas on the board.

4. Have students look at grammar chart **5.2** and compare their ideas. Clarify any confusion.

### EXERCISE 2  page 118

⏱ Time: 10–15 min.

**Answers: 1.** playing; **2.** making; **3.** hitting; **4.** suffering; **5.** cutting; **6.** admitting; **7.** trying; **8.** happening; **9.** staying; **10.** growing; **11.** hurrying; **12.** grabbing; **13.** raising; **14.** fixing; **15** rescuing; **16.** doing; **17.** breeding; **18.** losing; **19.** waiting; **20.** serving; **21.** visiting; **22.** occurring; **23.** dying; **24.** disappearing

---

**PRACTICE IDEA: WRITING**

Have students choose five verbs from Exercise 2 that they would use the most in their daily lives. Have them write five sentences using the present continuous. Encourage them to use a variety of subjects. Have them give peer feedback in pairs.

---

### EXERCISE 3  page 118

⏱ Time: 5–10 min.

**Answers: 1.** are suffering; **2.** 're losing; **3.** 're disappearing; **4.** is rescuing; **5.** are working; **6.** is having; **7.** are catching; **8.** selling; **9.** are stealing; **10.** 's trying

## 5.3 The Present Continuous— Use, page 119

⏱ Time: 5–10 min.

1. Have students close their books. Write the following matching exercise on the board:

   *1.* *We are watching a show on TV now.*

   *2.* *Steve Boyes is trying to teach people about parrots.*

   *3.* *The babies are sleeping now.*

   *a.* *to show a long-term action that is in progress*

   *b.* *to describe a state or condition*

   *c.* *to show that an action is in progress now, at this moment*

   Have students work in pairs to match the example with the rule. (**Answers: 1.** c; **2.** a; **3.** b)

2. Have students look at grammar chart **5.3** and compare their answers. Review additional examples.

---

**PRACTICE IDEA: WRITING**

Have students write two sentences for each of the three rules. Say: *Look at the classroom right now. What is happening?* Have volunteers write their sentences on the board.

---

### EXERCISE 4 page 119

⏱ Time: 5–10 min.

**Answers:** (Note: accept contracted and non-contracted forms.)

**1.** African parrots are losing their homes.

**2.** The teacher is not / The teacher isn't / The teacher's not showing us a video about lemurs.

**3.** We are / We're learning about animals in this lesson.

**4.** I am / I'm writing sentences about animals.

**5.** Steve Boyes isn't / is not studying lemurs.

**6.** Boyes is trying to rescue parrots.

**7.** Unhealthy baby lemurs aren't / are not gaining weight.

**8.** Many lemurs are living at the Lemur Center.

## 5.4 Questions with the Present Continuous, page 120

⏱ Time: 10–15 min.

1. Have students close their books. Write on the board:

   *1.* *I am teaching grammar.*

   *2.* *Juan is studying.*

   *3.* *The class is learning English.*

First, ask students what the subject and verb is in each sentence. Circle the subjects and underline the verbs. Then, ask students to work in pairs to make a *Yes/No* and *Wh-* question from each sentence. Have volunteers write questions on the board.

2. Have students look at grammar chart **5.4**. Review the examples for *Yes/No* questions and short answers and *Wh-* questions. Compare students' ideas with the chart.

3. Finally, review the subject questions. Provide additional examples as necessary.

## ADDITIONAL PRACTICE

1. If possible, have students exchange phone numbers and text each other using the present continuous. Provide examples on the board (e.g., *Hi! I am thinking about the weekend. Really? I'm not. I'm doing homework.*).

2. Have students get on social media and share information about their family and friends back home in pairs (e.g., *This is my cousin. Look at his picture! His name is Abdullah. Right now, he's studying mechanical engineering at the university. This is his mom. She's not working, but his dad is. He is teaching at the same university. I think he's teaching in the business department.*). Have volunteers share what they learned about their classmates.

3. Have students write an e-mail to a friend back home. Have them describe what they are doing right now and what their long-term actions are for the semester or course. Have students exchange e-mails for peer feedback. Have volunteers read their e-mails to the class.

---

**PRACTICE IDEA: WRITING**

Have students return to the reading on page 114 and choose four statements in the present continuous. Have them change these statements into either *Yes/No* or *Wh-* questions. Have them ask and answer the questions in pairs. Be sure that students are responding with short answers.

---

### EXERCISE 5 pages 121–122

⏱ Time: 5–10 min.

**Answers: 1. a.** Is he studying, **b.** is, **c.** 's studying, **d.** is he / Steve Boyes studying; **2. a.** Are you learning **b.** am, **c.** are you learning; **3. a.** are (some) parrots (or they) losing, **b.** Am I bothering; **4. a.** Are, **b.** reading, **c.** I'm not, **d.** are you reading; **5. a.** 's / is, **b.** 's, **c.** isn't he doing; **6. a.** taking, **b.** are scientists taking; **7. a.** Are, **b.** 're not / aren't, **c.** aren't they gaining; **8.** Are you writing, **b.** am, **c.** are you writing

## PRACTICE IDEA: SPEAKING

Have volunteers role-play all or part of the conversation in Exercise 5 in front of the class.

## EXERCISE 6 page 122

🕐 Time: 5–10 min.
**Answers will vary.**

## PRACTICE IDEA: SPEAKING

Have students stand in two concentric circles, with half the students standing in an outer ring around the classroom and the other half standing in an inner ring, facing each other. Instruct students to ask and answer the questions from Exercise 6. Call out *turn* every minute or so. Students in the inner ring should move one space clockwise. Now have students ask and answer with their new partner. Have students ask questions in random order. Make sure students look at each other when they're speaking.

READING

# Disappearing Birds, page 123

## PRE-READING

🕐 Time: 5–10 min.

1. Have students look at the photo and read the caption. Ask: *What is this animal?* (a puffin) *Where does it live?* (Iceland)
2. Have students read the title and then skim the reading. Ask: *What is the reading about? How do you know?* Have students make predictions.
3. Pre-teach any vocabulary words your students may not know, such as *desert, safe, to go down,* and *chemical.*
4. Ask: *Have you ever seen a puffin? What are some animals that are going extinct in your home country and region?* Have volunteers share their knowledge and personal experiences.

## READING GLOSSARY

**desert:** an area of very dry, hot land
**safe:** not in danger
**to go down:** to become smaller in size
**chemical:** a substance made by chemical process

## READING

🕐 Time: 10–15 min.
Go over the answers to the Comprehension Check on page 124: **1.** T; **2.** F; **3.** T.

## CONTEXT NOTE

Climate change is extremely dangerous to animals that struggle to adapt to new weather conditions. Species that have specialized in what they eat or where they live are the hardest hit as they are forced to change their strict behaviors in order to survive. Birds are among these species and have begun nesting, breeding, and migrating earlier as seasons become more irregular. Hundreds of different bird species have seen population decline in recent years. As of 2012, more than 1,300 bird species are facing extinction.

## ADDITIONAL COMPREHENSION QUESTIONS

*How do birds help human beings?* (they carry seeds, they control bugs) *How many birds migrate?* (one out of five) *What is causing the bird populations to go down?* (chemicals in the environment) *What do birds eat?* (insects, fish, dead animals) *What messages are birds sending to humans?* (messages about our health and the health of the planet)

## EXPANDING ON THE READING

The topic for this reading can be enhanced with the following items:

1. Maps of bird migration patterns and habitats
2. Lists of hints to help migrating and nesting birds
3. Photos and information about the four species of Puffin
4. Biography of Susan Schubel "Seabird Sue," the outreach educator for Audubon's Project Puffin and winner of Disney Conservation's Hero Award

## PRACTICE IDEA: LISTENING

Have students first listen to the audio alone. Have them count how many times they hear the present continuous verb tense (seventeen). If possible, have them write examples of the present continuous as they hear them. Repeat the audio if necessary. Then have students open their books and read along as they listen to the audio.

## PRESENTATION IDEA

Have students re-read paragraph four. On blank sheets of paper, have students work in pairs to draw a diagram illustrating how chemicals affect birds (e.g., 1. Insects, fish, and other animals take in chemicals from environment. 2. Birds eat insects and fish. / Some birds eat dead animals. 3. These animals give birds health problems.). Have volunteers present their diagrams and describe them to the class.

## 5.5 The Present Continuous vs. the Simple Present— Forms, page 124

🕐 Time: 10–15 min.

1. Have students look at grammar chart **5.5**. In pairs, have them discuss the differences between the present continuous and simple present verb form. Lead a class discussion comparing the verb tenses, and write students' ideas on the board.

**EXERCISE 7** pages 124–125

🕐 Time: 5–10 min.

**Answers: 1.** are losing; **2.** are taking; **3.** are suffering; **4.** is going down; **5.** are we doing; **6.** is working; **7.** is helping; **8.** are having; **9.** need; **10.** don't know; **11.** don't have; **12.** Do we want

### PRACTICE IDEA: SPEAKING

Have students cover up Exercise 7 after completing the task. Write on the board: *What is Luke Dollar doing? Why is he doing this?* Have students summarize and review the information in pairs. Remind them to use the present continuous in their responses.

## 5.6 The Present Continuous vs. the Simple Present—Use, page 125

🕐 Time: 5–10 min.

1. Have students close their books. Ask: *What do we use the simple present tense for?* (to talk about a habitual activity, a custom, or a general truth or fact) Solicit

example sentences in the simple present and write them on the board. *What do we use the present continuous for?* (to show actions in progress at this moment, to show long-term action in progress, to describe a state or condition) Solicit example sentences in the simple present and write them on the board.

2. Have students look at grammar chart **5.6** and compare their ideas and examples with the chart. Review additional examples and provide more if necessary.

## EXERCISE 8 page 125

🕐 Time: 10–15 min.

**Answers:** (Note: accept contracted and non-contracted forms.)

**1.** are you doing; **2.** 'm eating; **3.** eat; **4.** 'm also watching; **5.** are you watching; **6.** 'm taking; **7.** 're studying; **8.** are you learning; **9.** 'm learning; **10.** eat; **11.** 's diving; **12.** do pelicans live; **13.** live

### PRACTICE IDEA: WRITING

Write on the board:

1. a. *Every afternoon*    b. *This afternoon*
2. a. *Normally*           b. *Now*
3. a. *Usually*            b. *Right now*
4. a. *Always*             b. *At this moment*

Then, write a number of verbs on the board, such as *do, think, study, play, eat, drink*, etc. Have students work in pairs to write four sentences with the simple present and present continuous with four of the verbs from the list. Write an example on the board: *Every afternoon I eat a sandwich, but this afternoon I am eating soup.* Have volunteers share their sentences with the class.

## READING

# Climate Change, page 126

### PRE-READING

🕐 Time: 5–10 min.

1. Have students look at the photo and read the caption. Ask: *Who are the people in the photo?* (scientists) *What are they doing?* (in a boat, melting ice sheets) *Where are they?* (Antarctica)

2. Have students read the title and then skim the reading. Ask: *What is the reading about? How do you know?* Have students make predictions.

3. Pre-teach any vocabulary words your students may not know, such as *sheet, to be responsible, industry,* and *to be in danger.*

4. Ask: *Has the climate changed in recent years in your home country and region? What are some reasons why it has changed?* Have volunteers share their knowledge and personal experiences.

## READING GLOSSARY

**sheet:** a thin, flat, rectangular piece of something

**to be responsible:** to cause something to happen

**industry:** group of businesses that provide a particular product or service

**to be in danger:** to be in a situation where you may be hurt or killed

## READING  CD 1 TR 24

🕐 Time: 10–15 min.

Go over the answers to the Comprehension Check on page 127: **1.** T; **2.** T; **3.** T.

## CONTEXT NOTE

According to the U.S. Environmental Protection Agency (EPA), there are different ways humans can help prevent and slow climate change at home, at the office, on the road, and at school. Some of these include changing light fixtures and lightbulbs from standard to energy efficient brands, using public transportation or telecommuting, buying fuel-efficient or electric vehicles, and increasing recycling practices in our schools.

## ADDITIONAL COMPREHENSION QUESTIONS

*What is the size of ice sheets?* (very big) *What is happening to the temperature of the ocean?* (It is getting warmer) *What are some activities that warm the planet?* (transportation, electricity production, industry) *What places are in danger of being underwater?* (coastal cities)

## EXPANDING ON THE READING

The topic for this reading can be enhanced with the following items:

1. EPA's Household Carbon Footprint Calculator
2. Interactive maps of sea level rise and coastal cities affected
3. Free climate change mobile apps, such as Images of Change or Earth Now
4. NASA's Offset, a free iOS education game (mobile app)
5. Photos and diagrams of Antarctic ice sheets

## PRACTICE IDEA: LISTENING

Have students first listen to the audio alone. Have them count how many times they hear the simple present verb tense (seven). If possible, have them write examples of the simple present as they hear them. Repeat the audio if necessary. Then have students open their books and read along as they listen to the audio.

## PRESENTATION IDEA

Have students re-read paragraph three. On blank sheets of paper, have students work in pairs to draw a diagram illustrating how the climate is changing ice sheets (e.g., 1. The ocean warms. 2. Big pieces of ice break away. 3. These pieces go into the ocean. 4. This causes the ocean level to rise.). Have volunteers present their diagrams and describe them to the class. Hang the diagrams around the room and invite other classes to a poster fair.

## 5.7 Action and Nonaction Verbs, page 127

🕐 Time: 10–15 min.

1. Have students analyze the reading on page 126 in pairs. Have them underline all the verbs and guess if they are action or nonaction. Make two columns (*action* and *nonaction*) on the board and write students' ideas in the columns. Then, have students share the difference between action and nonaction verbs.

2. Have students look at grammar chart **5.7** and compare their ideas. Have volunteers read examples aloud and carefully review the explanations.

3. Point out the difference between *hear/see* and *listen/look*. (*Hear/see* are nonaction because they are involuntary—you do them without necessarily wanting to. *Listen/look* are action because they are voluntary actions.) Go over the examples.

4. Direct students' attention to the Language Note. Review the common nonaction verbs and have students make example sentences in the simple present (e.g., This coffee tastes delicious. I prefer to go to the mall during the week.).

---

**PRACTICE IDEA: SPEAKING**

Put students in groups. Have students brainstorm different ways humans can prevent climate change, focusing on action verbs. Write students' ideas on the board (e.g., recycle, use public transportation, eat less meat, ride their bikes). Have students play charades with the activities on the board. Say: *One student acts out an activity, and the other students in the group guess what it is.* If necessary, write activities on slips of paper and have students choose an activity. Model the activity first and remind students to use the present continuous tense to describe the activity (e.g., Pedro's recycling his coffee cup.).

---

**EXERCISE 9** page 128  CD 1 TR 25
⏱ Time: 10–15 min.

**Answers: 1.** think; **2.** say; **3.** happen; **4.** don't realize; **5.** are causing; **6.** need; **7.** understand; **8.** are starting; **9.** don't want; **10.** costs; **11.** care; **12.** are hurting; **13.** are; **14.** doing; **15.** say

**EXERCISE 10** pages 128–129
⏱ Time: 5–10 min.

**Answers:** (Note: accept contracted and non-contracted forms when correct.) **1. a.** are you reading, **b.** 'm not really reading, **c.** 'm just looking, **d.** Do you want, **e.** looks, **f.** has, **g.** has, **h.** do parrots live, **i.** live; **2. a.** Are you taking, **b.** have, **c.** 'm learning, **d.** are harming, **e.** are dying, **f.** need, **g.** don't understand, **h.** think, **i.** agree, **j.** 'm thinking, **k.** do you hope, **l.** sounds; **3. a.** is rising, **b.** is it rising, **c.** is melting, **d.** do scientists know, **e.** have,

**f.** is it melting, **g.** is getting, **h.** thinks, **i.** happens; **4. a.** are dying, **b.** don't know, **c.** does it mean, **d.** means, **e.** do you know, **f.** 'm watching, **g.** talk, **h.** do birds give, **i.** are they doing

---

**PRACTICE IDEA: SPEAKING**

Have volunteers role-play all or part of the conversation in Exercise 10 in front of the class.

---

**PRACTICE IDEA: SPEAKING**

Have students explain why they used the simple present or the present continuous in each statement in Exercise 10 (e.g., 1. *understand*— simple present because *understand* is a nonaction word).

---

# SUMMARY OF LESSON 5

◑ Time: 20–30 min.

## PART A  USE OF PRESENT CONTINUOUS (WITH ACTION VERBS ONLY)

Have students look around the classroom and write two additional sentences for each use of the present continuous. Be sure they use action verbs. If necessary, have students review:

**5.1**  The Present Continuous—Forms (page 115–116)

**5.3**  The Present Continuous—Use (page 119)

**5.6**  The Present Continuous vs. the Simple Present—Use (page 125)

**5.7**  Action and Nonaction Verbs (page 127)

## PART B  USES OF THE SIMPLE PRESENT

Have students write two additional sentences for each use of the simple present. They can write about their classmates and the English language. Be sure they use both action and nonaction verbs. If necessary, have students review:

**5.5**  The Present Continuous vs. the Simple Present—Forms (page 124)

**5.6**  The Present Continuous vs. the Simple Present—Use (page 125)

**5.7**  Action and Nonaction Verbs (page 127)

## PART C  ACTION AND NONACTION VERBS

Have students write four sentences about the topic of their choice: two using action verbs and two using nonaction verbs. If necessary, have students review:

**5.7**  Action and Nonaction Verbs (page 127)

## TEST/REVIEW

🕐 Time: 15 min.

Have students do the exercise on page 131. For additional practice, use the Assessment CD-ROM with Exam*View*® and the Online Workbook.

**Answers: 1.** are you doing; **2.** 'm looking; **3.** aren't you using; **4.** have; **5.** want; **6.** Do you want; **7.** don't have; **8.** 'm waiting; **9.** are / 're working; **10.** are you working; **11.** need; **12.** don't believe; **13.** is / 's happening; **14.** do you think; **15.** believe; **16.** am / 'm thinking; **17.** Does your teacher teach; **18.** think; **19.** Do you like; **20.** love; **21.** like; **22.** doesn't give; **23.** doesn't he give; **24.** prefers; **25.** thinks; **26.** agree; **27.** sounds; **28.** see; **29.** is / 's walking; **30.** know

## WRITING

## PART 1  EDITING ADVICE

🕐 Time: 10–15 min.

1. Have students close their books. Write the first few sentences without editing marks or corrections on the board. For example:

   *He working now.*

   *Where you're going?*

2. Ask students to correct each sentence and provide a rule or an explanation for each correction. This activity can be done individually, in pairs, or as a class.

3. After students have corrected each sentence, tell them to turn to page 132. Say: *Now compare your work with the Editing Advice in the book.* Have students read through all the advice.

## PART 2  EDITING PRACTICE

🕐 Time: 10–15 min.

1. Tell students they are going to put the Editing Advice into practice. Ask: *Do all the shaded words and phrases have mistakes?* (no) Go over the examples with the class. Then do #1 together.

2. Have students complete the practice individually. Then have them compare answers with a partner before checking answers as a class.

3. For the items students had difficulties with, have them go back and find the relevant grammar chart and review it. Monitor and give help as necessary.

**Answers: 1.** C; **2.** has; **3.** C; **4.** lives; **5.** C; **6.** are they; **7.** need; **8.** C; **9.** are they destroying; **10.** C; **11.** C; **12.** are killing; **13.** C; **14.** C; **15.** need

## PART 3  WRITE ABOUT IT

🕐 Time: 30–40 min.

1. Have students talk about the different classes they are taking in pairs, explaining what they are learning and why they think the classes are interesting or not. Encourage students to organize their thoughts and make notes before they begin to write. Remind them to include any useful and relevant vocabulary about climate change and extinction and to use the present continuous. If necessary, write model topic sentences on the board first.

2. Guide a class brainstorm about different wild animals. Solicit ideas from students and make a list on the board. Have students choose one wild animal and describe what they know about the animal in pairs. Then have them answer the questions and write their compositions individually. Encourage them to write as much as possible. If possible, encourage students to conduct online research to learn more about the animal. Collect for assessment and/or have students share their compositions in small groups.

## PART 4  EDIT YOUR WRITING

🕐 Time: 15–20 min.

Have students edit their writing by reviewing the Lesson Summary on page 130 and the Editing Advice on page 132. Collect for assessment and/or have students share their essays in small groups.

## EXPANSION ACTIVITIES

1. Have students make climate change prevention materials. Have them design and draw a pamphlet or poster that illustrates at least five ways humans can prevent climate change. Remind them to use the present continuous. Have a poster fair or informational session, and invite other classes to learn about climate change prevention.

2. Write on the board: *Cultural differences: behavior*. Ask questions such as: *What kind of things do Americans do that are strange in your culture?* Elicit one or two ideas and write them on the board. Then have students discuss behaviors that are strange to them in groups. Have groups report the results of their discussions to the class (e.g., *We think it's strange that Americans don't have much physical contact when they greet each other.*). If possible, put students from different countries together in the same group.

3. Ask students to observe behaviors in public places and write all the actions they see. Have students report their observations in groups or have volunteers report their observations to the class.

4. Tell students to use the Internet to find the Web site of a college in this city and answer the following questions:

    1. *Where is it?*
    2. *What's the tuition?*
    3. *Does this college have evening classes?*
    4. *Does this college have more than one location?*
    5. *Does it have a graduate program?*
    6. *Does it have dormitories?*
    7. *Does it have ESL classes?*
    8. *When is the next registration?*
    9. *What are the vacation days?*

Have students brainstorm a list of local colleges. Go over the questions to make sure that students understand everything.

# 6 OUR FUTURE

## GRAMMAR CHARTS

## LESSON OPENER

Have students look at the photo and read the caption. Ask: *What is the man in the picture doing?* (riding a jet pack over a city) *Where is he?* (Denver, Colorado) Have students read the quotation. Ask: *Do you agree with the quote? Why or why not? What do you most look forward to in the future?*

**Background:** Over the next fifty years, the American population will continue to grow, but experts predict it might look a little different. Immigration has long been the main force behind U.S. population growth. According to the Pew Research Center, in the future, immigrants will make up a record 18 percent of the U.S. population, compared with 14 percent today and 5 percent in 1965.

According to the U.S. Census Bureau statistics, 9 million people checked more than one race compared to 6.8 million people in 2000. This trend will not only change the way Americans look, but also the way Americans speak. Some believe that Spanish will overshadow English as a first language in the future. Other surveys have pointed to an American cynicism about the future in regard to stronger political divisions, an increasing wealth gap, and the falling behind of the United States as a superpower. But American cities will continue to grow, playing an important role in evolving American behaviors. By 2025, the top one hundred cities with the highest gross domestic products (GDPs) will produce 75 percent of the total U.S. GDP. Cities will also change, with mid-sized cities rising in population, size, and influence.

Abraham Lincoln was the sixteenth president of the United States. He began his term in a divided nation, but led the United States, also known as the Union, to victory against the Confederacy in the Civil War. This victory united the nation, abolished slavery, and led to modernization of the economy. On April 15, 1865, a confederate spy named John Wilkes Booth shot Lincoln while he attended a play, mortally wounding and killing the president.

## CONTEXT

This unit is about the future. Students will read about future careers, a futurist named Ray Kurzweil, and a colony on Mars.

1. Give students a few minutes to look through the lesson. Have them look at the photos and titles. How do they relate to the context?

2. Elicit the topics that will be discussed.

3. Have students discuss what they know about our future in pairs or small groups.

## GRAMMAR

Students will learn about future verb tenses.

1. To activate students' prior knowledge, ask what students know about the future verb tenses.

2. Give several examples of future verb tenses (e.g., *I will see you tomorrow. Next week, I'm going to travel to California.*).

3. Have volunteers give examples and write them on the board.

### EXPANDING ON THE CONTEXT

The context for this lesson can be enhanced with the following items:

1. Photos of old and new technologies

2. Images of what humans may look like in the far future

3. Charts and graphs that show the rate of technological growth and change

4. Clips from science fiction films about the future, such as *Back to the Future* and *Minority Report*

# Future Careers, page 136

## PRE-READING

⏱ Time: 5–10 min.

1. Have students look at the photo. Ask: *Who are these people?* (nurses and doctors) *What are they doing?* (surgery)

2. Have students read the title and then skim the reading. Ask: *What is the reading about? How do you know?* Have students make predictions.

3. Pre-teach any vocabulary words your students may not know, such as *to prepare, training, health care,* and *profession.*

4. Ask: *Are the common careers different in the United States than in your home country? Are the careers that your parents and grandparents had different from the jobs people commonly have today?* Have volunteers share their knowledge and personal experiences.

## READING GLOSSARY

**to prepare:** to make something or somebody ready for some purpose

**training:** a process by which someone is taught the skills needed for a job

**health care:** the prevention or treatment of illness

**profession:** a job that requires special training or education

## READING  CD 1 TR 26

⏱ Time: 10–15 min.

Go over the answers to the Comprehension Check on page 137: **1.** T; **2.** T; **3.** T.

## CONTEXT NOTE

According to projections from the U.S. Bureau of Labor Statistics on job growth from 2012 to 2022, the top ten fastest growing jobs are the following:

1. Industrial-organizational psychologists
2. Personal care aides
3. Home health aides
4. Interpreters and translators
5. Diagnostic medical sonographers
6. Helpers of brickmasons, blockmasons, stonemasons, and tile and marble setters
7. Mechanical insulation workers
8. Occupational and physical therapist assistants and aides
9. Skincare specialists
10. Physician assistants

## ADDITIONAL COMPREHENSION QUESTIONS

*What jobs will have the fastest growth?* (health care, health care support, construction, and personal care) *Why will health care occupations grow?* (because the U.S. population is aging) *How many openings will there be for nurses in 2022?* (over one-half million) *What do personal care helpers do?* (help people with disabilities take care of daily needs) *What does* STEM *stand for?* (Science, Technology, Engineering, and Mathematics) *What is an example of a job that will decrease?* (postal workers, farm workers)

### EXPANDING ON THE READING

The topic for this reading can be enhanced with the following items:

1. Photos of fastest-growing jobs
2. Graphs and tables of job growth projections in the United States
3. List of six high-paying jobs of the future from *Forbes*
4. Example job interview questions from the fastest-growing occupations
5. Free career placement tests

### PRACTICE IDEA: LISTENING

Have students first listen to the audio alone. Have students count how many times they hear the word *will* (fifteen). Then have students open their books and read along as they listen to the audio.

## 6.1 The Future with *Will—Forms,* page 137

⏱ Time: 10–15 min.

1. Have students look at the reading on page 136. Elicit examples of sentences with *will* and write them on the board. Have students analyze the sentences in pairs and state the form of the future with *will*. Ask:

*What do all the sentences have?* (subject + *will* + verb)
Write these labels above the sentences.

2. Have students look at grammar chart **6.1** (the first chart). Have volunteers read the examples aloud and review the explanations. Have students return to the sentences on the board and, in pairs, form contractions and make them into negative statements.

3. Direct students' attention to the Language Notes. Provide additional examples of adverbs with the future *will*.

4. Have students read through the second grammar chart to compare statements, questions, and short answers. Clarify any questions.

**EXERCISE 1** page 138

⏱ Time: 5–10 min.

Answers:

**1.** will be; **2.** will need; **3.** will find; **4.** will; **5.** mean; **6.** will; **7.** be; **8.** will affect; **9.** will be

---

**PRACTICE IDEA: SPEAKING**

Write on the board: *How will new technology affect jobs in the future?* First, write the example from Exercise 1 on the board: *More people are shopping online, so store workers will have fewer job opportunities.* Review the examples, pointing out that the 'new technology' is shopping online and that the effect will be fewer jobs. Do a class brainstorm about other new technology practices and write students' ideas on the board. Finally, have students discuss the question in pairs. Have volunteers share their ideas with the class.

---

**EXERCISE 2** page 138

⏱ Time: 5–10 min.

Answers:

**1.** 'll take; **2.** 'll find; **3.** 'll probably major; **4.** won't make; **5.** Will there be; **6.** will be; **7.** 'll show; **8.** will be; **9.** 'll make; **10.** 'll always remember

---

**PRACTICE IDEA: SPEAKING**

Have students read the conversation aloud in pairs. Have volunteers read part or all of the conversation in front of the class.

---

# 6.2 The Future with *Will*— Use, page 139

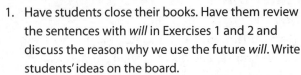

⏱ Time: 5–10 min.

1. Have students close their books. Have them review the sentences with *will* in Exercises 1 and 2 and discuss the reason why we use the future *will*. Write students' ideas on the board.

2. Have students turn to grammar chart **6.2** and compare their ideas with the explanations in the chart. Review additional examples and provide more examples if necessary.

**EXERCISE 3** page 139

⏱ Time: 5–10 min.

**Answers will vary.** (Note: accept non-contracted form and contracted form where correct.)

---

**PRACTICE IDEA: WRITING**

In pairs, have students turn sentences in Exercise 3 into questions (e.g., *1. Will technology replace teachers? 2. Will there always be a need for gardeners?*). Then have students mingle around the classroom, asking and answering the six questions.

---

**EXERCISE 4** page 139

⏱ Time: 5–10 min.

**Answers will vary.** *Possible answers:*

**1.** I'll show you the BLS website. You can find information there.

**2.** I'll help you fill out an application for financial aid.

**3.** I'll take you there. / I'll show you where it is.

**4.** I'll write one for you.

**5.** I'll explain it to you.

---

**PRACTICE IDEA: WRITING**

Have students work in pairs to write similar conversations between a student and a teacher, an American and an international student, or a parent and a child. Have volunteers act out the conversations in front of the class.

---

## READING

# Ray Kurzweil, Futurist, page 140

## PRE-READING

🕑 Time: 5–10 min.

1. Have students look at the photo. Ask: *Who is this man?* (Ray Kurzweil) *What is he holding?* (a laptop computer)

2. Have students read the title and then skim the reading. Ask: *What is the reading about? How do you know?* Have students make predictions.

3. Pre-teach any vocabulary words your students may not know, such as *inventor, prediction, wireless network,* and *technology.*

4. Ask: *What do you think a* futurist *is? How will life be different in the future?* Have volunteers share their knowledge and personal experiences.

## READING GLOSSARY

**inventor:** a person who creates something for the first time

**prediction:** a statement about what will or might happen in the future

**wireless network:** a system of computers that are connected to each other using wireless data connections

**technology:** use of science to invent useful things or solve problems

## READING  CD 1 TR 28

🕑 Time: 10–15 min.

Go over the answers to the Comprehension Check on page 141: **1.** T; **2.** F; **3.** T.

## CONTEXT NOTE

Ray Kurzweil, along with other futurists and scientists, uses the term *singularity,* or *technological singularity,* to refer to the coming of genuine artificial intelligence. According to this theory, computers and robots will be capable of designing themselves or building computers and robots on their own. Because of these new capabilities, humans will see an intelligence explosion where smart machines design smarter, more powerful machines—far more intelligent than humans. As a result, human intelligence will no longer be able to predict or control events in the future. In his research, Kurzweil has employed a mathematical equation to predict that the singularity will occur around 2045.

## ADDITIONAL COMPREHENSION QUESTIONS

*What kinds of jobs does Ray Kurzweil have?* (author, inventor, computer scientist, futurist) *What is an example of something he predicted in the 1980s that is now true?* (documents that include voice, music, and other sounds; computers are as common as pencils and books in schools; we have wireless networks to share information)

### EXPANDING ON THE READING

The topic for this reading can be enhanced with the following items:

1. Ray Kurzweil quotes
2. Clips from Ray Kurzweil's TED Talks
3. Videos of ASIMO, the world's most advanced humanoid robot
4. Photos of future technology based on artificial intelligence
5. Infographics, diagrams, and charts about the singularity and the evolution of technology

# 6.3 The Future with *Be Going To*—Forms, page 141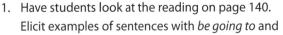

🕑 Time: 10–15 min.

1. Have students look at the reading on page 140. Elicit examples of sentences with *be going to* and

write them on the board. Have students analyze the sentences in pairs and state the form of the future with *be going to*. Ask: *What do all the sentences have?* (subject + form of *be* + *going to* + base verb) Write these labels above the sentences.

2. Have students look at grammar chart **6.3** (the first chart). Have volunteers read the examples aloud and review the explanations. Have students return to the sentences on the board and, in pairs, form contractions and make them into negative statements.

3. Direct students' attention to the Language Notes. Provide additional examples of adverbs with the future *be going to*. Review the Pronunciation Note. Have students practice saying *gonna* with the example sentences in pairs.

4. Have students read through the second grammar chart to compare statements, questions, and short answers. Clarify any questions.

**EXERCISE 5** page 142  CD 1 TR 29

🕐 Time: 5–10 min.

Answers:

**1.** 's going to be; **2.** is it going to be; **3.** 'm not going to watch; **4.** 'm going to record; **5.** aren't you going to watch; **6.** are going; **7.** 'm going to watch; **8.** Are you going to be; **9.** is going to be; **10.** are you going to be; **11.** 'm going to write; **12.** is going to help

---

**PRACTICE IDEA: SPEAKING**

Have students discuss their weekend plans in pairs. Remind them to use both *will* and *be going to*. Encourage the use of contractions and the informal use of *gonna*.

---

# 6.4 The Future with *Be Going To*—Use, page 142

🕐 Time: 5–10 min.

1. Have students close their books. Have them review the sentences with *be going to* in Exercise 5 and discuss the reason why we use the future *be going to*. Write students' ideas on the board.

2. Have students turn to grammar chart **6.4** and compare their ideas with the explanations in the chart. Review additional examples and provide more examples if necessary.

**EXERCISE 6** page 143

🕐 Time: 5–10 min.

**Answers will vary.**

**EXERCISE 7** page 143

🕐 Time: 5–10 min.

**Answers will vary.**

---

**PRACTICE IDEA: WRITING AND SPEAKING**

In pairs, have students turn sentences in Exercises 3 and 4 into questions. Then, have students stand in two concentric circles, with half the students standing in an outer ring around the classroom and the other half standing in an inner ring, facing each other. Instruct students to make offers of help using the statements in Exercise 9. Call out *turn* every minute or so. Students in the inner ring should move one space clockwise. Students now offer to help their new partners. Now have students say the problems from Exercise 9 in random order. Make sure students look at each other when they're speaking.

---

**EXERCISE 8** page 143

🕐 Time: 5–10 min.

**Answers will vary.**

# 6.5 Choosing *Will* or *Be Going To*, page 143

🕐 Time: 5–10 min.

1. Have students look at grammar chart **6.5**. Review the explanations and have volunteers read the example sentences aloud. For each use, have students write one or two examples of their own in pairs.

2. Direct students' attention to the Language Notes. Emphasize the formal/informal tone of *will* and *be going to*. Provide additional examples of *will* after the verb *think*.

**EXERCISE 9** page 144

🕐 Time: 10–15 min.

Answers:

(Note: accept non-contracted form and contracted form where correct.)

**1.** are you going to major; **2.** am going to start; **3.** Is it always going to be / will it always be; **4.** will become; **5.** will / 'll let; **6.** will / 'll enjoy; **7.** am / 'm not going to have / won't have; **8.** will / 'll tell; **9.** will be / are going to be; **10.** will / 'll borrow; **11.** will / 'll give; **12.** are you going to major; **13.** am / 'm going to be; **14.** will / 'll be

---

**PRACTICE IDEA: SPEAKING**

In small groups, have students share their plans for after they finish their English course (e.g., jobs, majors, going home). Remind them to use both *will* and *be going to*. Encourage the use of contractions and the informal use of *gonna*. Have volunteers share their group's plans with the class.

---

**PRACTICE IDEA: WRITING AND SPEAKING**

In pairs, have students write survey questions to interview their classmates about their future plans (e.g., *After this class, will you study at the university? What are you going to major in?*). Then have them switch partners and interview another classmate. Remind students to ask follow-up questions for more details (e.g., *How many years will you have to study that major?*). Have students share their partner's plans with the class.

---

READING

# Colony on Mars, page 145

## PRE-READING

🕐 Time: 5–10 min.

1. Have students look at the photo. Ask: *What do you see in the picture?* (dry desert, houses of some sort, an astronaut, a vehicle, solar panels) *Where is this place?* (the possible Mars One colony on Mars)

2. Have students read the title and then skim the reading. Ask: *What is the reading about? How do you know?* Have students make predictions.

3. Pre-teach any vocabulary words your students may not know, such as *application, to train,* and *colonist.*

4. Ask: *Do you believe there is life on other planets? Why or why not? Do you think humans will live on other planets in the future? Why or why not?* Have volunteers share their knowledge and personal experiences.

## READING GLOSSARY

**application:** a formal and written request for something
**to train:** to be taught the skills needed to do something
**colonist:** a person who helps create a colony

## READING  🎧  CD 1 TR 30

🕐 Time: 10–15 min.

Go over the answers to the Comprehension Check on page 141: **1.** T; **2.** T; **3.** F.

## CONTEXT NOTE

The nonprofit organization Mars One has received widespread criticism since its founders announced the concept in 2012. The criticism is multifaceted, including pointed attacks from academics, scientists, other astronauts, and even religious leaders. Some people say the proposed mission to Mars is a scam designed to take money from donors, investors, and the applicants themselves. Despite large donations, other critics call the project's budget far too low to be able to support a human colony on Mars. Still others claim that much of the media coverage has been inaccurate and hyperbolic. Finally, some former astronauts are against it, citing a probability of only 30 percent that inhabitants would reach Mars alive, and an even lower probability (20 percent) that they would survive more than 3 months even if they did.

## ADDITIONAL COMPREHENSION QUESTIONS

*By what year does Mars One want to put a human colony on Mars?* (2025) *How many people have applied to be part of the project?* (200,000) *How many years will people have to train to go on the mission?* (8) *Where will they train?* (in the Arctic region) *Why don't some people believe in the plan?* (They say that if the colonists have a problem, they will die.)

---

**EXPANDING ON THE READING**

The topic for this reading can be enhanced with the following items:

1. Profiles and videos of the Mars One shortlist of the top ten hopefuls
2. Additional photos of the Mars One colony
3. Infographics explaining the Mars One roadmap
4. Clips from the Mars One introduction film
5. Mars photos and maps from the United States Geological Survey (USGS)

---

## 6.6 The Future with Time Clauses and *If* Clauses,

page 146

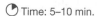

🕐 Time: 5–10 min.

1. Have students go back to the reading on page 145 and put brackets (e.g., [ ]) around all the sentences that start with the words *if* or *when*. Have students read them aloud in pairs.

2. Ask students if they know the meaning of *if*. Tell them that *if* creates a condition: Action *X* will happen *if* action *Y* happens. Review example sentences from the reading, pointing out the condition.

3. Have students look at grammar chart **6.6**. Point out that these sentences are made up of two clauses: the time clause and the main clause. Have students read examples aloud, and ask: *What tense is used in the time clause?* (simple present) *What tense is used in the main clause?* (future) With the bracketed sentences in the reading, have students circle the simple present verb and underline the verb in the future tense.

4. Direct students' attention to the Language Note. Point out that the main clause can come before or after the Time/*If* clause. Explain that when the Time/*If* clause goes first, they must use a comma. Have students change the word order in a couple of *If* sentences from the reading and rewrite them in pairs.

**EXERCISE 10** page 146
🕐 Time: 5–10 min.
**Answers will vary.**

**EXERCISE 11** page 147
🕐 Time: 5–10 min.
**Answers will vary.**

**EXERCISE 12** page 147
🕐 Time: 5–10 min.
**Answers will vary.**

## SUMMARY OF LESSON 6

🕐 Time: 20–30 min.

### PART A  THE FUTURE

1. Have students practice forms of *will and be going to* in pairs. Say: *One student says, "Affirmative." The other student gives an example such as, "Sally will wear a white wedding dress."* Instruct students to continue with the other forms of *will*. Then have pairs switch roles and repeat.

2. Have students close their books. Say various sentences in the future, and have students identify the use (e.g., *I will help you tomorrow.*). Students say: *promise*. On the board, write: *promise*. If necessary, have students review:

   **6.1**  The Future with *Will*––Forms (page 137)

## PART B THE FUTURE WITH TIME AND *IF* CLAUSES

Have students close their books. Copy the first column of the summary chart on the board and have students finish the sentences in pairs. Encourage students to finish them in as many different ways as possible. Once completed, have students open their books and compare their ideas with the chart. If necessary, have students review:

**6.6** The Future with Time Clauses and *If* Clauses (page 146)

### TEST/REVIEW

🕐 Time: 15 min.

Have students do the exercise on page 149. For additional practice, use the Assessment CD-ROM with Exam*View*® and the Online Workbook.

**Answers:**

(Note: accept non-contracted form and contracted form where correct.)

**1.** are you going to do; **2.** 'm / am going to watch; **3.** finish; **4.** is going to talk; **5.** 's / is going to be / will be; **6.** is it going to / will it start; **7.** 're / are going to have; **8.** are going to / will have; **9.** are going to / will use; **10.** will be / are going to be; **11.** won't be / aren't going to be; **12.** 're / are going to grow/will grow; **13.** won't get / aren't going to get; **14.** are there going to be / will there be; **15.** 'm / am going to attend; **16.** 'll / will send; **17.** 's / is not / isn't going to talk; **18.** isn't she going to discuss politics?; **19.** 'll / will come; **20.** 'll / will wait; **21.** 'll / will call; **22.** get

### WRITING

## PART 1 EDITING ADVICE

🕐 Time: 10–15 min.

1. Have students close their books. Write the first few sentences without editing marks or corrections on the board. For example:

   *I will be go.*

   *He will angry.*

2. Ask students to correct each sentence and provide a rule or an explanation for each correction. This activity can be done individually, in pairs, or as a class.

3. After students have corrected each sentence, tell them to turn to page 150. Say: *Now compare your work with the Editing Advice in the book.* Have students read through all the advice.

## PART 2 EDITING PRACTICE

🕐 Time: 10–15 min.

1. Tell students they are going to put the Editing Advice into practice. Ask: *Do all the shaded words and phrases have mistakes?* (no) Go over the examples with the class. Then do #1 together.

2. Have students complete the practice individually. Then have them compare answers with a partner before checking answers as a class.

3. For the items students had difficulties with, have them go back and find the relevant grammar chart and review it. Monitor and give help as necessary.

**Answers:**

**1.** C; **2.** will be; **3.** C; **4.** will be; **5.** will be / is going to be; **6.** C; **7.** C; **8.** C; **9.** aren't they going to do; **10.** C; **11.** are going to learn; **12.** are going to become; **13.** graduate; **14.** will have / are going to have; **15.** C; **16.** C; **17.** am still; **18.** C

## PART 3 WRITE ABOUT IT

🕐 Time: 30–40 min.

1. Review the topic with students, eliciting student ideas about predictions for the future and writing ideas on the board. Have students answer the questions in pairs, describing different future predictions. Remind them to include any useful and relevant vocabulary from this lesson on the future and to be careful with their use of *will* versus *be going to*. If necessary, write model topic sentences on the board first.

2. Have students make a list of plans or goals for the future. Have them share their lists in pairs and then write their paragraphs individually. Briefly model the activity by beginning a paragraph about your plans and concerns on the board using student ideas. Encourage them to use Time/*If* clauses and to write as much as possible. Collect for assessment and/or have students share their compositions with the group.

## PART 4  EDIT YOUR WRITING

🕐 Time: 15–20 min.

Have students edit their writing by reviewing the Lesson Summary on page 148 and the Editing Advice on page 150. Collect for assessment and/or have students share their essays in small groups.

## EXPANSION ACTIVITIES

1.  Have students work in pairs to create dialogues for each use of the future tense (a. prediction; b. promise; c. plan, promise; d. plan, promise; e. promise). Then have volunteers role-play the dialogues in front of the class.

2.  Have students debate whether humans should colonize other planets, or if we should just send robots. Divide the class into two teams. Tell each team to list five reasons supporting their views. Have each team present their arguments. Then give each team an opportunity to respond to the other team's arguments. At the end of the debate, survey the class to see which opinion is more popular.

3.  Tell students to interview an American about his or her concerns for the future. Students can choose to report their interview to the class or to hand in a written report.

4.  Have students watch short videos about new technology and choose one product to report on. Have them predict how this product will change our daily lives in the future and share this information in a short presentation using a high- or low-tech visual aid.

# 7 AVIATION

## GRAMMAR CHARTS

## LESSON OPENER

Have students look at the photo and read the caption. Ask: *What do you see in the photo?* (a seaplane, an airplane) *Where is it?* (over the ocean) Have students read the quotation. Ask: *Why was the airplane such an important invention? How can aviation bring together people, languages, ideas, and values?*

**Background:** Due to the vast size of the United States and the long distances between major cities, air transportation is the preferred travel method for many Americans. Business and holiday travelers alike use America's extensive aviation network, which was created due in part to 1917 legislation called the Aero Bill that dedicated $640 million toward aircraft production. As the federal government focused on production, big cities began to host air meets, held in Los Angeles, Boston, and New York, which drew top aviators from around the world. American aviators, such as the Wright brothers, also made history around that time by touring the country entertaining crowds and fostering public interest in aviation. In present-day America, there are eighty-six airports that handle more than one million passengers per year. However, since the terrorist attacks of September 11, 2001, the airline industry has had losses of between 1 and 2 billion dollars.

Bill Gates is an American businessman and investor. He co-founded the world's largest personal computer (PC) company, Microsoft, in 1975, where he held various top positions and was instrumental in starting the PC revolution. In 2000, Gates and his wife launched the Bill and Melinda Gates Foundation to reduce poverty and expand educational opportunities worldwide.

## CONTEXT

This unit is about aviation. Students will read about the Wright brothers, Charles Lindbergh, and Amelia Earhart, the "Rocket Man" Robert Goddard, and Evelyn Bryan "Mama Bird" Johnson.

1. Give students a few minutes to look through the lesson. Have them look at the photos and titles. How do they relate to the context?

2. Elicit the topics that will be discussed.

3. Have students discuss what they know about aviation in pairs or small groups.

## GRAMMAR

Students will learn about the simple past tense.

1. To activate students' prior knowledge, ask what students know about the simple past tense.

2. Give several examples of the simple past tense (e.g., *They dreamed about flying. They designed an airplane.*).

3. Have volunteers give examples and write them on the board.

### EXPANDING ON THE CONTEXT

The context for this lesson can be enhanced with the following items:

1. Books with photos of the Wright brothers, early airplanes, and famous aviators

2. Maps of famous flights

3. Diagrams showing different parts of airplanes

# The Wright Brothers, page 154

## PRE-READING

⏱ Time: 5–10 min.

1. Have students look at the photo and read the caption. Ask: *Who is this man?* (Wilbur Wright) *Where is he?* (Kitty Hawk, North Carolina) *What is happening in the photo?* (He is watching his brother's first flight)

2. Have students read the title and then skim the reading. Ask: *What is the reading about? How do you know?* Have students make predictions.

3. Pre-teach any vocabulary words your students may not know, such as *to dream, to design, to repair,* and *hero.*

4. Ask: *What kinds of airplanes have you flown in? How old were you the first time you flew on a plane? What was that experience like?* Have volunteers share their knowledge and personal experiences.

## READING GLOSSARY

**to dream:** to think about something you wish would happen

**to design:** to plan and make decisions about something

**to repair:** to put back into good condition

**hero:** a person who is admired for doing great things

## READING  CD 1 TR 31

⏱ Time: 10–15 min.

Go over the answers to the Comprehension Check on page 155: **1.** F; **2.** F; **3.** F.

## CONTEXT NOTE

The Wright Brothers National Memorial in North Carolina was founded in 1953 in honor of the Wright brothers' aviation achievements. It is run by the U.S. National Park System. According to history, the Wright brothers enjoyed working in the town of Kill Devil Hills, North Carolina, due to its privacy and distance from major population centers.

## ADDITIONAL COMPREHENSION QUESTIONS

*What kind of shop did the Wright brothers open?* (bicycle shop) *What were the three necessary things for flying that the Wright brothers studied?* (life, control, and power) *When did the brothers fly a small flying machine for the first time?* (December 17, 1903) *Who was the pilot?* (Orville

Wright) *Where did the brothers become celebrities?* (in Europe) *When did they sell their Wright Flyer to the U.S. Army?* (1909)

### EXPANDING ON THE READING

The topic for this reading can be enhanced with the following items:

1. Old photos of the Wright brothers
2. Blueprints of their flyer designs
3. A time line of important dates in the Wright brothers' trajectory
4. Excerpts from the Wright brothers' biographies and documentaries
5. Children's books about the Wright brothers

### PRACTICE IDEA: LISTENING

Have students first listen to the audio alone. Ask a few comprehension questions, such as: *Who were Wilbur and Orville Wright?* (inventors of the first successful airplane) *When did the Wright brothers first start thinking about flying?* (as young boys when they received a flying toy from their father) *Where did the Wright brothers go after not receiving support from the U.S. government?* (Europe) Repeat the audio if necessary. Then have students open their books and read along as they listen to the audio.

### PRESENTATION IDEA

Have students work in pairs to make a short time line of important dates from the reading on page 154. Encourage them to write complete sentences in the simple past tense when describing the events. Hang time lines on the wall and have volunteers present their work.

## 7.1 The Simple Past—Form, 
page 155

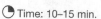

⏱ Time: 10–15 min.

1. Have students go back to the reading on page 154 and find *past verbs that end in -ed* (e.g., *dreamed, changed, received, started*). Write the verbs on the board. Then ask students to tell you the base form

of the verbs. Write them next to the past tense (e.g., *dream, change, receive, start*).

2. Have students look at grammar chart **7.1.** Have volunteers read the examples aloud and review explanations.

3. Direct students' attention to the Language Notes. Review the subject pronouns and give additional examples comparing the past tense of the verb *be* with other regular verbs. Give several examples of infinitives after the simple past tense and have students review the list of irregular past forms.

**EXERCISE 1** pages 155–156

🕐 Time: 10–15 min.

**Answers: 1.** was; **2.** was; **3.** came; **4.** included; **5.** were; **6.** cost; **7.** hoped; **8.** was; **9.** rained; **10.** waited; **11.** didn't succeed; **12.** hit; **13.** stopped; **14.** repaired; **15.** waited; **16.** needed; **17.** wasn't; **18.** flew; **19.** got

---

**PRACTICE IDEA: WRITING**

Have students write the base forms of the verbs in the box in Exercise 1. Have them compare their answers in pairs.

---

# 7.2 The Simple Past—Use,

page 156

🕐 Time: 5–10 min.

1. Have students close their books. Make a matching exercise on the board. Write the example sentences from grammar chart **7.2** in random order on the board. Then write the explanations in random order next to the examples. Have students work in pairs to match the example sentences to the appropriate explanations.

2. Have students look at grammar chart **7.2** and check their work. Review any errors.

3. Direct students' attention to the Language Note. Give additional examples of *ago*.

---

**PRESENTATION IDEA**

Have students write five to ten sentences about important events in their life using the simple past. Then, have them make a time line of the events and present it in pairs. Have volunteers present their time lines in front of the class.

---

**PRACTICE IDEA: SPEAKING IDEA**

Have students choose one important event from their childhood and share the story in small groups (i.e., *My father gave me a soccer ball. I started to play soccer when I was 5 years old. I played soccer until I was 20.*). Have volunteers share their stories with the class.

---

**EXERCISE 2** page 156

🕐 Time: 5–10 min.

**Answers:** December 17, 2003, was the hundredth anniversary of the Wright bothers' first flight. There was a 6-day celebration at Kitty Hawk, North Carolina, the location of the first flight. A crowd of 35,000 people <u>came</u> to see the flight of a model of the first airplane. The audience <u>included</u> some famous people, such as Neil Armstrong and Buzz Aldrin. They were the first men to walk on the moon.

It <u>cost</u> $1.2 million to make a copy of the original plane. People <u>hoped</u> to see the Flyer go up in the air. The weather was bad that day. It <u>rained</u> hard. The crowd <u>waited</u> with excitement in the rain. But the Flyer didn't <u>succeed</u>. A wing <u>hit</u> the ground, and the plane <u>stopped</u>. Mechanics <u>repaired</u> the engine and wing. The crowd <u>waited</u> again for a second try. The plane <u>needed</u> wind to lift off, but there wasn't enough that day. The Flyer <u>flew</u> for 12 seconds in 1903. It didn't <u>fly</u> at all in 2003.

**EXERCISE 3** page 156

🕐 Time: 10–15 min.

**Answers: 1.** rain R; **2.** write I; **3.** open R; **4.** sell I; **5.** start R; **6.** happen R; **7.** make I; **8.** die R; **9.** study R; **10.** come I; **11.** give I; **12.** fly I; **13.** be B; **14.** need R; **15.** be B; **16.** live R

---

**READING**

# Amazing Aviators, page 157

## PRE-READING

🕐 Time: 5–10 min.

1. Have students look at the photo and read the caption. Ask: *Who are these people?* (Charles Lindbergh and Amelia Earhart) *What are they doing?* (flying in planes)

2. Have students read the title and then skim the reading. Ask: *What is the reading about? How do you know?* Have students make predictions.

3. Pre-teach any vocabulary words your students may not know, such as *adventurous, historic, intelligence, and ability.*

4. Ask: *Are you adventurous? Why or why not? How can you describe the most adventurous person you know?* Have volunteers share their knowledge and personal experiences.

## READING GLOSSARY

**adventurous:** daring; bold
**historic:** famous or important in history
**intelligence:** the ability to learn or understand things
**ability:** the power or skill to do something

## READING   CD 1 TR 33

⏱ Time: 10–15 min.

Go over the answers to the Comprehension Check on page 158: **1.** T; **2.** F; **3.** T.

## ADDITIONAL COMPREHENSION QUESTIONS

*What kind of people flew in airplanes at the beginning of the twentieth century?* (adventurous people) *Whom did Charles Lindbergh work for?* (the U.S. Mail Service) *Why did he become famous?* (He was the first person to fly alone across the Atlantic Ocean) *How old was Earhart when she flew across the Atlantic alone?* (34 years old) *Where did she disappear?* (somewhere over the Pacific Ocean)

### EXPANDING ON THE READING

The topic for this reading can be enhanced with the following items:

1. Old newspaper clippings about Lindbergh and Earhart
2. Clips from documentaries about Lindbergh and Earhart
3. Excerpts from biographies about Lindbergh and Earhart
4. Map of Earhart's flight path
5. Educational videos and children's books about Earhart

### PRACTICE IDEA: LISTENING

Have students first listen to the audio alone. Have students listen for verbs in the simple past tense and take note of as many verbs as they can. Repeat the audio if necessary. Then have students open their books and read along as they listen to the audio.

### PRESENTATION IDEA

Have students review simple present tense by working in pairs to make a newspaper article reporting on either Lindbergh or Earhart. Have volunteers pretend to be reporters in a news show and present their work to the class.

## 7.3 The Simple Past of *Be*— Forms, pages 158–159

⏱ Time: 10–15 min.

1. Have students go back to the reading on page 157. Have them find all the past forms of the verb *be* (*was, were*) and circle the subject that comes before the verb. Have volunteers write the subjects and verbs they found on the board. Have students analyze the examples from the reading in pairs and look for patterns (e.g., *was* follows *I, he, she, it*; *were* follows *we, you, they*).

2. Have students look at grammar chart **7.3** and compare their ideas. Review the example sentences in the tables in the chart, and have students write their own examples. After reviewing the final table, have students ask and answer additional questions about the reading on page 157 using the table as a model.

## ADDITIONAL PRACTICE

1. Have students write sentences about a famous historical person from their country. Instruct students to use the past form of *be*. If possible, have students from the same country work together in pairs or groups. Ask volunteers to share their information with the class.

2. Write the sentence starter on the board: *When you arrived in the United States, …* Elicit *Yes/No* or *Wh-* questions from students to finish the question (e.g. *When you arrived in the United States, were you scared? When you arrived in the United States, how many people*

*did you know?*). Have students work in pairs to write five more questions. Then, have students find a new partner and interview their classmates with the five questions. Have volunteers talk about how their partners felt when they arrived in the United States.

3. Do a survey with the class. Have students report the results of their interviews in small groups. Then have the groups report their results to the class (e.g., Three students were excited when they arrived. One student was scared.). Record the results on the board.

## EXERCISE 4 pages 159–160
🕐 Time: 10–15 min.

**Answers: 1.** Were; **2.** was; **3.** were; **4.** weren't; **5.** were; **6.** were; **7.** Was; **8.** was; **9.** Was; **10.** wasn't; **11.** was; **12.** was; **13.** was; **14.** was; **15.** were; **16.** wasn't; **17.** wasn't

---

### PRACTICE IDEA: SPEAKING IDEA

Have students practice the conversation in Exercise 4 in pairs. Then, have them write their own short conversation between two friends using Exercise 4 as a model. Have volunteers role-play their conversation in front of the class.

---

# 7.4 The Simple Past of *Be*— Uses, page 160

🕐 Time: 10–15 min.

1. Have students close their books. Make a matching exercise on the board. Write the example sentences from grammar chart **7.4** in random order on the board. Then write the explanations in random order next to the examples. Have students work in pairs to match the example sentences to the appropriate explanations.

2. Have students look at grammar chart **7.4** and check their work. Review any errors.

## EXERCISE 5 pages 160–161
🕐 Time: 5–10 min.

**Answers: 1.** were D; **2.** wasn't C; **3.** was L; **4.** was L; **5.** wasn't D; **6.** wasn't D; **7.** was C; **8.** wasn't B; **9.** Were D; **10.** was O; **11.** was A; **12.** weren't T

## EXERCISE 6 page 161
🕐 Time: 5–10 min.
**Answers:**

1. Earhart and Lindbergh weren't inventors.
2. The airplane wasn't a method of transportation in the early 1900s.
3. Lindbergh wasn't from Kansas.
4. Earhart wasn't an inventor.
5. There weren't a lot of reporters at Kitty Hawk in 1903.
6. The Wright brothers weren't born in the twentieth century.

## EXERCISE 7 pages 161–162
🕐 Time: 5–10 min.
**Answers:**

1. Was Lindbergh an inventor? No, he wasn't.
2. Was the telephone an important invention? Yes, it was.
3. Were there airplanes 100 years ago? Yes, there were.
4. Were the Wright brothers adventurous? Yes, they were.
5. Was Lindbergh (an)American? Yes, he was.
6. Was travel by plane common 100 years ago? No, it wasn't.
7. Were you interested in the story about aviators? Yes, I was. / No, I wasn't.

---

### PRACTICE IDEA: SPEAKING IDEA

Have students return to the readings on pages 154 and 157 and work in pairs asking and answering questions using the simple past of *be*. For example, Student A: *Was Robert Goddard 17 years old?* Student B: *Yes, he was.*

---

## EXERCISE 8 page 162
🕐 Time: 5–10 min.
**Answers:**

1. **A:** Why was Charles Lindbergh famous? **B:** He was one of the first aviators.
2. **A:** Why was Lindbergh a hero? **B:** (He was a hero) because he was the first person to fly across the Atlantic Ocean alone.
3. **A:** What nationality was Earhart? **B:** She was American (too).
4. **A:** How old was Lindbergh when he crossed the ocean? **B:** He was 25 years old.
5. **A:** Who were the Wright brothers? **B:** They were the inventors of the airplane.
6. **A:** When was Earhart born? **B:** She was born in 1897.
7. **A:** Why wasn't it / the flight (at Kitty Hawk) successful (in 2003)? **B:** (It wasn't successful) because of rain / weather.

**PRACTICE IDEA: SPEAKING IDEA**

Display images of different internationally famous figures such as Mother Theresa, Madonna, or Barack Obama. Write on the board: *Why is/was* _____ *famous?* Have students answer the question in pairs. Model answers in front of the class first.

**EXPANDING ON THE READING**

The topic for this reading can be enhanced with the following items:

1. Quotes by Robert Goddard
2. Old photos of Goddard with his rockets and designs
3. News clippings about Goddard
4. Excerpts of short biographies or mini-documentaries about Goddard

## READING

# The Rocket Man, page 163

## PRE-READING

🕐 Time: 5–10 min.

1. Have students look at the photo and read the caption. Ask: *Who is this man?* (Robert Goddard) *What is he holding?* (one of his rocket designs)
2. Have students read the title and then skim the reading. Ask: *What is the reading about? How do you know?* Have students make predictions.
3. Pre-teach any vocabulary words your students may not know, such as *rocket, to imagine, space,* and *invention.*
4. Ask: *Are you interested in science? Why or why not? Have you ever seen a rocket take off?* Have volunteers share their knowledge and personal experiences.

## READING GLOSSARY

**rocket:** a powerful engine powered by gases that are released from burning fuel

**to imagine:** to think of or create in your mind

**space:** the region beyond Earth's atmosphere where there are stars and planets

**invention:** a useful new device or process

## READING

🕐 Time: 10–15 min.

Go over the answers to the Comprehension Check on page 164: **1.** T; **2.** F; **3.** T.

## ADDITIONAL COMPREHENSION QUESTIONS

*Why didn't Goddard graduate from high school until he was 21?* (He was a sick child.) *What did Goddard teach at the university?* (physics) *How long did the first rocket flight in 1926 last?* (2.5 seconds) *When did the first men land on the moon?* (1969)

**PRACTICE IDEA: LISTENING**

Have students first listen to the audio alone. Have students listen for both regular and irregular verbs in the simple past tense and take note of as many verbs as they can. Repeat the audio if necessary. Then have students open their books and read along as they listen to the audio.

**PRACTICE IDEA: WRITING AND SPEAKING**

Put students in groups of four. Give each group one of the famous aviators in the lesson to report on (the Wright brothers, Charles Lindbergh, Amelia Earhart, or Robert Goddard). Have the group work together to make a time line of their famous aviator's life, based on the information in the readings. Students should include important dates and events. They can supplement information from the Internet if possible. Although they are working in a group, each student needs to draw his or her own time line. Then, jigsaw the groups so each new group of four has one student to report on each famous aviator. Have students hold up their time line and retell the biography of their chosen aviator to the group.

# 7.5 The Simple Past of Regular Verbs, page 164

🕐 Time: 5–10 min.

1. Have students look at grammar chart **7.5** and read the examples aloud in pairs. Review the base forms and examples in the simple past.

2. Then have students go back to the reading on page 163 and circle all the regular verbs in the past tense. Have them work in pairs to make a list of their base forms. Review answers as a class and address any questions.

### EXERCISE 9 page 164
🕐 Time: 5–10 min.

**Answers: 1.** graduated; **2.** studied; **3.** wanted; **4.** experimented; **5.** ignored; **6.** laughed; **7.** continued; **8.** died

## 7.6 The Simple Past of Regular Verbs—Spelling, page 165

🕐 Time: 10–15 min.

1. Copy the lists of verbs (base form and simple past) from grammar chart **7.6** on the board. Make sure you separate the eight sets of verbs. For example:

| | |
|---|---|
| *start* | *started* |
| *die* | *died* |
| *carry* | *carried* |
| *stay* | *stayed* |
| *stop* | *stopped* |
| *show* | *showed* |
| *refer* | *referred* |
| *open* | *opened* |

2. Have students close their books and analyze the lists on the board. Say: *There are eight rules for spelling the past tense of regular verbs. Can you list them?* If students have difficulty, give them hints. For example, say: *Look at the endings of these two verbs*: die *and* live. *What do you add?* (d) *So what's the rule?* (When the base form ends in *e*, add *d*)

3. Have students look at grammar chart **7.6** and compare their rules with the chart. Review the rules and examples as a class. Provide additional examples as necessary.

### EXERCISE 10 page 165
🕐 Time: 10–15 min.

**Answers: 1.** played; **2.** worried; **3.** hoped; **4.** wanted; **5.** liked; **6.** showed; **7.** looked; **8.** shopped; **9.** happened; **10.** carried; **11.** prayed; **12.** dragged; **13.** dropped; **14.** voted; **15.** followed; **16.** preferred; **17.** tied; **18.** mixed; **19.** admitted; **20.** propelled

## 7.7 The Simple Past of Regular Verbs—Pronunciation, page 166

🕐 Time: 10–15 min.

1. Have students close their books. Write the following on the board, and pronounce each sound:

    *1.* /t/

    *2.* /d/

    *3.* /əd/

2. Give an example of each from the chart. Remind students that this is about pronunciation, not spelling or writing. Then say: *Listen to each word as I say it. Tell me which sound I'm making.* Carefully pronounce the examples from the grammar chart **7.7** in random order, and have students hold up their fingers for sound one, two, or three.

3. Have students look at chart **7.7**. Review the rules and have volunteers pronounce the words.

---

**PRACTICE IDEA: SPEAKING**

Have students work in pairs. Student A points to one of the past tense verbs in the reading or the grammar chart. Student B pronounces it. After 3 minutes, students switch roles. Then, Student A pronounces one of the past tense verbs, and Student B points to the correct sound.

---

### EXERCISE 11 page 166
🕐 Time: 5–10 min.

**Answers:** (See pronunciation guide in grammar chart **7.7**.)

### EXERCISE 12 page 166
🕐 Time: 5–10 min.

**Answers: 1.** received; **2.** played; **3.** lived; **4.** dreamed; **5.** studied; **6.** opened; **7.** liked; **8.** wanted; **9.** graduated; **10.** worked; **11.** believed; **12.** used

## 7.8 The Simple Past of Irregular Verbs, page 167

🕐 Time: 10–15 min.

1. Have students close their books. Have them go back to the reading on page 163 and circle any verbs they think are irregular. Have volunteers write students'

ideas on the board. Point out the irregular past tense form of the verb *be* they already learned.

2. Have students work in pairs to guess the base form of the irregular verbs on the board. Review answers as a class. Have volunteers write the base forms next to the irregular verbs on the board.

3. Ask students if they notice any patterns, and have them discuss how to form the simple past of irregular verbs. Then have them look at grammar chart **7.8** and compare their ideas with the rules in the tables.

## ADDITIONAL PRACTICE

1. Read students a short poem using irregular simple past verbs from the chart (e.g., *The ball he hit. He would not quit. He played baseball until it was time to split.*). In pairs, have students choose one category of verbs in grammar chart **7.8** that has vowel change similarities and work to write a short poem. Provide help with vocabulary as needed. Have volunteers share their poems with the class.

2. Provide students with sentence starters on the board. For example:

   > When I got on a plane for the first time, I _felt_…
   > Last night, I _slept_ for … hours.
   > This morning, I _woke up_ at …

   Have students complete the sentences with their own information. Then, have students write five more of their own complete sentences using the past tense irregular verbs in the chart.

### EXERCISE 13  page 168
⏱ Time: 10–15 min.
**Answers: 1.** gave; **2.** had; **3.** became; **4.** read; **5.** sold; **6.** built; **7.** flew; **8.** saw; **9.** made; **10.** sold; **11.** were; **12.** brought; **13.** went

### EXERCISE 14  page 168
⏱ Time: 5–10 min.
**Answers: 1.** became; **2.** was; **3.** thought; **4.** put; **5.** flew; **6.** saw; **7.** wrote; **8.** took

## 7.9 Negative Statements with the Simple Past, page 169 ⭐
⏱ Time: 10–15 min.

1. Have students go back to the reading on page 163 and circle any negative verbs in the simple past tense.

Have volunteers write them on the board (*didn't graduate, didn't fly, didn't show, didn't live, didn't stop*).

2. Have students look at grammar chart **7.9** and review the examples. Have students return again to the reading on page 163. Have them choose five affirmative sentences and work in pairs to turn them into negative sentences by changing the past tense verb.

3. Direct students' attention to the Language Notes. Explain that this is how the negative is formed for all verbs—regular and irregular—except for the verb *be*. Provide examples showing this difference (e.g., *The student <u>didn't study</u>. He <u>wasn't</u> a student.*).

### EXERCISE 15  page 169
⏱ Time: 10–15 min.
**Answers: 1.** didn't believe; **2.** didn't dream; **3.** didn't sell; **4.** didn't have; **5.** didn't want; **6.** didn't build; **7.** didn't think; **8.** didn't write; **9.** didn't fly; **10.** didn't stay; **11.** didn't see; **12.** didn't go; **13.** wasn't

### READING

## "Mama Bird" Johnson, pages 170–171

### PRE-READING
⏱ Time: 5–10 min.

1. Have students look at the photo and read the caption. Ask: *Who is this woman?* (Evelyn Johnson) *Where is she?* (at the Moore-Murrell Airport in Tennessee)

2. Have students read the title and then skim the reading. Ask: *What is the reading about? How do you know?* Have students make predictions.

3. Pre-teach any vocabulary words your students may not know, such as *special, lonely, helicopter,* and *to race*.

4. Ask: *What are some of your favorite hobbies? Have you ever been interested in flying? Why or why not?* Have volunteers share their knowledge and personal experiences.

### READING GLOSSARY
**special:** different from what is normal
**lonely:** sad from being apart from other people
**helicopter:** an aircraft that can stay in the air without moving forward
**to race:** to be in a competition

🕐 Time: 10–15 min.

Go over the answers to the Comprehension Check on page 171: **1.** T; **2.** F; **3.** T.

## ADDITIONAL COMPREHENSION QUESTIONS

*When was Evelyn born?* (1909) *Why is 1909 a special year?* (It is 6 years after the Wright brothers' first flight.) *When did Evelyn begin flying?* (1944) *Why did she begin flying?* (because she was lonely) *How many flying hours did she have?* (about 57,000) *How many miles did she travel?* (over 5 million) *How many pilots did she train?* (over 5,000)

---

### EXPANDING ON THE READING

The topic for this reading can be enhanced with the following items:

1. Excerpts from the NPR story on "Mama Bird" Johnson's death
2. Photos of Evelyn Johnson through the years
3. Excerpts from Evelyn Johnson's biography in the National Aviation Hall of Fame
4. Video interviews with Evelyn Johnson

---

### PRACTICE IDEA: LISTENING

Have students first listen to the audio alone. Ask a few comprehension questions, such as: *What was Evelyn Johnson's hobby?* (flying planes) *What different careers in aviation did she have?* (She trained pilots, worked as a flight examiner, raced planes, and ran a tourist flight service.) *Who gave her the nickname "Mama Bird"?* (one of her students) Repeat the audio if necessary. Then have students open their books and read along as they listen to the audio.

## 7.10 Questions with the Simple Past, pages 171–172

🕐 Time: 10–15 min.

1. Have students close their books. Elicit *Yes/No* questions and *Wh-* questions from students. Review the word order as volunteers write them on the board.
2. Write the following sentences on the board: *The pilot landed the plane. The plane lost power.*

Have students write six sentences in pairs:

1. Write a *Yes/No* question and short answer for each of the two sentences.
2. Write a *Wh-* question for each of the two sentences.
3. Write a negative question for each of the two sentences.

Have volunteers share their sentences on the board.

3. Have students look at grammar chart **7.10** and compare their sentences with the examples in the chart. Have them fix any word order mistakes and label the subjects and base forms in their sentences.
4. Review the examples in the chart and address any questions that come up. Review subject questions and point out that the word order pattern is the same for subject questions and statements. Compare all statements, questions, and answers in the final table.
5. Direct students' attention to the Language Note. Provide additional examples as necessary.

---

### PRACTICE IDEA: SPEAKING

Come up with several questions to ask somebody the first time you meet them (e.g., *Where were you born? How long have you lived in the United States? How long have you studied English? When did you decide to study abroad?*). Write the questions on the board. Have students mingle and ask each other as many of the questions as possible.

---

## EXERCISE 16 page 172–173

🕐 Time: 5–10 min.

**Answers:** (Note: accept first and last names.) **1. a.** Did she graduate, **b.** she did.; **2. a.** Did she work, **b.** she did; **3. a.** Did she train, **b.** she did.; **4. a.** Did she teach, **b.** she didn't; **5. a.** Did she have, **b.** she did; **6. a.** Did she win, **b.** she did.; **7. a.** Did she know, **b.** she didn't

---

### PRACTICE IDEA: SPEAKING

Have students practice asking and answering the questions in pairs. Have volunteers read the dialogs in front of the class.

---

## EXERCISE 17 pages 173–174

🕐 Time: 5–10 min.

**Answers:** (Note: accept appropriate pronouns and first and last names.)

**1.** Did Goddard have a dream? Yes, he did.

**2.** Did Wilbur Wright die in an airplane crash? No, he didn't.

**3.** Did Goddard build an airplane? No, he didn't.

**4.** Did Lindbergh love to fly? Yes, he did.

**5.** Did Earhart cross the ocean? Yes, she did.

**6.** Did Earhart work for the U.S. Mail Service? No, she didn't.

**7.** Was Earhart famous? Yes, she was.

**8.** Was Earhart born in the twentieth century? No, she wasn't.

**9.** Did they / people believe Goddard at first? No, they didn't.

### EXERCISE 18 pages 174–175
🕑 Time: 5–10 min.

**Answers: 1.** did Johnson train; **2.** were female; **3.** did she rescue; **4.** gave her; **5. a.** did she become the manager (of an airport)?, **b.** was she; **6.** did she love; **7. a.** happened, **b.** Was she; **8. a.** was she born, **b.** Did she meet; **9. a.** did she retire, **b.** did she have; **10.** did she die

---

**PRACTICE IDEA: SPEAKING**

Have students practice asking and answering the questions in pairs. Have volunteers read the dialogs in front of the class.

---

### EXERCISE 19 pages 176–177
🕑 Time: 10–15 min.

**Answers: 1.** did the first airplane have; **2.** did the Wright brothers build; **3.** didn't newspapers report; **4.** did Lindbergh work; **5.** did he cross; **6.** did he win?; **7.** was he / Lindbergh; **8.** was Earhart born; **9.** did Earhart's / her plane disappear; **10.** happened; **11.** flew; **12.** wasn't the U.S. government interested; **13.** did the first man walk; **14.** didn't Goddard see

### EXERCISE 20 page 177
🕑 Time: 5–10 min.

**Answers:**

1. When did you fly in a plane for the first time?

2. Who was with you?

3. What was your first impression of flying?

4. What was your longest trip?

5. Did you like the articles about aviation in this lesson?

6. Which article did you like the best?

7. Did you know about Robert Goddard before you read the story?

8. Did you know anything about Amelia Earhart before you read the story?

9. Did you see the first moon landing?

---

**PRACTICE IDEA: SPEAKING**

Have students stand in two concentric circles, with half the students standing in an outer ring around the classroom and the other half standing in an inner ring, facing each other. Instruct students to ask and answer the questions from Exercise 20. Call out *turn* every minute or so. Students in the inner ring should move one space clockwise. Now have students ask and answer with their new partners. Have students ask questions in random order. Make sure students look at each other when they're speaking.

---

## SUMMARY OF LESSON 7

🕑 Time: 20–30 min.

### PART A  THE SIMPLE PAST OF *BE*
Review the forms of the simple past tense of *be*. Have students close their books.

Write on the board:      *was      were*

1. *affirmative*
2. *negative*
3. *Yes/No question*
4. *short answer*
5. *Wh- question*
6. *negative question*
7. *subject question*

Have students work in pairs to make sentences with *was* and *were*. Then have students open their books and compare their sentences with the sentences in the chart. If necessary, have students review:

**7.1**  The Simple Past—Form (page 155)

**7.2**  The Simple Past—Use (page 156)

**7.3**  The Simple Past of *Be*—Forms (pages 158–159)

**7.4**  The Simple Past of *Be*—Uses (page 160)

**7.9**  Negative Statements with the Simple Past (page 169)

**7.10**  Questions with the Simple Past (pages 171–172)

### PART B  THE SIMPLE PAST OF OTHER VERBS
Review the simple past tense of other verbs—regular and irregular. Have students close their books.

Write on the board: *regular* (work) *irregular* (fly)

1. *affirmative*
2. *negative*

3. Yes/No *question*

4. *short answer*

5. Wh- *question*

6. *negative question*

7. *subject question*

Have students work in pairs to make sentences with *work* and *fly*. Then have students compare their sentences with the sentences in the chart. If necessary, have students review:

**7.1** The Simple Past—Form (page 155)

**7.2** The Simple Past—Use (page 156)

**7.5** The Simple Past of Regular Verbs (page 164)

**7.6** The Simple Past of Regular Verbs—Spelling (page 165)

**7.7** The Simple Past of Regular Verbs—Pronunciation (page 166)

**7.8** The Simple Past of Irregular Verbs (page 167)

**7.9** Negative Statements with the Simple Past (page 169)

**7.10** Questions with the Simple Past (pages 171–172)

## TEST/REVIEW

🕐 Time: 15 min.

Have students do the exercise on page 179. For additional practice, use the Assessment CD-ROM with Exam*View*® and the Online Workbook.

**Answers: 1.** didn't come; **2.** was; **3.** wasn't; **4.** did you go; **5.** went; **6.** Did you go; **7.** didn't; **8.** went; **9.** Did you drive; **10.** didn't; **11.** flew; **12.** didn't you drive; **13.** found; **14.** didn't want; **15.** took; **16.** did you stay; **17.** stayed; **18.** did you do; **19.** visited; **20.** was; **21.** loved; **22.** saw; **23.** were; **24.** were

## WRITING

## PART 1 EDITING ADVICE

🕐 Time: 10–15 min.

1. Have students close their books. Write the first few sentences without editing marks or corrections on the board. For example:

   *I wanted to bought a new car.*
   *I studyed for the last test.*
   *He droped his pencil.*

2. Ask students to correct each sentence and provide a rule or an explanation for each correction. This activity can be done individually, in pairs, or as a class.

3. After students have corrected each sentence, tell them to turn to page 180. Say: *Now compare your work with the Editing Advice in the book.* Have students read through all the advice.

## PART 2 EDITING PRACTICE

🕐 Time: 10–15 min.

1. Tell students they are going to put the Editing Advice into practice. Ask: *Do all the shaded words and phrases have mistakes?* (no) Go over the examples with the class. Then do #1 together.

2. Have students complete the practice individually. Then have them compare answers with a partner before checking answers as a class.

3. For the items students had difficulties with, have them go back and find the relevant grammar chart and review it. Monitor and give help as necessary.

**Answers: 1.** had; **2.** C; **3.** did you write; **4.** wrote; **5.** C; **6.** C; **7.** wasn't; **8.** C; **9.** did he go; **10.** Did he go; **11.** C; **12.** were; **13.** died; **14.** was he born?; **15.** born; **16.** was; **17.** C; **18.** saw; **19.** was / happened; **20.** C; **21.** die; **22.** happened; **23.** was

## PART 3 WRITE ABOUT IT

🕐 Time: 30–40 min.

1. In pairs, have students look back at Part 2 and make a list of important pieces of information about Yuri Gagarin. Encourage students to organize their ideas in a simple outline before writing. Have students write their paragraph individually. Remind them to include any useful and relevant vocabulary from this lesson on aviation and to double-check their use of the simple past verb tense. Have them exchange for peer feedback.

2. Review the topic with students, allowing them time to research other famous people from aviation or space exploration. Write students' ideas on the board. Encourage students to organize their thoughts and make notes before they begin to write. If necessary, write model topic sentences on the board first.

## PART 4 EDIT YOUR WRITING

🕐 Time: 15–20 min.

Have students edit their writing by reviewing the Lesson Summary on page 178 and the Editing Advice on page 180. Collect for assessment and/or have students share their essays in small groups.

## EXPANSION ACTIVITIES

1. Have students interview a classmate about his or her experiences before and after they came to the United States. Brainstorm interview questions as a class first, and help students as they write their own interview questions. Have volunteers report back to the class.

2. Write *space exploration* on the board. Elicit from students any words or phrases they think of when they hear the phrase, and write them on the board. Put students in small groups or pairs to discuss their opinions about space exploration. Monitor group work. Give help as needed. Have volunteers share their group's opinions with the class.

3. Tell students to interview an American about a vacation he or she took. Tell them to find out where he or she went, with whom, for how long, and other related information. Brainstorm the questions they can ask in class beforehand. Students can report their interviews to the class or hand in a written report.

4. Tell students to interview an older person about a pivotal moment in history he or she remembers. Tell them to find out as many details as possible about this historical event. Brainstorm the questions they can ask in class beforehand. Students can report their interviews to the class or hand in a written report.

5. Tell students to use the Internet to find out something about one of the following famous people (or have students research a famous person from their countries). They should answer these questions: *What did he or she do? When did he or she do it? When was he or she born? Is he or she still alive? If not, when did he or she die?*

   a. Marie Curie
   b. Alexander Fleming
   c. Thomas Edison
   d. Alexander Graham Bell
   e. Bill Gates
   f. Henry Ford
   g. Jonas Salk
   h. Edwin Hubble
   i. Enrico Fermi
   j. John Von Neumann
   k. Leo Baekeland
   l. Ian Wilmut

Ask volunteers to make a brief presentation in front of the class. Encourage students to include time lines and photos.

6. Tell students to find a Web site with information about the 2004 landing on Mars. Find a picture of Mars. Have volunteers present their information to the class.

7. Tell students to find a Web site with information about the 2003 anniversary of the Wright brothers' first flight. Have them find out what events took place. Have volunteers present their information to the class.

# 8 SHOPPING

## GRAMMAR CHARTS

## LESSON OPENER

Have students look at the photo and read the caption. Ask: *What do you see in the photo?* (people shopping, eating) *Where do you think these people are?* (outdoor shopping center, Las Vegas) Have students read the quotation. Ask: *Do you agree with the quote? Can money buy you happiness? Why or why not?*

**Background:** Retail is one of America's largest industry sectors and private employers. It drives the national economy and supports one out of every four jobs. According to the U.S. Department of Commerce, in 2009 the retail industry generated about $155 billion in earnings for the business services sector, $147 billion for manufacturing, $97 billion for real estate, and $89 billion for the financial services sector. Retail's gross domestic product (GDP) impact accounted for nearly one-fifth (17.6 percent) of U.S. GDP. The United States has several shopping and outlet malls, the largest of which is the Mall of America in Bloomington, Minnesota. Luxury shopping is also popular; Saks Fifth Avenue in New York City is known as one of the fashion capitals of the world. High quality products are also available at low prices alongside generic products from retailers like Target and

Costco. Online shopping is also incredibly popular in the United States, with 191.1 million Americans browsing and buying merchandise online in 2013, and the trend is only growing. The most commonly purchased products in the United States are global positioning system (GPS) technology, instant coffee products, and the most popular and most sold soda in the world, Coca-Cola.

Joshua Becker is an American writer and film director. He has worked as a production assistant on the movie *The Evil Dead* (1981) and is well known for his work with the TV show *Xena: Warrior Princess* (1995–2001).

## CONTEXT

This unit is about shopping. Students will read about shopping in the digital age, if free trials are really free, smart shopping tips, and a typical conversation at the customer service counter.

1. Give students a few minutes to look through the lesson. Have them look at the photos and titles. How do they relate to the context?

2. Elicit the topics that will be discussed.

3. Have students discuss what they know about shopping in pairs or small groups.

## GRAMMAR

Students will learn about infinitives, modals, and imperatives.

1. To activate students' prior knowledge, ask what students know about infinitives, modals, and imperatives.

2. Give several examples of infinitives, modals, and imperatives (e.g., infinitives [*to go, to buy*], modals [*can, could, will, would*], or imperatives [*stand, walk, stop*]).

3. Have volunteers give examples and write them on the board.

### EXPANDING ON THE CONTEXT

The context for this lesson can be enhanced with the following items:

1. Store flyers

2. Store coupons, rebates, and rain checks

# Shopping in the Digital Age,
page 184

## PRE-READING

🕐 Time: 5–10 min.

1. Have students look at the photo and read the caption. Ask: *What is this woman doing?* (taking a picture of a price tag on her cell phone) *Where is the she?* (in a clothes store)

2. Have students read the title and then skim the reading. Ask: *What is the reading about? How do you know?* Have students make predictions.

3. Pre-teach any vocabulary words your students may not know, such as *product, habit, social, attention,* and *electronics.*

4. Ask: *Do you usually shop at a mall or online? Why? What are the benefits of shopping online?* Have volunteers share their knowledge and personal experiences.

## READING GLOSSARY

**product:** something that is made to be sold or used

**habit:** something a person does in a regular, repeated way

**social:** involving activities where people spend time talking to other people

**attention:** special care or treatment

**electronics:** devices that operate using small electronic parts

## READING 🎧

🕐 Time: 10–15 min.

Go over the answers to the Comprehension Check on page 185: **1.** F; **2.** T; **3.** T.

## CONTEXT NOTE

As of July 2015, Bloomberg reported that Amazon passed Walmart as the world's biggest retailer by market value. Amazon has a value of about $272 billion while Walmart has about $233 billion. Although Walmart continues to top Internet retailer lists in terms of sales, with about five times Amazon's annual revenue, Amazon has proven to dominate all other e-commerce competitors in market value.

## ADDITIONAL COMPREHENSION QUESTIONS

*What makes somebody a "smart" shopper?* (ability to use different methods to get the best price) *What is "reverse showrooming"?* (when customers go online and do research before they go into a store to get the product on the same day) *Why do teens prefer to shop at the mall?* (it's a social experience) *What do in-store shoppers want?* (salespeople to give attention, be polite, and be knowledgeable about the product) *What is the number one online purchase?* (electronics)

---

### EXPANDING ON THE READING

The topic for this reading can be enhanced with the following items:

1. Screenshots of top online retailers like Amazon, Ebay, and Alibaba

2. Best showrooming phone apps, like Amazon Price Check, Flow, and Red Laser

3. How-to articles about shopping online

---

### PRACTICE IDEA: LISTENING

Have students first listen to the audio alone. Ask a few comprehension questions, such as: *What do businesses have to do to make money these days?* (understand the habits of today's shoppers) *What is "showrooming"?* (when customers go into a store, look at a product, talk to a salesperson, and then use their phones to find a better price) Repeat the audio if necessary. Then have students open their books and read along as they listen to the audio.

---

## 8.1 Infinitives—Overview,
page 185

🕐 Time: 10–15 min.

1. Have students close their books. Write the example sentences from grammar chart **8.1** on the board:

   *Do you like to shop online?*
   *It's important to compare prices.*
   *Are you surprised to know about shopping apps?*
   *Stores needs to understand shoppers' habits to stay in business.*

   Ask: *What words are the infinitives in these sentences?* If students need help, give them hints (e.g., *What's the subject? What's the verb? What words are left?*). Make notes on the board as students share their ideas.

2. Have students look at grammar chart **8.1** and compare their ideas. Review the explanations providing additional examples as necessary.

3. Direct students' attention to the Language Notes. Emphasize that an infinitive never has an ending and does not show tense.

**EXERCISE 1** pages 185–186  CD 2 TR 4

🕐 Time: 5–10 min.

**Answers: 1.** to get; **2.** to try; **3.** to buy; **4.** to buy; **5.** to take; **6.** to tip; **7.** to do; **8.** to use; **9.** to get; **10.** to shop

# 8.2 Verbs + Infinitives, page 186

🕐 Time: 10–15 min.

1. Have students go back to the reading on page 184 and circle all the verbs (other than *be*) that come before the infinitives (e.g., *like, prefer, need*). Have volunteers give you examples and write them on the board.

2. Then have students look at grammar chart **8.2.** Review the verbs often followed by infinitives and give example sentences in different tenses. Remind students that an infinitive can follow a verb that's in the past, present, and future.

3. Direct students' attention to the Pronunciation Notes. Demonstrate the informal pronunciation of *want to* ("wanna"). Explain that most native speakers say *wanna*—but it's not written that way in academic English.

4. Explain that often the *to* in infinitives is pronounced "ta" or "da" (after a vowel sound as in *try "ta" get*) or "a" (after a /d/ sound as in *decided "a" buy*). Demonstrate the pronunciation. Go over the example sentences. Read the sentences in the top part of the chart as well. Have students practice the pronunciation in pairs.

---

**PRACTICE IDEA: WRITING**

Have students choose five verbs commonly followed by infinitives, and write five sentences using their own information. Have students peer edit and share their sentences in pairs.

---

**EXERCISE 2** page 186

🕐 Time: 5–10 min.

**Answers: 1.** to buy; **2.** to spend; **3.** to compare; **4.** to get; **5.** to read; **6.** to be; **7.** to shop; **8.** to wait

---

**PRACTICE IDEA: SPEAKING**

In pairs, have students discuss which statements in Exercise 2 are true for them. Be sure students ask follow-up questions and explain why. Have volunteers share their partner's preferences with the class.

---

**EXERCISE 3** page 187

🕐 Time: 5–10 min.

**Answers will vary.**

**EXERCISE 4** page 187

🕐 Time: 5–10 min.

**Answers will vary.**

---

**PRACTICE IDEA: WRITING**

Have students write a short paragraph about their partners using some of the information from Exercises 3 and 4. Then have volunteers share interesting information about their partner with the class, if appropriate.

---

# 8.3 *It* + *Be* + Adjective + (Noun) + Infinitive, page 187

🕐 Time: 10–15 min.

1. Have students look at grammar chart **8.3.** Say: *We often use an infinitive with sentences beginning with an impersonal it.* Go over the examples. Point out the list of adjectives that are often followed by an infinitive.

2. Have students work in pairs to make sentences following the word order in the chart. Address questions as they come up. Have volunteers share sentences with the class.

**EXERCISE 5** pages 187–188

🕐 Time: 5–10 min.

**Answers will vary.**

---

**PRACTICE IDEA: SPEAKING**

Have students discuss their answers in Exercise 5 in groups. Ask: *Did anyone have the same ideas you had? Do you agree or disagree with what your groups members wrote?*

---

## 8.4 *Be* + Adjective + Infinitive, page 188

⏱ Time: 5–10 min.

Have students look at grammar chart **8.4**. Review the examples and explanation. Point out the list of adjectives that are often followed by an infinitive. Provide additional examples as necessary.

### EXERCISE 6  pages 188–189

⏱ Time: 5–10 min.

**Answers: 1.** to buy; **2.** to make; **3.** to do; **4,** to spend; **5.** to bother; **6.** to help; **7.** to go; **8.** to use; **9.** to have

---

**PRACTICE IDEA: WRITING AND SPEAKING**

In pairs, have students write a similar conversation as Exercise 6 about a new electronic device, such as a phone or tablet. Then have volunteers to role-play their conversations in front of the class.

---

## 8.5  Object + Infinitive, page 189

⏱ Time: 5–10 min.

1.  Have students close their books. Write on the board: *You want the employees to be polite.* Have students analyze the sentence in pairs and label the parts of the sentence. Ask: *What is the subject? What is the verb? What is the object? What is the infinitive?*

2.  Have students look at grammar chart **8.5** and compare their ideas. Review additional examples, and read the explanation. If necessary, briefly review object pronouns.

### EXERCISE 7  pages 189–190

⏱ Time: 5–10 min.

**Answers:**

**Conversation 1**
**1.** me; **2.** to help; **3.** us to buy; **4.** her to use; **5.** you to consider; **6.** her

**Conversation 2**
**1.** you to; **2.** me to

**Conversation 3**
**1.** me to get; **2.** us

**Conversation 4**
**1.** me; **2.** to help; **3.** to pay; **4.** to help

---

### EXERCISE 8  page 190

⏱ Time: 5–10 min.

**Answers: 1.** expect me to save; **2.** want them to leave; **3.** wanted them to buy; **4.** want you to talk; **5.** encourage you to be; **6.** expected them to buy; **7.** wanted him to buy; **8.** expect you to graduate

---

**PRACTICE IDEA: SPEAKING**

Have students compare answers to Exercise 8 in pairs and discuss any differences. Then, have them read the conversation aloud in pairs.

---

**PRACTICE IDEA: SPEAKING**

Put students in small groups with classmates from similar cultures. Write on the board: *Who has expectations of you? What do they expect you to do?* Clarify the word *expectations* before students begin. Then, have students share stories and compare expectations. Have volunteers share if their group had similar or different experiences.

---

## 8.6 Infinitives to Show Purpose, page 190

⏱ Time: 5–10 min.

1.  Have students close their books. Write on the board: *I teach English in order to make a difference.* Ask: *Why do I teach English?* Point to the phrase *in order to make a difference* and elicit student responses. Put parentheses around the phrase *in order* and underline the phrase *to make a difference.* Write *purpose* above it. Say: *I teach English for this reason, for this purpose.*

2.  Ask: *Why do you study English?* Have students share their answers in pairs. Have volunteers write their answers on the board. Be sure they use an infinitive phrase.

3.  Have students look at grammar chart **8.6.** Explain that the use of *to* in order to show purpose is a short form of *in order to.* Read through the example sentences and explanations. Then go back to the top of the chart and ask volunteers to substitute *in order to* for *to* in the other example sentences.

4.  Have students go back to the reading on page 184. Say: *Underline the infinitives that show purpose or why something is being done.*

## EXERCISE 9  page 191

🕐 Time: 5–10 min.

**Answers: 1.** to talk; **2.** to compare; **3.** to look for; **4.** to print; **4.** to learn; **6.** to change; **7.** to make

## EXERCISE 10  page 191

🕐 Time: 5–10 min.

**Answers will vary.**

READING

# Are Free Trials Really Free?,
page 192

## PRE-READING

🕐 Time: 5–10 min.

1.  Have students look at the photo. Ask: *What is a "free trial"?* (a test of a product or service at no cost)

2.  Have students read the title and then skim the reading. Ask: *What is the reading about? How do you know?* Have students make predictions.

3.  Pre-teach any vocabulary words your students may not know, such as *service, app, bill,* and *period*.

4.  Ask: *Have you ever done a free trial? Was it a good experience? Why or why not?* Have volunteers share their knowledge and personal experiences.

## READING GLOSSARY

**service:** work done that doesn't involve producing goods

**app:** a computer program designed to run on mobile devices like smartphones

**bill:** a document that says how much money you owe for something

**period:** length of time in which a series of events takes place

## READING

🕐 Time: 10–15 min.

Go over the answers to the Comprehension Check on page 193: **1.** T; **2.** T; **3.** T.

## ADDITIONAL COMPREHENSION QUESTIONS

*Is it easier to start or cancel a free trial?* (start) *Why is it so hard to cancel a free trial?* (hard to find phone number, have to cancel online) *Where might they charge the free trial?* (your credit card) *What should you read before you sign up?* (cancellation policy) *What are other tips for signing up for a free trial?* (mark your calendar to cancel; use a credit card, not debit card; don't sign up just because it's free)

### EXPANDING ON THE READING

The topic for this reading can be enhanced with the following items:

1.  Sample free trial Web pages
2.  Phone number and basic information of local consumer protection agency
3.  How-to articles about canceling free trials

## 8.7 Modals and Phrasal Modals—Overview, page 193

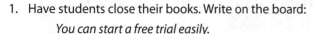

⏱ Time: 10–15 min.

1. Have students close their books. Write on the board:

   *You can start a free trial easily.*

   *You should read the cancellation policy.*

   Have students analyze the sentences in pairs. Ask: *What's the subject? What's the verb? What's the object?* Have volunteers share their ideas with the class. Circle the words *can* and *should* and underline the verb that follows.

2. Have students look at grammar chart **8.7.** Have volunteers read the examples aloud. Review the explanations. Point out that modals don't have an -s form and aren't followed by infinitives.

3. Direct students' attention to the Language Note. Compare the word order in the different sentences.

4. Review the three phrasal modals and their examples. Provide more examples if necessary.

**EXERCISE 11** pages 193–194  CD 2 TR 6

⏱ Time: 10–15 min.

**Answers: 1.** might; **2.** should; **3.** can't; **4.** can't; **5.** don't have to; **6.** can; **7.** should; **8.** can't; **9.** can; **10.** must; **11.** can; **12.** have to; **13.** have to; **14.** may; **15.** should

---

**PRACTICE IDEA: LISTENING**

To practice listening skills, have students first listen to the audio alone. Ask a few comprehension questions, such as: *Why do manufacturers send coupons to shoppers?* (They want people to try their products.) *What does a rain check do?* (It allows you to buy an item at the sale price even after the sale is over.) Then have students open their books and read along as they listen to the audio.

---

## 8.8 *Can, Be Able To, Be Allowed To,* pages 194–195

⏱ Time: 10–15 min.

1. Have students close their books. Write a matching exercise on the board:

   *1. I'm not able to find the phone number.*

---

*2. Free trials can sometimes cost money.*

*3. Can I download music for free?*

*4. You can't buy more than two of this sale item.*

   a. permission

   b. prohibition

   c. ability

   d. possibility

   Have students match the examples with the explanations in pairs. (**Answers: 1.** c; **2.** d; **3.** a; **4.** b)

2. Have students look at grammar chart 8.8 and check their work. Go over additional examples and address any questions.

3. Direct students' attention to the Language Notes. Provide additional examples of *be permitted* and *be allowed to.*

4. Direct students' attention to the Pronunciation Notes. Tell students to listen for the sound of the vowel and not the ending because the final *t* in *can't* is difficult to hear.

5. Demonstrate the pronunciation with the sentences in the grammar chart. Ask students to hold up their hands if they hear *can* and to keep their hands down if they hear *can't.* Then have students practice the pronunciation in pairs.

## ADDITIONAL PRACTICE

1. Do a class brainstorm of sports and other physical activities and games. Write as many ideas as possible on the board. Have students discuss in pairs what activities they can and cannot do.

2. Have students get in small groups and brainstorm the rules and regulations of the school. Have them make a list of things students can do and things students can't do. Have the groups compare their lists. Have volunteers present their group's ideas with the class. Encourage them to use *be permitted* and *be allowed to* in their presentations.

3. Have students get in small groups with classmates from another country or culture. If appropriate, ask them to share federal laws according to their governments of things they can or can't do in their country (e.g., *Women can't drive cars, but they can vote in elections. Parents can only have one child.*).

## PRACTICE IDEA: SPEAKING

Have students write one thing they do well on a small piece of paper. Tell students not to write their names. Put all the pieces of paper into a bag. Pass around the bag and have students pick a paper from the bag. Instruct students to mingle with classmates and ask *Yes/*No questions to find the person who wrote it (e.g., *Can you swim well? Can you ride a bike well?*).

**EXERCISE 12** page 195

🕐 Time: 5–10 min.

**Answers will vary.**

## PRACTICE IDEA: SPEAKING

Have students discuss their answers in small groups. Go through the items in Exercise 12, one by one, and do a class survey. Have volunteers share their reactions to and experiences with U.S. supermarkets.

**EXERCISE 13** page 196

🕐 Time: 5–10 min.

**Answers: 1.** can help; **2.** 'm not able to finish; **3.** can give; **4.** can't wait; **5.** 're not allowed to apply; **6.** can say

## 8.9 *Should,* page 196

🕐 Time: 5–10 min.

1. Have students look at grammar chart **8.9.** Say: *We use* should *to give or ask for advice.* Read the examples in the chart.
2. Go over the negative and the contraction *shouldn't.* Point out that the negative is used to give advice or a warning.

## PRACTICE IDEA: WRITING

Have students write their own "I should" lists. Say: *What do you think you should do?* Make a list: *I should exercise more, I should eat more vegetables, etc.*

**EXERCISE 14** page 196

🕐 Time: 5–10 min.

**Answers will vary.**

## PRACTICE IDEA: SPEAKING

Have students compare advice in groups. Then have them compile the best advice from the group and present it to the class.

**EXERCISE 15** page 197

🕐 Time: 5–10 min.

**Answers: 1.** Should we buy; **2.** shouldn't buy; **3.** shouldn't eat; **4.** should use; **5,** should be; **6.** should look at; **7.** should take; **8.** should come; **9.** should bring; **10.** Should we pay

## PRACTICE IDEAS: SPEAKING

In pairs, have students discuss what else parents should or should not buy for their children at the supermarket. Have them write a list of five to ten statements. Then have groups exchange lists and say whether they agree or disagree with the statements.

## 8.10 *Must* and *Have To,*
pages 197–198

🕐 Time: 10–15 min.

1. Have students look at grammar chart **8.10.** Have students read the examples aloud. Review the explanations and address any questions.
2. Direct students' attention to the Language Note. Give additional examples of sentences expressing necessity with *have got to* and contractions.

## PRACTICE IDEA: WRITING

In pairs, have students discuss and write rules for what they *must* or *have to* do in particular situations in the United States (e.g., hospitals, restaurants, embassies, schools).

**EXERCISE 16** page 198

🕐 Time: 5–10 min.

**Answers: 1.** have to return; **2.** have to use; **3.** have to buy; **4.** has to send; **5.** has to show; **6.** has to go

## 8.11 *Not Have To* and *Must Not*, page 198

🕐 Time: 5–10 min.

1. Have students look at grammar chart **8.11.** Point out that the affirmative *must* and *have to* have similar meanings, but the negatives *mustn't* and *don't have to* are very different. Go over the examples.

2. Review the explanations emphasizing that *must not* means something is prohibited or against the law while *don't have to* simply means something is not necessary.

3. Direct students' attention to the Language Note. Provide additional examples where we use *can't* rather than *must not* (e.g., *Students can't turn homework in late. Dogs can't eat human food.*).

---

### PRESENTATION IDEA

Have students make a poster with things you have to or don't have to do when you visit their countries as tourists. If possible, have pairs or groups from the same country work together. Display the posters around the classroom. Have a class discussion comparing the posters.

---

**EXERCISE 17** page 199

🕐 Time: 5–10 min.

**Answers: 1.** buy; **2.** use / take; **3.** take; **4.** go; **5.** carry / take; **6.** pay; **7.** go

## 8.12 *May, Might,* and *Will,* page 199

🕐 Time: 5–10 min.

1. Have students look at grammar chart **8.12.** Have volunteers read examples aloud.

2. Review the explanations. Explain that the negative of *may* is *may not* and the negative of *might* is *might not*, and there are no contractions for *may not* or *might not*.

3. Direct students' attention to the Language Note. Tell students not to confuse *maybe* (adverb) and *may be* (verb—e.g., *I may be free tomorrow night.*).

**EXERCISE 18** page 200

🕐 Time: 5–10 min.

**Answers: 1.** may receive; **2.** might want; **3.** may be; **4.** might get; **5.** might not be; **6.** may try

**EXERCISE 19** page 200

🕐 Time: 5–10 min.

**Answers will vary.**

---

### PRACTICE IDEA: WRITING

Have students rewrite the *If* clauses in sentences 1–6 in Exercise 19, changing them from affirmative to negative (e.g., 1. *If you don't shop online, _____.*). Have them write new endings for the sentences and share their new ideas with a partner.

---

### PRACTICE IDEA: READING

Have students go back to the reading on page 192. Have them re-read the text aloud in pairs and notice the modals and phrasal modals. Ask students to identify the use for each modal or phrasal modal (ability, permission, prohibition, etc.).

---

**READING**

## Shopping Tips, page 201

### PRE-READING

🕐 Time: 5–10 min.

1. Have students look at the photo. Ask: *What is this woman doing?* (completing a purchase) *Where is she?* (at a retail store) *What objects do you see in the photo?* (necklaces, belts, shoes, bags, other jewelry)

2. Have students read the title and then skim the reading. Ask: *What is the reading about? How do you know?* Have students make predictions.

3. Pre-teach any vocabulary words your students may not know, such as *coupon, item, policy, discount,* and *senior citizen.*

4. Ask: *Do you like to go shopping? Why or why not? What have you learned to make shopping a good experience?* Have volunteers share their knowledge and personal experiences.

## READING GLOSSARY

**coupon:** piece of paper that lets you get a service or product for a lower price

**item:** an individual thing

**policy:** an officially accepted set of rules

**discount:** an amount taken off a regular price

**senior citizen:** an older person

## READING  CD 2 TR 7

🕐 Time: 10–15 min.

Go over the answers to the Comprehension Check on page 201: **1.** T; **2.** T; **3.** T.

## ADDITIONAL COMPREHENSION QUESTIONS

*How can you find a coupon for your favorite store?* (Google the store name with the word *coupon*) *Why should you use a gift card as soon as possible?* (some have expiration dates) *Why shouldn't you shop when you are hungry?* (Hungry shoppers often buy a lot of junk food) *Who are some people who often get discounts?* (teachers, college students, and senior citizens)

---

### EXPANDING ON THE READING

The topic for this reading can be enhanced with the following items:

1. Web sites for store coupons
2. Sample receipts from local retail stores
3. Student ID cards and an explanation of discounts

---

### PRACTICE IDEA: LISTENING

To practice listening skills, have students first listen to the audio alone. Ask students to remember and repeat as many of the tips as they can in pairs. Repeat the audio if necessary. Then have students open their books and read along as they listen to the audio.

---

## 8.13 Imperatives, page 202

🕐 Time: 10–15 min.

1. Have students close their books. Write a matching exercise on the board:

   1. *Please sign your name at the bottom.*

2. *Stand up!*
3. *Watch out! There's a car coming.*
4. *Always do your best.*
5. *Have a nice day.*
6. *Go away.*

   a. *to give a warning or suggestion*
   b. *in some impolite expressions*
   c. *to give a demand*
   d. *to give instructions*
   e. *to give encouragement*
   f. *in certain social expressions*

   Have students match the examples with the explanations. (**Answers: 1.** d; **2.** c; **3.** a; **4.** e; **5.** f; **6.** b)

2. Tell students to look at grammar chart **8.13** and check their work. Review the example sentences and explanations. Explain that an imperative is the base form of the verb. Provide additional social expressions (e.g., *Sleep well. Break a leg!*). Have students discuss additional examples of instructions, suggestions, demands, and encouragements in pairs.

3. Direct students' attention to the Language Notes. Review the word order when using *always* and *never*. Look back at the examples in the chart and point out that the subject is *you* even though we don't say or write it.

## EXERCISE 20 page 202

🕐 Time: 5–10 min.

**Answers: 1.** compare; **2.** find; **3.** Ask; **4.** Don't buy; **5.** Don't lose; **6.** Take; **7.** don't forget; **8.** train

## EXERCISE 21 page 202

🕐 Time: 5–10 min.

**Answers will vary.**

---

### PRACTICE IDEA: SPEAKING

Survey the class. Have groups report their answers to Exercise 21 to the class (e.g., *Everyone in our group said you must bring your own bag to the supermarket.*).

---

# At The Customer Service Counter, page 203

## PRE-READING

⏱ Time: 5–10 min.

1.  Have students look at the photo. Ask: *Who is the woman in the photo?* (a store employee, a customer service worker, cashier) *Where is she?* (at a customer service counter, in a store)

2.  Have students read the title and then skim the reading. Ask: *What is the reading about? How do you know?* Have students make predictions.

3.  Pre-teach any vocabulary words your students may not know, such as *to cash, to fill out, application, driver's license,* and *customer.*

4.  Ask: *What are different things you can do at a customer service counter at a supermarket in the city where you used to live?* Have volunteers share their knowledge and personal experiences.

## READING GLOSSARY

**to cash:** to exchange a check for currency

**to fill out:** to complete

**application:** a formal and written request for something

**driver's license:** a card that shows you have the legal right to drive

**customer:** somebody who buys good or services from a business

## READING

CD 1
TR 8

⏱ Time: 10–15 min.

Go over the answers to the Comprehension Check on page 204: **1.** T; **2.** F; **3.** F.

## ADDITIONAL COMPREHENSION QUESTIONS

*Where is there a check-cashing service?* (at the customer service counter) *What does person A have to fill out to get a check-cashing card?* (an application) *What does person A need to cash a check?* (a driver's license) *What mistakes did person A make in filling out the application?* (wrote in the gray box) *When will person A get the check-cashing card?* (7 to 10 days)

## EXPANDING ON THE READING

The topic for this reading can be enhanced with the following items:

1.  Online and paper applications to cash a check
2.  Stamps

### PRACTICE IDEA: WRITING

Bring in sample paper applications to cash a check from your local supermarket. Have students fill them out and then practice the conversation in the reading on page 203 in pairs. Have volunteers role-play the conversation in front of the class.

## 8.14 Modals and Other Expressions for Politeness, page 204 ⭐

⏱ Time: 10–15 min.

1.  Have students close their books. Tell one student: *Stand up.* Then say to another student: *Could you stand up?* Explain that imperatives like *stand up, sit down, don't run,* etc., can be used to make a request, but modals can also be used for requests. They sound softer and more polite. Say: *Could you stand up? Could you sit down?*

2.  Have students look at grammar chart **8.14**. As you review the examples and explanations, have volunteers give additional examples for each row. Draw special attention to the contraction of *would* and the use of *let's* to make suggestions that include the speaker.

### PRACTICE IDEA: WRITING

In pairs, have students write a short dialog for one of the following uses of modals:

1.  *To make and answer a request*
2.  *To ask and give permission*
3.  *To state a need with the same meaning as want*
4.  *To offer and take a suggestion that includes the speaker*
5.  *To offer and accept help as a salesperson*

Encourage them to use contractions. Have volunteers role-play their dialogs in front of the class.

**EXERCISE 22** pages 204–205

⏱ Time: 5–10 min.

**Answers: 1.** May I; **2.** I'd like; **3.** Could you; **4.** Would you like; **5.** Could you / Would you; **6.** Why don't we; **7.** Could you; **8.** Can I; **9.** Do you want / Would you like; **10.** Why don't you think about it?

---

**PRACTICE IDEA: SPEAKING**

Have students practice the conversation or create similar conversations in pairs. Ask volunteers to role-play the conversation in front of the class.

---

## SUMMARY OF LESSON 8

⏱ Time: 20–30 min.

## PART A  INFINITIVES

Review infinitive patterns. Have students write about sports or other physical activities. Have them write a sentence for each infinitive pattern:

Sentence 1: verb followed by an infinitive
Sentence 2: *it* + *be* + adjective + infinitive
Sentence 3: *be* + adjective + infinitive
Sentence 4: object before an infinitive
Sentence 5: using an infinitive to show purpose

If necessary, have students review:

**8.1**  Infinitives—Overview (page 185)

**8.2**  Verbs + Infinitives (page 186)

**8.3**  It + *Be* + Adjective + (Noun) + Infinitive (page 187)

**8.4**  *Be* + Adjective + Infinitive (page 188)

**8.5**  Object + Infinitive (page 189)

**8.6**  Infinitives to Show Purpose (page 190)

## PART B  MODALS

Review modals. Go over examples and explanations in the chart. Have students write about their experiences living, studying, and/or working in the United States. Have them work in pairs to write sentences for each modal. Monitor pair work. Give help as needed. If necessary, have students review:

**8.7**  Modals and Phrasal Modals—Overview (page 193)

**8.8**  *Can, Be Able To, Be Allowed To* (pages 194–195)

**8.9**  *Should* (page 196)

**8.10**  *Must* and *Have To* (pages 197–198)

**8.11**  *Not Have To* and *Must Not* (page 198)

**8.12**  *May, Might,* and *Will* (page 199)

## PART C  PHRASAL MODALS

Review phrasal modals. Go over examples and explanations in the chart. Have students work individually to write about a specific experience where they weren't able to do something in the United States. Give help as needed. If necessary, have students review:

**8.7**  Modals and Phrasal Modals—Overview (page 193)

**8.8**  *Can, Be Able To, Be Allowed To* (pages 194–195)

**8.10**  *Must* and *Have To* (pages 197–198)

**8.11**  *Not Have To* and *Must Not* (page 198)

## PART D  IMPERATIVES

Remind students that for an imperative, you use the base form of the verb. In groups, have students take turns giving each other commands (e.g., *Sit down. Write your name.*). If necessary, have students review:

**8.13**  Imperatives (page 202)

## PART E  SUGGESTIONS

Remind students that *let's* is the contraction of *let us* and that it is used for making suggestions. Have students make a list of things to do and places to go in their countries. Then have students work in pairs to plan a trip and itinerary to each country (e.g., *Let's go to Bogotá. Let's visit the Museum of Gold. Then let's see a bullfight.*). If necessary, have students review:

**8.14**  Modals and Other Expressions for Politeness (page 204)

---

## TEST/REVIEW

⏱ Time: 15 min.

Have students do the exercise on page 207. For additional practice, use the Assessment CD-ROM with Exam*View*® and the Online Workbook.

**Answers: 1.** to get; **2.** would / 'd; **3.** to follow; **4.** is; **5.** to compare; **6.** get; **7.** it's; **8.** to take; **9.** to have; **10.** don't have to; **11.** go; **12.** may / might; **13.** him to match; **14.** should; **15.** might; **16.** to call; **17.** to; **8.** it's; **19.** to get; **20.** have to wait; **21.** to wait; **22.** should; **23.** can you; **24.** wants us to; **25.** might not; **26.** would; **27.** to learn

# WRITING

## PART 1 EDITING ADVICE
🕐 Time: 10–15 min.

1. Have students close their books. Write the first few sentences without editing marks or corrections on the board. For example:

   *I must to go.*

   *They like play.*

2. Ask students to correct each sentence and provide a rule or an explanation for each correction. This activity can be done individually, in pairs, or as a class.

3. After students have corrected each sentence, tell them to turn to page 130. Say: *Now compare your work with the Editing Advice in the book.* Have students read through all the advice.

## PART 2 EDITING PRACTICE
🕐 Time: 10–15 min.

1. Tell students they are going to put the Editing Advice into practice. Ask: *Do all the shaded words and phrases have mistakes?* (no) Go over the examples with the class. Then do #1 together.

2. Have students complete the practice individually. Then have them compare answers with a partner before checking answers as a class.

3. For the items students had difficulties with, have them go back and find the relevant grammar chart and review it. Monitor and give help as necessary.

**Answers: 1.** C; **2.** get; **3.** me to help; **4.** you to be; **5.** It's; **6.** C; **7.** to look; **8.** can look; **9.** C; **10.** try to use; **11.** C; **12.** C; **13.** easy to make; **14.** C; **15.** happy to help; **16.** can you; **17.** want you to help

## PART 3 WRITE ABOUT IT
🕐 Time: 30–40 min.

1. Review the topic with students clarifying any questions that students don't understand. Lead a class brainstorm of purchases to write about, and write students' ideas on the board. Have students choose a purchase and discuss the experience in small groups. Encourage students to organize their thoughts and make notes before they begin to write. If necessary, write model topic sentences on the board first. Remind them to include any useful and relevant vocabulary from this lesson on shopping and to use infinitives. Have students peer edit and pay attention to the use of the simple past tense.

2. Repeat the procedure for the second topic. Have students share their food shopping experiences in pairs. Then have them write their compositions. Encourage students to use modals and phrasal modals. If necessary, write model topic sentences on the board first.

## PART 4 EDIT YOUR WRITING
🕐 Time: 15–20 min.

Have students edit their writing by reviewing the Lesson Summary on page 206 and the Editing Advice on page 208. Collect for assessment and/or have students share their paragraphs in small groups.

## EXPANSION ACTIVITIES

1. Have students share and then write about what any rules, regulations, or activities in their last school using modals such as *I had* to and *I didn't have to.* Briefly review the past tense if necessary.

2. Elicit from students ways to save money when you shop and write their ideas on the board. Have students get in small groups and make a poster or pamphlet for "smart shoppers." Remind them to use imperatives, modals, and phrasal modals in their suggestions and advice. Have students hang their posters or pamphlets on the walls and invite other classes to ask questions about their work.

3. Have students write a letter or e-mail to a family member or friend who wants to live in the United States, giving advice about shopping in the United States.

4. Tell students: *You're going to comparison shop for electronics on the Internet.* Suggest products such as a DVD player, TV, digital camera, or computer. Ask students to find prices for two items. Have students make a chart of the products they looked for and the prices they found. Survey the class. Who found the best prices? What product do they suggest buying?

5. Have students give advice, suggestions, or warnings to people who are getting married (*should, have to/ don't have to,* imperatives).

# 9 HEALTHY LIVING

## GRAMMAR CHARTS

## LESSON OPENER

Have students look at the photo and read the caption. Ask: *Where is this man?* (at a juice bar) *What is his job?* (owner of a juice bar, restaurant owner) *How is he feeling?* (happy, proud) Have students read the quotation. Ask: *How has the food we eat changed in the past 100 years? What advice do your grandparents or parents give you about food and cooking?*

**Background:** The United States is among the wealthiest nations in the world and prides itself on a high standard of living. According to the National Institutes of Health (NIH), the United States. has some of the top medical care in the world, leading to lower cancer death rates, greater control of blood pressure and cholesterol levels, and longer life expectancies when compared with other peer countries. The United States, however, ranks low in other health areas, such as infant mortality, drug-related deaths, and obesity and diabetes rates. Explanations for these discrepancies point to health behaviors like higher rates of drug and alcohol abuse, and a culture designed around automobile use that discourages physical activity. But the American health care system is by far the largest indicator of the health status of the United States. While the United States spends more on health care as percentage of gross domestic product (GDP) than any other nation, it has a relatively large uninsured population and more limited access to primary care. The federal government is focusing on improving these issues. In 2010, the United States passed the Patient Protection and Affordable Care Act (PPACA), sometimes known as ObamaCare, to help hospitals and primary physicians update their financial, technological, and clinical practices and provide a healthier life for all Americans.

Michael Pollan is an American author, activist, and professor of journalism. His research and work critiques the industrial food chain, agribusiness, and factory farming in the United States. He is the author of books advocating for local eating and farming practices such as *The Omnivore's Dilemma* (2006) and *In Defense of Food* (2008).

## CONTEXT

This unit is about healthy living. Students will read about organic food, the importance of water, and cultures that eat less and live longer.

1.  Give students a few minutes to look through the lesson. Have them look at the photos and titles. How do they relate to the context?

2.  Elicit the topics that will be discussed.

3.  Have students discuss what they know about healthy living in pairs or small groups.

## GRAMMAR

Students will learn about count and noncount nouns and quantity words and phrases.

1.  To activate students' prior knowledge, ask what students know about count and noncount nouns and quantity words and phrases.

2.  Give several examples of count and noncount nouns and quantity words and phrases. Say: *Name two articles that we've already studied.* (a, an) *Do you know any quantity words?* (some, many)

3.  Have volunteers give examples and write them on the board.

## EXPANDING ON THE CONTEXT

The context for this lesson can be enhanced with the following items:

1. Dietary guidelines from the USDA
2. Online information and pamphlets about farmer's markets
3. Healthy living magazines
4. Rankings of the healthiest states in the United States

## READING

# Organic Food, page 212

## PRE-READING

🕐 Time: 5–10 min.

1. Have students look at the photo. Ask: *Where is this picture taken?* (in a supermarket) *What kinds of food do you see?* (vegetables like carrots, lettuce, beets, celery, radishes, etc.)

2. Have students read the title and then skim the reading. Ask: *What is the reading about? How do you know?* Have students make predictions.

3. Pre-teach any vocabulary words your students may not know, such as *product, farmer,* and *chemical.*

4. Ask: *Is it common for people to grow and buy organic food in your hometown? Do you eat organic food? Why or why not?* Have volunteers share their knowledge and personal experiences.

## READING GLOSSARY

**product:** something made or grown to be sold or used
**farmer:** a person growing living things for food
**chemical:** a substance made by a chemical process

## READING  CD 2 TR 9

🕐 Time: 10–15 min.

Go over the answers to the Comprehension Check on page 213: **1.** F; **2.** T; **3.** T.

## CONTEXT NOTE

Organic farming has become quite popular in the United States. Within this area are two notable movements: the slow food movement and the farm-to-table movement. The slow food movement juxtaposes itself with the industrial speed of fast food. The goal is preserve

traditional farming and cuisine. Likewise, the farm-to-table movement focuses on local, sustainable agriculture. It refers to and promotes the natural production cycle of food, from the farm (harvesting) to the table (consumption).

## ADDITIONAL COMPREHENSION QUESTIONS

*Why does it take longer for organic animals to grow?* (They aren't given growth hormones) *Why are organic products more expensive?* (Farming without chemicals takes more work) *Why is organic farming better for the planet?* (It doesn't harm the soil, water, and air) *Why is organic farming better for farmers?* (They don't have to breathe pesticides) *What are some nonorganic foods to avoid?* (apples, spinach, lettuce, etc.) *Is all organic food healthy?* (no)

## EXPANDING ON THE READING

The topic for this reading can be enhanced with the following items:

1. Nutrition labels
2. Infographics or diagrams comparing organic and conventional foods
3. Examples of organic food labels and packaging
4. Charts or graphs with statistics about organic food and farming
5. Paper flyers from stores carrying organic products

## PRACTICE IDEA: LISTENING

Have students first listen to the audio alone. Ask a few comprehension questions, such as: *What is different about organic meat, eggs, and dairy products?* (The animals are raised without growth hormones) *What is different about organic fruits and vegetables?* (They don't have pesticides) *Why are organic products better for you?* (They are better for your health and the health of the planet) Repeat the audio if necessary. Then have students open their books and read along as they listen to the audio.

## 9.1 Count and Noncount Nouns—An Overview, page 213

🕐 Time: 10–15 min.

1. Have students close their books. Write on the board:

| count nouns | noncount nouns |
|---|---|
| an apple / apples | meat |
| an egg / eggs | corn |
| a banana / bananas | bread |
| an onion / onions | rice |

2. Say: *There are two groups of nouns in English: count and noncount.* Ask: *What is the difference between the two?* In pairs, have students analyze the lists and make rules to answer the question. Have volunteers share their ideas with the class.

3. Have students look at grammar chart **9.1** and compare their ideas. Have volunteers read the examples aloud. Review the explanations, and address any confusion about articles.

---

**PRACTICE IDEA: SPEAKING**

Put a number of light, small objects in two bags (e.g., pen, garlic, lipstick, phone charger). Put students into two teams, and have them sit in two small circles. One by one, students should pull an object from a bag and guess what each object is. The student to their left says whether that object is count or noncount. Each correct guess gets one point.

---

**EXERCISE 1** pages 213–214   CD 2 TR 10

🕐 Time: 10–15 min.

**Answers: 1.** foods; **2.** information; **3.** choices; **4.** food; **5.** calories; **6.** fat; **7.** fats; **8.** nuts; **9.** oil; **10.** avocados; **11.** cookies; **12.** chips; **13.** snacks; **14.** salt; **15.** beans; **16.** vegetables; **17.** fruits; **18.** grains; **19.** rice; **20.** bread; **21.** pasta; **22.** flour; **23.** Sugar; **24.** Fruit; **25.** vitamins; **26.** minerals; **27.** Fish; **28.** chicken; **29.** eggs; **30.** beans; **31.** meat

---

**PRACTICE IDEA: SPEAKING**

Ask students to bring in packages of food they eat on a daily basis (e.g., breakfast foods, snack items). Put students in small group to analyze the different categories on the packages. Have a volunteer from each group share their group's findings with the class. Take a class survey and decide which foods are the healthiest and least healthy.

---

## 9.2 Groups of Noncount Nouns, pages 214–215

🕐 Time: 10–15 min.

1. Have students look at grammar chart **9.2**. Explain that there are many different types of noncount nouns. Review the examples group by group. Have volunteers read the noncount nouns aloud.

2. After each group, have students draw three to five of the noncount nouns in that group on a blank sheet of paper. Be sure they draw a whole picture for the nouns in Group A, separate parts for the nouns in Group B, and different categories for the nouns in Group C. For Group D, encourage students to be creative and draw whatever the abstract noun means to them.

3. Have students get in pairs and compare drawings. Have them explain their drawings from Group D in small groups.

4. Direct students' attention to the Language Notes. Review instances when nouns can be both count and noncount nouns. Stress the importance of context when deciding if a noun should be count or noncount.

**EXERCISE 2** page 215

🕐 Time: 10–15 min.

**Answers:**

| Noncount Nouns | Count Nouns | |
|---|---|---|
| information | choices | minerals |
| oil | nuts | eggs |
| chicken | avocados | |
| salt | cookies | |
| sugar | (potato) chips | |
| rice | snacks | |
| fish | beans | |
| meat | vegetables | |
| bread | grains | |
| pasta | calories | |
| flour | vitamins | |

🕐 Time: 5–10 min.

**Answers: 1.** milk; **2.** candy; **3.** coffee; **4.** Oliver oil; **5.** salt;
**6.** sugar; **7.** information; **8.** advice

**EXERCISE 4**  pages 216–217

🕐 Time: 10–15 min.

**Answers: 1.** vegetable; **2.** potatoes; **3.** sugar; **4.** fries;
**5.** cholesterol; **6.** carrots; **7.** broccoli; **8.** corn; **9.** peas;
**10.** fruit; **11.** bananas; **12.** strawberries; **13.** cherries;
**14.** milk; **15.** yogurt; **16.** beans; **17.** almonds; **18.** oranges;
**19.** vitamins; **20.** minerals; **21.** food; **22.** pills

---

**PRACTICE IDEA: SPEAKING**

Have students practice the conversations in
Exercise 4 in pairs. Have volunteers role-play all or
part of the conversation in front of the class.

---

**PRACTICE IDEA: SPEAKING**

Have students make lists of the healthiest and
least healthy foods they eat. Then have them get
in small groups and share their list, explaining
why they think each item on their list is healthy or
unhealthy.

---

# 9.3 Units of Measure with Noncount Nouns, page 217

🕐 Time: 10–15 min.

1. Have students look at grammar chart **9.3**. Write on
the board:

   ~~a water~~ → [a bottle of] water
   ~~two breads~~ → [two slices of] bread
   ~~an advice~~ → [a piece of] advice

   Read through the examples on the board. Point out
   that we can't use articles like *a/an*, number words, or
   add an *-s* to noncount nouns.

2. Review the examples in the chart. As you read
   through the units of measure, display as many
   images of the examples as possible to help students
   understand new terminology like *container*, *portion*,
   *measurement*, and *piece*.

3. Direct students' attention to the Language Note.
   Provide additional examples using *a helping of* or *a
   serving of* (e.g., *Would you like a serving of potatoes?*).

---

**PRACTICE IDEA: READING**

Bring in units of measure conversion tables. Have
students read through the different measurement
systems in pairs and compare the terms for
customary units used in the United States with
metric units used in other countries. Have them
calculate their weight and height using the tables.

---

## ADDITIONAL PRACTICE

1. Have students bring in a recipe for their favorite
   dish. Ask them to bring in accompanying images
   if possible. Have students get in pairs and read the
   recipes aloud. Have volunteers share the recipes with
   the class.

2. Print off a number of recipes, and have each student
   choose one. Have the students underline the units of
   measure in each recipe.

3. Have students draw a plate on a blank sheet of paper.
   Use the My Plate template from the USDA Web site as a
   model. Have students divide their plate into helpings or
   servings and label each category (e.g., *fruits, vegetables,
   proteins, grains, dairy*). Be sure to have them draw a
   bigger section for *proteins* if they eat more protein. Have
   them compare their plates in pairs. Then, have students
   brainstorm and write which food items would go in
   each serving. Put the plates up on the wall for display.

4. Help students find a calorie counter on a phone
   app or Web site. Have them calculate the calories
   for different meals. For example, 4 mini muffins and
   1 cup fresh fruit is 240 calories plus 90 calories: total
   breakfast is 330 calories. Have students compare their
   meals and decide which are healthiest.

**EXERCISE 5**  page 217

🕐 Time: 5–10 min.

**Answers: 1.** cups of; **2.** piece of / slice of; **3.** pounds of
/ kilos of; **4.** loaf of; **5.** slices of / pieces of; **6.** bag of /
pound of / kilo of; **7.** bowl of; **8.** teaspoon of / spoonful of;
**9.** bowl of; **10.** ears of

**READING**

# The Importance of Water, page 218

## PRE-READING

🕐 Time: 5–10 min.

1. Have students look at the photo. Ask: *Where is the woman in the photo?* (in nature, on a mountain) *What is she doing?* (drinking water, exercising, hiking)

2. Have students read the title and then skim the reading. Ask: *What is the reading about? How do you know?* Have students make predictions.

3. Pre-teach any vocabulary words your students may not know, such as *source, humid, sweat,* and *athlete.*

4. Ask: *What do you use water for on a daily basis? How many glasses of water do you normally drink in a day?* Have volunteers share their knowledge and personal experiences.

## READING GLOSSARY

**source:** something that provides what is wanted or needed

**humid:** having a lot of moisture in the air

**sweat:** the clear liquid that forms on your skin when you are hot or nervous

**athlete:** a person who is trained at sports

## READING

🕐 Time: 10–15 min.

Go over the answers to the Comprehension Check on page 219: **1.** F; **2.** T; **3.** T.

## CONTEXT NOTE

Supermarkets, colleges, and even whole cities are beginning to ban plastic bottles in the United States. In November of 2015, San Francisco, California, was the first city to ban the sale of plastic water bottles. The city aims to achieve zero net waste by 2020, and the ban helps advocates move closer to this goal. Violators of the ban—people who sell or buy plastic water bottles—can be fined up to $1,000.

## ADDITIONAL COMPREHENSION QUESTIONS

*How much water should you drink a day?* (eight 8-ounce glasses of water) *What foods have water?* (watermelon, milk, juice, etc.) *What percent of your body is made up of water?* (60 percent) *What are three factors that determine your need for water?* (your health, your physical activity, and where you live) *Why do athletes lose more water?* (They sweat more)

## EXPANDING ON THE READING

The topic for this reading can be enhanced with the following items:

1. Water footprint online calculator

2. Infographics or diagrams showing the water composition of the human body

3. Different brands of water bottles and nutrition facts

4. Weather maps from different parts of the world

5. Graphs and charts showing water consumption patterns

### PRACTICE IDEA: LISTENING

Have students first listen to the audio alone. Write across the top of the board: *much/many; a lot of; a few/a little; some.* Have students copy the columns on a sheet of paper. Have them make a mark in the appropriate column each time they hear one of these words or phrases. Model the first sentence of the reading. Repeat the audio if necessary. Then have students open their books and read along as they listen to the audio.

### PRESENTATION IDEA

Have students open a water footprint calculator on their smart device or a computer. Walk them through calculating their water footprint, clarifying new vocabulary. Have students share results in pairs. Have volunteers share their water footprint with the class.

# 9.4 *Many, Much,* and *A Lot Of* with Large Quantities,
page 219

🕐 Time: 10–15 min.

1. Have students close their books. Write on the board:

    1. *Do you spend <u>a lot of</u> money when you buy food?*

    2. *How <u>much</u> money do you spend?*

    3. *How <u>many</u> days a week do you eat out?*

Have students ask and answer the questions in pairs. Then ask: *What is the difference between* many, much, *and* a lot of? *When do we use them?* Have students analyze the sentences in pairs. Have volunteers share their answers with the class.

2. Have students look at grammar chart **9.4** and compare their ideas. Read through the examples and have students circle the noun after the quantity words (e.g., *people, water, calories, coffee, oranges, water*).

3. Have students work in pairs to rewrite the affirmative and negative statements as questions with short answers (e.g., *Do you drink a lot of water? Yes, I do. / No, I don't.*).

4. Direct students' attention to the Language Notes. Provide additional examples of sentences that omit nouns.

### EXERCISE 6 page 219

🕐 Time: 5–10 min.

**Answers: 1.** a lot of; **2.** A lot of / Many; **3.** a lot, much; **4.** many / a lot of; **5.** a lot of, much / a lot; **6.** a lot of / much; **7.** many; **8.** much; **9.** many / a lot of; **10.** a lot of

---

**PRACTICE IDEA: SPEAKING**

In pairs, have students ask and answer items 5, 6, and 7 from Exercise 6. Have them also say whether the other items in the exercise are true for them.

---

## 9.5 *A Few* and *A Little* with Small Quantities, page 220

🕐 Time: 5–10 min.

1. Have students look at grammar chart **9.5**. Have students circle the nouns after the quantity words as volunteers read through the examples. Provide additional examples as necessary.

---

**PRESENTATION IDEA**

Write on the board: *Habits of _____ People (healthy, successful, productive, happy)* Have students choose one of the adjectives and make a list of relevant habits for that type of person (e.g., Habits of Productive People: drink a cup of coffee in the morning, do a lot of exercise, only check e-mail a few times a day, etc.). Have volunteers present their ideas to the class.

---

### EXERCISE 7 page 220

🕐 Time: 5–10 min.

**Answers: 1.** a little; **2.** a few; **3.** a little; **4.** a little; **5.** a few; **6.** a little; **7.** a little; **8.** a few; **9.** a few

## 9.6 *A/An, Some, No,* and *Any,* page 220

🕐 Time: 10–15 min.

1. Have students close their books. Write the following nouns on the board: *peach, apple, banana, water, salt, raisin, grape, watermelon, potato,* and *oil*. Have students work in pairs to divide them into count and noncount nouns. Write the two lists on the board.

2. Then have students work in pairs to make the singular count nouns plural. Have volunteers write the plural nouns next to the singular nouns on the board.

3. Have students look at grammar chart **9.6** and compare their ideas. Have students circle the nouns following the quantity words as you review the statements and questions.

4. Direct students' attention to the Language Notes. Provide several additional examples of sentences using *any* or *some* in statements and questions.

---

**PRACTICE IDEA: SPEAKING**

Have students sit or stand in a circle. Start the activity by saying: *Let's go shopping! I'm going to buy some _____ (e.g., some apples, some rice).* The student to your left has to continue the shopping list by saying, *I'm going to buy some _____ (what you just said) and some _____ (something new).* Then the next student to the left continues by adding another item to the list: *I'm going to buy some _____ and some _____ and some _____.* Repeat the activity as long as possible. When a student forgets, the next student starts over with a new single item. Be sure to correct students' grammar when necessary.

---

### EXERCISE 8 page 221

🕐 Time: 5–10 min.

**Answers: 1.** an; **2.** some / any; **3.** any; **4.** some / any; **5.** any; **6.** some; **7.** no; **8.** an; **9.** any / some; **10.** any

## PRACTICE IDEA: SPEAKING

Have students get in pairs to ask and answer questions about what they ate that day.

**EXERCISE 9** page 221

⏱ Time: 5–10 min.

**Answers: 1.** a lot of; **2.** a lot of; **3.** no; **4.** any; **5.** some / a little; **6.** a lot of; **7.** a little / some; **8.** much / a lot of / any; **9.** a little / some; **10.** any / some; **11.** any

## PRACTICE IDEA: SPEAKING

Have students compare answers to Exercises 8 and 9 in pairs. For the items where more than one answer is possible, have students explain why.

**EXERCISE 10** page 222

⏱ Time: 10–15 min.

**Answers will vary.**

## PRACTICE IDEA: SPEAKING

Have students repeat Exercise 10 with new partners. This time, have them provide explanations for their answers (e.g., *I don't drink much milk because it makes my stomach hurt. I drink a lot of water because I exercise a lot.*). Take a class survey and record similarities among the students' eating habits.

**EXERCISE 11** pages 222–223

⏱ Time: 10–15 min.

**Answers: 1.** many; **2.** a lot of; **3.** a few; **4.** a lot of; **5.** any; **6.** some; **7.** a; **8.** much; **9.** a lot of; **10.** a lot of / many; **11.** a lot of; **12.** a lot of; **13.** much; **14** any; **15.** a lot of

## PRACTICE IDEA: SPEAKING

Have students practice the conversation in Exercise 11 in pairs. Have volunteers role-play all or part of the conversation in front of the class.

**EXERCISE 12** pages 223–224

⏱ Time: 10–15 min.

**Answers: 1.** some; **2.** some / a cup of; **3.** any / some; **4.** some; **5.** any; **6.** a few; **7.** a piece of / a slice of; **8.** some

/ a glass of; **9.** any / some; **10.** some; **11.** any / some; **12.** any/some; **13.** a slice of / a piece of; **14.** scoop; **15.** any / some; **16.** some; **17.** serving / plate / bowl; **18.** some; **19.** any

## PRACTICE IDEA: WRITING

Have students practice the conversation in Exercise 12 in small groups. Then have them write their own dialog between a server and customers in a restaurant. Remind them to use the appropriate quantity words. Have volunteers role-play the scene in front of the class.

## PRESENTATION IDEA

Bring in menus from different restaurants. Put students in small groups and have them act out a dialog similar to that in Exercise 12. Have volunteers role-play in front of the class.

## READING

# Eat Less, Live Longer, page 225

## PRE-READING

⏱ Time: 5–10 min.

1. Have students look at the photo. Ask: *Where is the woman in the photo from?* (Japan, Okinawa) *What is she doing?* (harvesting seaweed)

2. Have students read the title and then skim the reading. Ask: *What is the reading about? How do you know?* Have students make predictions.

3. Pre-teach any vocabulary words your students may not know, such as *typical, calorie,* and *diet.*

4. Ask: *Who is your oldest family member? How did he or she live for so long? How long do you want to live?* Have volunteers share their knowledge and personal experiences.

## READING GLOSSARY

**typical:** normal for a person, thing, or group

**calorie:** a unit used to tell how much energy foods produce in humans

**diet:** food that a person or animal usually eats

## READING

🕐 Time: 10–15 min.

Go over the answers to the Comprehension Check on page 226: **1.** T; **2.** T; **3.** T.

## CONTEXT NOTE

A "blue zone" is a region of the world where people live longer and are healthier than anywhere else on earth. Here, living a healthy life to 90 or 100 years, without medications or disabilities, is common. The five blue zones are the Italian island of Sardinia, Okinawa in Japan, Loma Linda in California, the Nicoya Peninsula in Costa Rica, and the island of Ikaria in Greece. Journalist Dan Buettner, in partnership with National Geographic, researched the secrets to longevity in these communities and found that lifestyle choices around physical activity, nutrition, stress, and spirituality are among the top factors affecting how long someone will live.

## ADDITIONAL COMPREHENSION QUESTIONS

*How many Americans are overweight?* (88 percent) *Why are many American children obese?* (They spend too many hours watching TV and don't get enough exercise) *What percent of food commercials during children's TV are for sugary foods?* (98 percent) *How can we live longer and healthier lives?* (eat less and exercise more)

### EXPANDING ON THE READING

The topic for this reading can be enhanced with the following items:

1. Map of the world's blue zones
2. Graphs and charts comparing obesity rates worldwide
3. Food commercials
4. Photos of typical American school lunches

### PRACTICE IDEA: LISTENING

Have students first listen to the audio alone. Write on the board: *too many, too much, a lot of.* Say the phrases aloud and have students repeat. As they listen, have them count how many times they hear the phrases on the board (*too many*: three; *too much*: one; *a lot of*: three). Repeat the audio if necessary. Then have students open their books and read along as they listen to the audio.

## 9.7 *A Lot of* and *Too Much/ Too Many,* page 226

🕐 Time: 5–10 min.

1. Have students close their books. Write on the board:
   1. *There are <u>a lot of</u> people on the bus today. It must be rush hour.*
   2. *There are <u>too many</u> people on the bus today. I can't get on!*
   3. *These shoes cost <u>a lot of</u> money, but the quality is very good.*
   4. *These shoes cost <u>too much</u> money. I won't buy them!*

2. Have students analyze the sentences in pairs. Ask: *What is the difference between examples 1 and 2, and examples 3 and 4?* Have volunteers share their ideas with the class.

3. Have students look at grammar chart **9.7** and compare their ideas. Have volunteers read the examples aloud. Review the explanations.

### EXERCISE 13 pages 226–227

🕐 Time: 10–15 min.

**Answers: 1.** many; **2.** much; **3.** a lot of; **4.** a lot; **5.** a lot of; **6.** many; **7.** a lot of; **8.** a lot of; **9.** a lot of; **10.** a lot; **11.** a lot of; **12.** a lot of; **13.** too much

### PRACTICE IDEA: SPEAKING

Have students practice the conversation in Exercise 13 in pairs. Have volunteers role-play all or part of the conversation in front of the class.

### EXERCISE 14 page 227

🕐 Time: 5–10 min.

**Answers will vary.**

## 9.8 *Too* and *Too Much/ Too many*, page 227

🕐 Time: 5–10 min.

1. Have students look at grammar chart **9.8**. Have students circle the adjectives, adverbs, and nouns after the quantity words as volunteers read through the examples. Provide additional examples as necessary.

2. Direct students' attention to the Language Note. Remind students that *too, too much,* and *too many* are often used to complain about something. Give students alternative expressions to use.

### EXERCISE 15 page 227

🕐 Time: 5–10 min.

**Answers: 1.** too; **2.** too many; **3.** too; **4.** too; **5.** too much; **6.** too much

### EXERCISE 16 page 228

🕐 Time: 5–10 min.

**Answers: 1.** too; **2.** too much; **3.** a lot of; **4.** too many; **5.** too much; **6.** too much; **7.** a lot of; **8.** a lot; **9.** A lot of

### EXERCISE 17 pages 228-229

🕐 Time: 10–15 min.

**Answers: 1.** too; **2.** a lot of; **3.** a lot of; **4.** a cup of; **5.** a lot of / much; **6.** a few / some; **7.** a can of; **8.** no; **9.** much;

**10.** any; **11.** a lot of; **12.** piece of; **13.** too; **14.** some / a lot of

### EXERCISE 18 page 229

🕐 Time: 5–10 min.

**Answers will vary.**

## SUMMARY OF LESSON 9

🕐 Time: 20–30 min.

### PART A QUANTITY WORDS AND PHRASES WITH COUNT AND NONCOUNT NOUNS

Have students imagine their perfect world. Have them discuss what this world would have and not have in pairs. Then have students write a short paragraph about their perfect world. Circulate and give help as needed. Encourage students to use as many different quantity words and count/noncount nouns as possible. Write model sentences on the board if necessary (e.g., *In my perfect world, there are a lot of nice people. There are a few cars but not too many because they cause pollution.*). Have volunteers present their perfect worlds to the class. If necessary, have students review:

**9.1** Count and Noncount Nouns—An Overview (page 213)

**9.2** Groups of Noncount Nouns (pages 214–215)

**9.3** Units of Measure with Noncount Nouns (page 217)

**9.4** *Many, Much,* and *A Lot Of* with Large Quantities (page 219)

**9.5** *A Few* and *A Little* with Small Quantities (page 220)

**9.6** *A/An, Some, No,* and *Any* (page 220)

**9.7** *A Lot Of* and *Too Much/Too Many* (page 226)

**9.8** *Too* and *Too Much/Too Many* (page 227)

## TEST/REVIEW

🕐 Time: 15 min.

Have students do the exercise on page 231. For additional practice, use the Assessment CD-ROM with Exam*View*® and the Online Workbook.

**Answers: 1.** some; **2.** much; **3.** A few; **4.** some; **5.** an; **6.** some; **7.** any; **8.** a few; **9.** a; **10.** no; **11.** a lot; **12.** any; **13.** a lot of; **14.** a cup of coffee; **15.** some; **16.** too many; **17.** a little

## PART 1 EDITING ADVICE

🕐 Time: 10–15 min.

1. Have students close their books. Write the first few sentences without editing marks or corrections on the board. For example:
   *My doctor gave me an advice about nutrition.*
   *He drank three waters today.*

2. Ask students to correct each sentence and provide a rule or an explanation for each correction. This activity can be done individually, in pairs, or as a class.

3. After students have corrected each sentence, tell them to turn to page 232. Say: *Now compare your work with the Editing Advice in the book.* Have students read through all the advice.

## PART 2 EDITING PRACTICE

🕐 Time: 10–15 min.

1. Tell students they are going to put the Editing Advice into practice. Ask: *Do all the shaded words and phrases have mistakes?* (no) Go over the examples with the class. Then do #1 together.

2. Have students complete the practice individually. Then have them compare answers with a partner before checking answers as a class.

3. For the items students had difficulties with, have them go back and find the relevant grammar chart and review it. Monitor and give help as necessary.

**Answers: 1.** good advice; **2.** C; **3.** very; **4.** advice; **5.** any / enough; **6.** a lot; **7.** a cup of coffee; **8.** a little sugar; **9.** C; **10.** friends; **11.** q; **12.** too / much too; **13.** C

## PART 3 WRITE ABOUT IT

🕐 Time: 30–40 min.

1. Review the first topic with students and review the meaning of *habit* and *typical*. Have students share their eating habits in pairs or small groups. Have volunteers share their ideas and write them on the board. Encourage students to organize their thoughts and make notes before they begin to write. Remind them to include any useful and relevant vocabulary from this lesson on healthy living and to use quantity words and phrases. If necessary, write model topic sentences on the board first.

2. Repeat the exercise for the second topic. Have students get in small groups with classmates from the same country or culture and brainstorm food

and eating habits. Then jigsaw the groups and have students from different countries or cultures share their food and eating habits. Encourage students to organize their ideas before writing. Write model topic sentences on the board first.

## PART 4 EDIT YOUR WRITING

🕐 Time: 15–20 min.

Have students edit their writing by reviewing the Lesson Summary on page 230 and the Editing Advice on page 232. Collect for assessment and/or have students share their essays in small groups.

## EXPANSION ACTIVITIES

1. Have students make a welcome pamphlet for newcomers to the United States. In the pamphlet, ask them to give advice and suggestions about how to stay healthy in the United States. Be sure they use quantity words and units of measure. Find a local newcomer organization, if possible, and have students meet new people and share their pamphlets.

2. Ask students to choose one thing they like about their lifestyle and one thing they'd like to change. Have them write a short paragraph about these habits. Encourage them to end the paragraph with how they will change their bad habits.

3. Show students a map of local farmer's markets. Have them go to a farmer's market and take notes on their experience (e.g., *How many people were there? How much was the food? Do you think it cost too much? Why?*). Have students report back on their experience.

4. Have students get in small groups and choose a kind of party to plan (e.g., a dinner party, birthday party, baby shower, New Year's Eve party). Each group needs to plan who will be in charge of what (e.g., food, music, decorations, invitations). Each group member needs to write a shopping list including specific quantities of the items they'll buy. The groups should share their party plans with the class.

# LESSON

# **10** GREET WOMEN

GREAT WOMEN

## GRAMMAR CHARTS

**10.1** Adjectives; Adverbs of Manner (page 237)

**10.2** Adjectives (page 238)

**10.3** Noun Modifiers (page 241)

**10.4** Adverbs (page 243)

**10.5** Spelling of -ly Adverbs (page 244)

**10.6** Very and Too (page 248)

**10.7** Enough (page 249)

## LESSON OPENER

Have students look at the photo and read the caption.
Ask: *Who is this woman in the photo?* (Dr. Pardis Sabeti)
*Where is she?* (in a lab) Have students read the quotation.
Ask: *Are men and women equal in this world? Why or why
not? In what areas do women have to try harder than men?*

**Background:** The role of women in the American
workforce, military, and politics has grown significantly
over the years thanks to the struggles and contributions
of several notable female figures. In the early 1800s,
many young American women worked as servants or
in shops and factories but were typically expected to
become full-time housewives after marrying young. This
trend continued until the mid-1900s when World Wars
I and II necessitated women work in industries such as
manufacturing. Around this same time, women's access
to and enrollment in universities increased, and in 1963,
President Kennedy signed the Equal Pay Act to prohibit
gender discrimination in the workplace. Today, there
are more women than men studying in the American
university system, and women are represented in almost
every industry. During the American Civil War, it is
estimated that between 400 and 750 women disguised
themselves as men to serve in the military. During World
Wars I and II, women were able to serve as nurses in
military hospitals as well as in other support roles, such as
telephone operators. During the Iraq War and operations
in Afghanistan in the early 2000s, women began to serve
in active-duty military roles. Today more than 200,000
women serve in active roles, including 69 female generals
and admirals. Also, women have long been vocal in the

political sphere. Their voice was first recognized in print
through books and newspapers but soon became vocal
in public debates and reform movements, particularly
abolitionism. Organization and activism intensified
during the Progressive Era around issues like prohibition,
suffrage, education, and public health, and the U.S.
government officially granted women the right to vote by
establishing the nineteenth amendment in 1920. Today,
women such as Nancy Pelosi, the first female Speaker of
the House, and Hillary Clinton, the first woman to win a
presidential primary, represent the progress women have
made in American politics.

Amelia Earhart was the first woman to complete a
nonstop solo flight across the Atlantic Ocean in 1932.
Two years later, she became the first person to fly solo
across the Pacific Ocean between Honolulu and Northern
California. She completed other notable flights during her
life, including an around-the-world-attempt in 1937. It
was during this journey that she vanished and was never
found again.

## CONTEXT

This unit is about great women. Students will read about
Helen Keller, Lilly Ledbetter, and Grandma Moses.

1. Give students a few minutes to look through the
   lesson. Have them look at the photos and titles. How
   do they relate to the context?
2. Elicit the topics that will be discussed.
3. Have students discuss what they know about great
   women in pairs or small groups.

## GRAMMAR

Students will learn about adjectives, noun modifiers, and
adverbs.

1. To activate students' prior knowledge, ask what
   students know about adjectives, noun modifiers, and
   adverbs.
2. Give several examples of adjectives (e.g., *healthy,
   intelligent, blind*) and adverbs (e.g., *patiently, quickly*).
3. Have volunteers give examples and write them on the
   board.

**READING**

# Helen Keller, page 236

## PRE-READING

Time: 5–10 min.

1. Have students look at the two photos and read the captions. Ask: *Who are the people in the top photo?* (Helen Keller and her teacher Anne Sullivan) *What are they doing?* (Anne Sullivan is "talking" to Helen using her fingers) *What do you see in the bottom photo?* (hands, paper) *What is this person doing?* (reading a book using Braille)

2. Have students read the title and then skim the reading. Ask: *What is the reading about? How do you know?* Have students make predictions.

3. Pre-teach any vocabulary words your students may not know, such as *remarkable, wild, patient,* and *equally.*

4. Ask: *Do you know anyone who is blind? Do you know anyone who is deaf? What is his or her life like? How do you imagine you would feel if you were blind and/ or deaf?* Have volunteers share their knowledge and personal experiences.

## READING GLOSSARY

**remarkable:** worthy of attention, noticeable
**wild:** unruly, uncontrolled
**patient:** having or showing patience, calm, or being undisturbed
**equally:** in an even manner

## READING  CD 2 TR 13

Time: 10–15 min.

Go over the answers to the Comprehension Check on page 237: **1.** F; **2.** T; **3.** T.

## CONTEXT NOTE

Gallaudet University was the first school established for the advanced education of the deaf and hard of hearing. Founded in 1864, it began as a grammar school and grew to become the most prominent private university in the world to specifically cater to and provide services to deaf and hard of hearing students. It is federally funded and authorized to grant and confirm college degrees to both undergraduate and graduate students. The institution is bilingual with both American Sign Language and English used for course instruction and among members of the college community. Hearing students are also admitted; in fact, the university was named after an advocate for deaf education who was not deaf, Thomas Hopkins Gallaudet.

## ADDITIONAL COMPREHENSION QUESTIONS

*Was Helen Keller deaf and blind at birth?* (No, she became deaf and blind after an illness at 19 months) *What happened when she couldn't understand anything*? (She became frustrated and angry) *Who taught Helen to communicate?* (Anne Sullivan) *How old was Helen when she graduated from college?* (24 years old)

# 10.1 Adjectives; Adverbs of Manner, page 237

Time: 10–15 min.

1. Have students close their books. Write on the board: *The young girl ran quickly*. Ask students what the subject and verb are. Underline and label *the*, *girl*, and *ran*. Circle the words *young* and *quickly* and ask students what these words are. Give students time to discuss in pairs.

2. Elicit student ideas and then label *young* (adj.) and *quickly* (adv.) on the board. Ask students what an adjective does and what an adverb does. Give students time to discuss in pairs.

3. Elicit student ideas and then tell students: *Adjectives describe nouns. We can use adjectives before nouns or after the verbs be, become, look, seem, and other sense-perception verbs*. Elicit additional adjectives and write student ideas on board. Then say: *Adverbs tell how or in what way we do things. They usually follow the verb phrase*. Elicit additional adjectives and write student ideas on board.

4. Write the sentences from the grammar chart on the board. Have volunteers come to the board and underline the adverb or adjective and explain their choice.

5. Then have students look at grammar chart **10.1** and compare their work. Point out that there are different kinds of adverbs, and these adverbs are *of manner*, or how we do things. Address any additional questions.

**EXERCISE 1** page 237

Time: 10–15 min.

**Answers: 1.** popular; **2.** annually; **3.** simple; **4.** beautiful; **5.** dead; **6.** black; **7.** beautiful; **8.** famous; **9.** national; **10.** carefully; **11.** honestly; **12.** perfect; **13.** excited; **14.** strongly; **15.** unusual; **16.** traditional; **17.** America; **18.** major

**EXERCISE 2** page 238

Time: 5–10 min.

**Answers: 1.** adj; **2.** adv; **3.** adj; **4.** adj; **5.** adj; **6.** adj; **7.** adj; **8.** adj; **9.** adj; **10.** adv; **11.** adv; **12.** adj; **13.** adj; **14.** adv; **15.** adj; **16.** adj; **17.** adj; **18.** adj

# 10.2 Adjectives, page 238

Time: 10–15 min.

1. Have students close their books. Say: *I'm going to read you some statements about adjectives; tell me if they are true or false*. Read these statements:
   a. *Adjectives describe verbs*. (false)
   b. *Adjectives are always singular*. (true)
   c. *Some words that end in -ed are adjectives—for example*, married. (true)
   d. *We can never put two adjectives before a noun*. (false)

2. Then have students look at grammar chart **10.2** and check their answers. Have volunteers read the examples aloud. Review the explanations and provide additional examples as necessary.

---

**PRACTICE IDEA: WRITING**

Have students share in pairs about a teacher from their past they remember and why. Remind them to use adjectives to describe this teacher's appearance and actions. Then, have students write a five to seven sentence paragraph about this teacher's impact on their life. Have volunteers share their short writings with the class.

---

**PRACTICE IDEA: SPEAKING AND WRITING**

Collect a number of images. Display the images to the class, one by one, leaving each image up for only 2 minutes. After time is up, display the next image. During this time, the students need to think of as many adjectives as they can that describe each image in pairs and write them. After all images have been shown, have students write one sentence describing each image. Display the images a final time and elicit sentences about each image.

---

**EXERCISE 3** pages 238–239
🕐 Time: 5–10 min.
**Answers: 1.** healthy; **2.** frustrated; **3.** wild; **4.** patient; **5.** excited; **6.** intelligent; **7.** Blind; **8.** equal; **9.** young; **10.** unusual; **11.** traditional; **12.** dead

---

**PRACTICE IDEA: SPEAKING AND WRITING**

In pairs, have students share what they were like when they were younger. Ask them to pick five adjectives and write three sentences describing themselves in the simple past tense.

---

**EXERCISE 4** page 239
🕐 Time: 5–10 min.
**Answers will vary.**

---

**PRESENTATION IDEA**

Have students collect more information and photos about the popular place or beautiful monument they named in Exercise 4. Have them prepare a short presentation (PowerPoint or poster) with visual aids on the place to present to the class.

---

**EXERCISE 5** page 239
🕐 Time: 5–10 min.
**Answers: 1. a.** serious, **b.** ones; **2. a.** long, **b.** one; **3. a.** great, **b.** one; **4. a.** patient, **b.** ones; **5. a.** simple, **b.** ones; **6. a.** new, **b.** one

---

**PRACTICE IDEA: SPEAKING**

Have students bring in pictures of their family or pull up pictures on their phones. In small groups, have students describe their family members using the adjectives from pages 236–239.

---

READING

# Lilly Ledbetter, page 240

## PRE-READING
🕐 Time: 5–10 min.

1. Have students look at the photo and read the caption. Ask: *Who is this woman?* (Lilly Ledbetter) *Where is she?* (in front of the tire company she worked for, Goodyear Tires)

2. Have students read the title and then skim the reading. Ask: *What is the reading about? How do you know?* Have students make predictions.

3. Pre-teach any vocabulary words your students may not know, such as *salary, performance, expenses,* and *retirement.*

4. Ask: *Do you think certain jobs are better for women and certain jobs are better for men? Which ones? Do women and men get paid the same amount of money for the same job in your country?* Have volunteers share their knowledge and personal experiences.

## READING GLOSSARY
**salary:** amount of money a worker is paid each year
**performance:** how well someone works

**expenses:** amount of money needed to pay for something

**retirement:** the act of ending your working career

## READING

Go over the answers to the Comprehension Check on page 241: **1.** F; **2.** T; **3.** F.

## ADDITIONAL COMPREHENSION QUESTIONS

*How much less money does a college-educated woman make than a college-educated man?* (7 percent) *How much more money were Lilly Ledbetter's male co-workers making than her?* (40 percent more) *What were Lilly Ledbetter's expenses at the time?* (house and car payments, college tuition) *Why did she lose her case in the Supreme Court in 2006?* (The Supreme Court said it was past the limit of 180 days) *What is the Lilly Ledbetter Fair Pay Act passed by President Barack Obama?* (a law that says employees can report discrimination 180 days after any paycheck)

---

### EXPANDING ON THE READING

The topic for this reading can be enhanced with the following items:

1. Photos of President Barack Obama signing the Lilly Ledbetter Fair Pay Act
2. Charts and graphs comparing wage gaps of males and females in different areas
3. Excerpts from Lilly Ledbetter's video telling her story

---

### PRACTICE IDEA: LISTENING

Have students first listen to the audio alone. Ask a few comprehension questions, such as: *Do women get paid more or less than men in the United States?* (less) *What was Lilly Ledbetter's job in 1979?* (manager at a tire company) *How did she find out her male co-workers made more money than her?* (another co-worker told her) *What did she do when she found out?* (sued the company) Repeat the audio if necessary. Then have students open their books and read along as they listen to the audio.

---

## 10.3 Noun Modifiers, page 241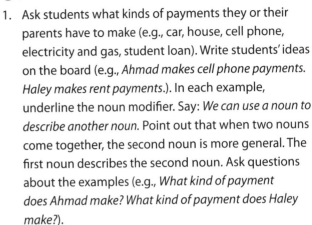

🕐 Time: 10–15 min.

1. Ask students what kinds of payments they or their parents have to make (e.g., car, house, cell phone, electricity and gas, student loan). Write students' ideas on the board (e.g., *Ahmad makes cell phone payments. Haley makes rent payments.*). In each example, underline the noun modifier. Say: *We can use a noun to describe another noun.* Point out that when two nouns come together, the second noun is more general. The first noun describes the second noun. Ask questions about the examples (e.g., *What kind of payment does Ahmad make? What kind of payment does Haley make?*).

2. Have students look at grammar chart **10.3.** Have volunteers read the examples aloud. Review the explanations, asking questions about the examples (e.g., *What kind of information can workers not discuss? What other kinds of information might people talk about in the workplace?*).

3. Direct students' attention to the Language Note. Have students read through the list in pairs and look in their dictionaries for the meaning of words or phrases they don't know.

## ADDITIONAL PRACTICE

1. Have students share their education experience in pairs. Encourage them to talk about what types of degrees they have (e.g., *high school diploma, bachelor's, master's, doctorate*) and what courses they took at their various institutions (e.g., *math course, English course*).

2. Have students draw simple blueprints of their apartments or houses. In pairs, have them describe their apartment or house. Encourage them to notice all the different noun modifiers they use to describe the different rooms and machines they have.

3. Have students research what kinds of museums are in their current city or a city close to them. Assign each student one museum to describe and present to the class. As a follow-up activity, students could choose one piece of artwork from their museum to describe to the class using adjectives.

### EXERCISE 6 pages 241–242

🕐 Time: 5–10 min.

(Note: accept answers without hyphens at this level)

**Answers: 1.** war memorial; **2.** college student; **3.** sign language; **4.** eyesight; **5.** stone wall; **6.** tire company; **7.** day limit; **8.** mailbox; **9.** twelve-hour shift / 12-hour shift; **10.** honor student / honors student

---

**PRACTICE IDEA: WRITING**

Have students read the sentences from Exercise 6 aloud in pairs. Have them write five more sentences using the noun + noun combinations in the Language Note of grammar chart **10.3** (e.g., *A license so somebody is allowed to drive a vehicle is a driver's license.*).

---

**EXERCISE 7** pages 242–243

🕒 Time: 5–10 min.

**Answers: 1.** TV program; **2.** wheelchair; **3.** basketball player; **4.** ten-year-old child / 10-year-old child; **5.** college team; **6.** bachelor's degree; **7.** community health / Community Health; **8.** gold medal; **9.** car accident; **10.** silver medal; **11.** athletic director

---

**PRACTICE IDEA: SPEAKING**

Ask students if they have an event similar to the Paralympic Games in their home countries. Have them describe this event in pairs or discuss how an event like this can benefit their society.

---

## 10.4 Adverbs, page 243

🕒 Time: 10–15 min.

1. Have students look at grammar chart **10.4**. Review the examples and explanations row by row. Have volunteers read the examples aloud. For the adverbs of manner, ask questions about the examples to point out the adverbs and to review the reading (e.g., *How did Lilly Ledbetter act? What is an example of how she was responsible? How did the company treat women? Why?*).

2. Review the adjectives and adverbs that have the same form. Elicit additional examples for *fast* and *late*.

3. Point out the word order in the examples. Explain that an adverb comes before the verb or after the verb phrase. An adverb cannot come between the verb and the object. Point out that you can use *very* before an adverb of manner.

4. Direct students' attention to the Languages Notes and provide additional examples as necessary.

---

**EXERCISE 8** page 244

🕒 Time: 5–10 min.

**Answers: 1. A:** great, **B:** patiently; **2. A:** quickly, **B.** clearly; **3. A:** well, **B:** excellent; **4. A:** beautiful, **B:** honestly; **5. A:** directly, **B:** unfortunately, late; **6. A:** hard, **B:** happy, finally, fast; **7. A:** hardly, **B:** certainly

---

**PRACTICE IDEA: WRITING**

Have students compare their answers to Exercise 8. Then, have them write sentences using the opposite answer. For example, opposite sentences for item 1: *A. Helen admired Anne greatly. B. Anne was a patient teacher.* Have students share sentences with the class.

---

## 10.5 Spelling of *-ly* Adverbs, page 244

🕒 Time: 10–15 min.

1. Have students close their books. Copy the lists of adjectives and adverbs from grammar chart **10.5** on the board. Make sure to separate the four sets of adjectives and adverbs. Have students analyze the adjective and adverb spelling changes in pairs and try to guess the spelling rules.

2. Have students look at grammar chart **10.5** and compare their rules. Point out the exception in the Language Note.

---

**EXERCISE 9** page 245

🕒 Time: 10–15 min.

**Answers: 1.** badly; **2.** well; **3.** lazily; **4.** truly; **5.** bravely; **6.** fully; **7.** probably; **8.** politely; **9.** fast; **10.** constantly; **11.** terribly; **12.** beautifully; **13.** responsibly; **14.** early

---

**EXERCISE 10** page 245

🕒 Time: 5–10 min.

**Answers: 1.** finally; **2.** equally; **3.** hard; **4.** easily; **5.** fully; **6.** carefully; **7.** simply; **8.** annually; **9.** strongly; **10.** probably; **11.** really

## EXERCISE 11 pages 245-246

Time: 10–15 min.

**Answers: 1.** constant; **2.** happy; **3.** impolite; **4.** rudely; **5.** well; **6.** late; **7.** angry; **8.** completely; **9.** hard; **10.** positive; **11.** active; **12.** frequently; **13.** fluently; **14.** quickly; **15.** curious; **16.** frequently; **17.** good

## EXERCISE 12 page 246

Time: 10–15 min.

**Answers: 1.** small child; **2.** wildly; **3.** well; **4.** good; **5.** poor; **6.** hard; **7.** year; **8.** clearly; **9.** elementary school; **10.** intelligent; **11.** sign; **12.** quickly; **13.** college classes; **14.** eyesight; **15.** completely

`READING`

# Grandma Moses, page 247

## PRE-READING

Time: 5–10 min.

1. Have students look at the photo and read the caption. Ask: *Who is this woman?* (Grandma Moses) *What is she doing?* (painting a picture)

2. Have students read the title and then skim the reading. Ask: *What is the reading about? How do you know?* Have students make predictions.

3. Pre-teach any vocabulary words your students may not know, such as *housekeeper, arthritis,* and *gallery.*

4. Ask: *What is one activity or hobby you always wanted to do but haven't done yet? Do you think people can have a successful career later in life? Why or why not?* Have volunteers share their knowledge and personal experiences.

## READING GLOSSARY

**housekeeper:** a person hired to take care of a private house

**arthritis:** inflammation of one or many joints, resulting in pain

**gallery:** a room or building used to display or sell art

## READING  CD 2 TR 16

Time: 10–15 min.

Go over the answers to the Comprehension Check on page 248: **1.** F; **2.** F; **3.** T.

## ADDITIONAL COMPREHENSION QUESTIONS

*What did Grandma Moses do before she became a painter?* (She was a farmer's wife) *Why didn't she start painting earlier?* (She was too busy) *What kind of pictures did she paint?* (pictures of farm life) *Are her paintings well known?* (Yes, some hang in major art museums)

## PRACTICE IDEA: LISTENING

Have students first listen to the audio alone. Write on the board: *very, too, enough.* Say the words aloud and have students count how many times they hear the words in the audio (seven). Repeat the audio if necessary. Then have students open their books and read along as they listen to the audio.

## 10.6 *Very* and *Too*, page 248

⏱ Time: 5–10 min.

1. Have students close their books. Write on the board:
   *1. The bus was <u>very</u> full this morning.*
   *2. There were <u>too</u> many people! I couldn't get on.*
   Have students analyze the sentences in pairs. Point out the use of *too* and *very.* Ask: *Which shows that there's a problem:* too *or* very? (too)

2. Have students look at grammar chart **10.6** and check their answer. Have volunteers read examples aloud. Review the explanations.

3. Direct students' attention to the Language Note. Provide several more examples of *much* before *too.*

## PRACTICE IDEA: LISTENING

Find the lyrics to a popular song that has the title or uses the phrase *much too much.* Create a cloze exercise, omitting specific words in the lyrics. Play the song in class several times. As students listen, have them fill in the missing words. As a follow-up, have a class discussion about the meaning of the phrase and provide additional examples of its use in popular American culture.

## EXERCISE 13 page 248

⏱ Time: 5–10 min.

**Answers: 1.** very; **2.** too; **3.** very; **4.** too; **5.** very; **6.** very; **7.** very; **8.** too; **9.** very

## PRACTICE IDEA: WRITING

Have students work in pairs to write five more sentences from their daily lives using *very* or *too.* Have volunteers share their sentences with the class.

## 10.7 *Enough,* page 249

⏱ Time: 5–10 min.

1. Have students close their books. Write on the board:
   *1. The bus was <u>very</u> full this morning.*
   *2. There were <u>too</u> many people! I couldn't get on.*
   *3. Because of this, I didn't have <u>enough</u> time to get to work.*
   Have students analyze the sentences in pairs. Ask: How are *very, too,* and *enough* used differently?

2. Have students look at grammar chart **10.7** and check their answer. Have volunteers read examples aloud. Review the explanations.

## EXERCISE 14 page 249

⏱ Time: 5–10 min.

**Answers: 1.** intelligent enough; **2.** patient enough; **3.** enough time; **4.** good enough; **5.** enough information; **6.** strong enough; **7.** enough money; **8.** well enough

## PRACTICE IDEA: WRITING

Have students work in pairs to write five more sentences from their daily lives using *enough.* Have volunteers share their sentences with the class.

## SUMMARY OF LESSON 10

◑ Time: 20–30 min.

### PART A ADJECTIVES AND ADVERBS

Have students close their books. On the board, write:

*patient*

*beautiful*

*good*

*late*

*unfortunate*

Say: *Write eight sentences with these words. Use each word as an adjective and as an adverb.* Then have students compare their work with the summary. If necessary, have students review:

**10.1** Adjectives; Adverbs of Manner (page 237)

**10.2** Adjectives (page 238)

**10.4** Adverbs (page 243)

**10.5** Spelling of *-ly* Adverbs (page 244)

## PART B ADJECTIVE MODIFIERS AND NOUN MODIFIERS

Have students close their books. Create an exercise on the board. Write:

*hard*

*tire*

*good*

*college*

*7-year-old*

*factory*

*new*

*eye*

*expensive*

*young*

Then write the following in two columns:

*Adjective Modifier*

*a _____ job*

*a _____ company*

*_____ sight*

*_____ tuition*

*a _____ child*

*Noun Modifier*

*a _____ job*

*a _____ company*

*_____ sight*

*_____ tuition*

*a_____ child*

Say: *Fill in the blanks with the appropriate word.* Then have students compare their work with the summary. If necessary, have students review:

**10.2** Adjectives (page 238)

**10.3** Noun Modifiers (page 241)

## PART C *VERY, TOO,* AND *ENOUGH*

Have students close their books. Create an exercise on the board.
Write:

*Lilly Ledbetter was brave.*

*She worked hard.*

*You're never old to learn something new.*

*Some workers work slowly.*

*Ledbetter was brave to fight for her rights.*

*Helen Keller spoke clearly. People understood her.*

*Ledbetter didn't make money.*

Say: *Complete these sentences with* very, too, *or* enough. Then have students compare their work with the summary. If necessary, have students review:

**10.6** *Very* and *Too* (page 248)

**10.7** *Enough* (page 249)

---

# TEST/REVIEW

⏲ Time: 15 min.

Have students do the exercise on page 251. For additional practice, use the Assessment CD-ROM with Exam*View*® and the Online Workbook.

**Answers: 1.** too old; **2.** year; **3.** health problems; **4.** paintbrush; **5.** oil paintings; **6.** very; **7.** too old; **8.** foreign language; **9.** English class; **10.** very; **11.** quickly; **12.** fast; **13.** classmates; **14.** hardly; **15.** busy; **16.** old enough; **17.** proud; **18.** very; **19.** history degree; **20.** very; **21.** probably; **22.** late; **23.** hard; **24.** hard; **25.** very; **26.** certainly; **27.** good

---

# WRITING

## PART 1 EDITING ADVICE

⏲ Time: 10–15 min.

1. Have students close their books. Write the first few sentences without editing marks or corrections on the board. For example:

   *Grandma Moses painted beautifuls art.*

   *Someone gave Anna Mary materials art.*

2. Ask students to correct each sentence and provide a rule or an explanation for each correction. This activity can be done individually, in pairs, or as a class.

3. After students have corrected each sentence, tell them to turn to page 252. Say: *Now compare your work with the Editing Advice in the book.* Have students read through all the advice.

## PART 2 EDITING PRACTICE

⏲ Time: 10–15 min.

1. Tell students they are going to put the Editing Advice into practice. Ask: *Do all the shaded words and phrases have mistakes?* (no) Go over the examples with the class. Then do #1 together.

2. Have students complete the practice individually. Then have them compare answers with a partner before checking answers as a class.

3. For the items students had difficulties with, have them go back and find the relevant grammar chart and review it. Monitor and give help as necessary.

**Answers: 1.** really; **2.** C; **3.** married; **4.** adult; **5.** old enough; **6.** computer programming; **7.** too (can also accept *much too*); **8.** C; **9.** flower shop; **10.** very interesting job; **11.** nice; **12.** C; **13.** kindly; **14.** C; **15.** C; **16.** English quickly; **17.** well; **18.** C

## PART 3 WRITE ABOUT IT

🕐 Time: 30–40 min.

1. Review the topic with students. Have students conduct research online and record their sources. Give your own example of a person you know that accomplished something great at an older age or with disabilities. Have students help you write the beginning of a paragraph as an example on the board. Then have students write their own paragraph following the model. Remind them to include any useful and relevant vocabulary from this lesson on great women and to double-check their use of adjectives, adverbs, and noun modifiers. Have them exchange for peer feedback.

2. Have students think of a woman they admire and make a list of things they could write about that woman. Have them tell a partner about the person they are thinking of. Say: *You can write about anyone whom you admire—the woman can be famous or just someone you know.* Then have them write their paragraphs individually. Collect for assessment and/or have students present their paragraphs to a group.

## PART 4 EDIT YOUR WRITING

🕐 Time: 15–20 min.

Have students edit their writing by reviewing the Lesson Summary on page 250 and the Editing Advice on page 252. Collect for assessment and/or have students share their essays in small groups.

## EXPANSION ACTIVITIES

1. Have students work individually to complete a personality survey online. Check whether students know the meaning of all the adverbs. Then put students in pairs to compare. If possible, have students from different countries work together.

2. Have students work in pairs to talk about what they do well. Each partner should name at least three to five things that he or she does well. Have volunteers tell the class what their partners can do.

3. Ask students to rent the movie *The Miracle Worker*. Tell them it's the story of Helen Keller and Anne Sullivan. Tell them to watch it at home and then be prepared to talk about the movie in class.

4. Have students use the Internet to find information about the following people. They should find out who they are and what extraordinary things they did.
   a. Erik Weihenmayer
   b. Sherman Bull
   c. Enrique Oliu
   d. Melissa Stockwell

5. Have students use the Internet to find the American Sign Language fingerspelling alphabet and find out how to spell their names.

6. Tell students to use the Internet to find some paintings by Grandma Moses. Have them bring a picture of one to class; have volunteers describe the painting they chose.

# 11 AMERICAN EXPERIENCES

## GRAMMAR CHARTS

**11.1** Comparatives and Superlatives--An Overview (page 257)

**11.2** Comparatives and Superlatives--Adjective and Adverb Forms (page 258)

**11.3** Short Adjectives and Adverbs--Spelling of Comparatives and Superlatives (page 259)

**11.4** Using Superlatives (page 260)

**11.5** Word Order with Superlatives (page 262)

**11.6** Using Comparatives (page 264)

**11.7** Word Order with Comparatives (page 266)

## LESSON OPENER

Have students look at the photo and read the caption. Ask: *How would you describe what you see in the photo?* (a geyser) *Where do you think it is?* (Black Rock Desert, Nevada) Have students read the quotation. Ask: *Do you agree with the quote? Why or why not?*

**Background:** American culture is characterized by individuality, strength, and an urge for adventure. It is also characterized by opportunities for unique experiences that represent this American spirit. One of those experiences is the American road trip. In the early 1900s, Americans didn't have the mobility they have today. Roads were unstable, and horses and steam locomotives were unable to traverse the long distances in any reasonable amount of time. With the invention of the automobile, Americans had a chance to harness adventure and drive straight through the nation's heartland from one side of the country to the other. Since then, a road trip on Route 66, the country's most famous old highway, has been the quintessential activity for tourists and locals alike. Another classic American experience is a visit to a national park, monument, trailhead, or other historical property. In 1916, the U.S. Congress established the National Park Service (NPS) and designated properties all across the country as federally protected and conserved land. Each year, thousands of visitors enjoy the outdoors while learning more about American culture. Other distinctive American experiences include state fairs, rodeos, Las Vegas, and the jazz scene of

New Orleans. Each one of these experiences embodies an important side of American history, society, and culture. Classic American drinks include bourbon, an alcohol specific to the United States that forms the base of many definitive cocktails, and classic American foods including barbecue, which is typically provided at festivals, restaurants, and in backyards across the country.

Oscar Wilde was an Irish author, playwright, and poet. He was one of London's most popular playwrights, known for his flamboyant personality and quick wit, which he used in comedies such as *The Importance of Being Earnest, A Trivial Comedy for Serious People*, a play that made satire out of social obligations and institutions. He was also an accomplished author. His most famous novel was *The Picture of Dorian Gray,* a story of a vain young man named Dorian Gray who wished for his portrait to age while he remained young and beautiful, so he could continue living his decadent lifestyle.

## CONTEXT

This unit is about American experiences. Students will read about climbing Mount Denali and an unusual trip across the United States.

1. Give students a few minutes to look through the lesson. Have them look at the photos and titles. How do they relate to the context?

2. Elicit the topics that will be discussed.

3. Have students discuss what they know about American experiences in pairs or small groups.

## GRAMMAR

Students will learn about comparatives and superlatives.

1. To activate students' prior knowledge, ask what students know about comparatives and superlatives.

2. Give several examples of comparatives and superlatives (e.g., comparatives: *taller, faster*; superlatives: *tallest, fastest*).

3. Have volunteers give examples and write them on the board.

## CONTEXT NOTES

**The Willis Tower** (formerly the Sears Tower): Built in 1973, it was the tallest building in the world until 1998. It is 1,450 feet tall, covers 2 city blocks, and has more than 4 million square feet of office and commercial space. It is still one of the tallest buildings in the world.

**The Empire State Building:** Construction on the Empire State Building began in 1930. The building took only 1 year and 45 days to build. It is 1,250 feet tall and is currently the tallest building in New York City.

**The Space Needle:** The Space Needle was built in 1962. It is 605 feet tall and has a revolving restaurant at the top. Every year, more than a million people visit the Space Needle. It is the biggest tourist attraction in the Northwest.

`READING`

# Climbing Denali, page 256

## PRE-READING

⏱ Time: 5–10 min.

1. Have students look at the photo and read the caption. Ask: *Where is this place?* (Mount Denali, Alaska) *What do you see in the picture?* (snow, clouds, and a man on top of the mountain)

2. Have students read the title and then skim the reading. Ask: *What is the reading about? How do you know?* Have students make predictions.

3. Pre-teach any vocabulary words your students may not know, such as *thin, busy,* and *deadly.*

4. Ask: *What is the tallest mountain you know about in the world? Are you interested in climbing to the top of these mountains? What is one challenging thing you want to do before you die?* Have volunteers share their knowledge and personal experiences.

## READING GLOSSARY

**thin:** having less oxygen than normal
**busy:** actively doing something
**deadly:** causing or able to cause death

## READING  CD 2 TR 17

⏱ Time: 10–15 min.

Go over the answers to the Comprehension Check on page 267: **1.** F; **2.** F; **3.** F.

## CONTEXT NOTE

The name *Denali* is a word borrowed from the Koyukon people, an indigenous Alaskan group. The word means "the high one" in Koyukon. Beginning in 1986, the mountain was known as Mount McKinley, a name first given by a gold prospector and then officially established by the U.S. government to recognize President William McKinley. However, in 1975 the Alaskan legislature changed the name to *Denali* and requested the federal government to follow suit. But it wasn't until August 2015 that the Secretary of the Interior and President Barack Obama announced the name would be changed to *Denali* in all federal documents. Although officially changed, the name of the mountain is still under public scrutiny and dispute.

## ADDITIONAL COMPREHENSION QUESTIONS

*How many feet above sea level is the base of Denali?* (2,000 feet) *What happens to the environment near the North Pole that makes Denali difficult to climb?* (The air gets thinner, and it's hard to breathe) *What is the busiest month for climbers?* (June) *When was the deadliest season?* (May 1992) *How many climbers died?* (eleven) *What did the Washburns become known for?* (making the most detailed, accurate map of Mount Everest in history)

## PRACTICE IDEA: LISTENING

Have students first listen to the audio alone. Ask a few comprehension questions, such as: *What state is Denali in?* (Alaska) *Why is Denali so difficult to climb?* (It's closer to the North Pole than other tall mountains) *When did the first group of climbers reach the top?* (in 1909) Repeat the audio if necessary. Then have students open their books and read along as they listen to the audio.

# 11.1 Comparatives and Superlatives—An Overview, page 257

🕐 Time: 10–15 min.

1. Have students close their books. Make two lists side-by-side on the board:

   *Comparatives*

   1. *The new smartphone is <u>more expensive than</u> the older smartphone.*
   2. *China has <u>more people than</u> the United States.*

   *Superlatives*

   1. *This new smartphone is <u>the most expensive</u> cell phone in the whole store.*
   2. *China is <u>the most populated</u> country in the world.*

   Have students analyze the sentences. Ask: *How are comparatives and superlatives different?*

2. Have students look at grammar chart **11.1** and compare their ideas. Have volunteers read the examples aloud. Review the explanations.

## PRACTICE IDEA: READING

Have students go back to the reading on page 266 and underline five comparatives and five superlatives. Ask volunteers to name the adjectives in the phrases, and ask them to explain how they identified them as a comparative or superlative (e.g., *The highest mountain in the world—there are many mountains in the world, not just two, so it's a superlative.*).

🕐 Time: 5–10 min.

**Answers: 1.** largest, larger; **2.** biggest, bigger; **3.** most populated, more populated;
**4.** highest, higher; **5.** tallest, more famous; **6.** most populated, more; **7.** least populated, less populated;
**8.** largest, larger; **9.** most, least; **10.** oldest, newest

## PRACTICE IDEA: SPEAKING

Have students read the statements in Exercise 1 aloud in pairs and discuss whether or not they already knew that fact. Then have students discuss the one place they most want to visit in the United States and why. Write on the board: *What place in the United States do you like the most? Why?* Have volunteers share their answers with the class.

# 11.2 Comparatives and Superlatives—Adjective and Adverb Forms, page 258

🕐 Time: 10–15 min.

1. Have students close their books. Write the following adjectives on the board: *tall, fast; easy, deadly; frequent, active; important, difficult; tired, worried; quickly, brightly. Have students analyze the words in pairs. Ask: What is similar about each pair of adjectives?* If students have difficulty, give them a hint: *Look at the syllables and spelling.*

2. Then have students look at grammar chart **11.2** and compare their answers. Go over the examples and explanations for each kind of adjective.

3. Direct students' attention to the Language Note. Explain that some two-syllable adjectives have two forms.

4. Assign students one of the adjectives in the chart and have them write three sentences each using the different forms (e.g., *The building is tall. My apartment building is taller than this school. The Burj Kahlifa in Dubai is the tallest building in the world.*). Have students share their sentences in pairs.

**EXERCISE 2** page 259

🕐 Time: 5–10 min.

**Answers: 1.** C; **2.** C; **3.** S; **4.** C; **5.** C; **6.** C; **7.** S; **8.** S

# 11.3 Short Adjectives and Adverbs—Spelling of Comparatives and Superlatives, page 259

🕐 Time: 10–15 min.

1. Have students look back at grammar chart **11.2**. Have them analyze the forms in pairs. Ask: *What are the spelling rules to form comparatives and superlatives?*

2. Have students look at grammar chart **11.3** and compare their ideas. Review the rules and examples, providing more examples as necessary. Have students look back at grammar chart **11.2**. Remind them that some forms are irregular; they must be memorized.

3. Direct students' attention to the Language Note. Provide additional examples as necessary.

---

**PRACTICE IDEA: WRITING**

Have students get in pairs or small groups with classmates from the same country, if applicable. Have them write five sentences comparing important places, people, or dates in their country. Suggest they use Exercise 2 as a model. Then put students in pairs or small groups with classmates from a different country. If applicable, give students time to pull up photos of the places and people on their phones as they share their country. Have volunteers share their sentences with the class.

---

**EXERCISE 3** pages 259–260

🕐 Time: 10–15 min.

**Answers: 1.** more interesting / most interesting; **2.** younger / youngest; **3.** more beautiful / most beautiful; **4.** better / best; **5.** more quiet or quieter / most quiet or quietest; **6.** thinner / thinnest; **7.** more carefully / most carefully; **8.** prettier / prettiest; **9.** worse / worst; **10.** more famous / most famous; **11.** luckier / luckiest; **12.** simpler or more simple / simplest or most simple; **13.** higher / highest; **14.** more important delicious / most important; **15.** farther / farthest; **16.** more foolishly / most foolishly

**EXERCISE 4** page 260

🕐 Time: 10–15 min.

**Answers will vary.**

---

**PRACTICE IDEA: WRITING**

Have students choose three of the words from Exercise 3 and use them to write sentences with comparatives or superlatives about their personal preferences. Have students share their sentences in pairs.

---

# 11.4 Using Superlatives, page 260

🕐 Time: 10–15 min.

1. Have students look at grammar chart **11.4**. Have volunteers read examples aloud.

2. Have students underline the prepositional phrases in the examples and circle the preposition in the phrases. Further explain the form and function of a prepositional phrase as necessary.

3. Direct students' attention to the Language Note. Review possessive adjectives if necessary and provide additional examples.

4. Have students work in pairs to change the example statements into questions. Review the questions as a class.

## ADDITIONAL PRACTICE:

1. Do a class brainstorm of feeling adjectives (e.g., *happy, sad, relaxed, stressed, busy, annoyed, joyful*). Write them on the board. Then, write the following sentence starter on the board: *The _____ I've ever been in my life was when…* Have students share their life experiences in pairs using the superlative forms of the adjectives and this sentence starter. Have volunteers share their experiences with the class.

2. Have students collect and bring in store advertisements or coupon books. Have them make superlative statements about the products (e.g., *The most expensive cereal is Big Oats. This pair of running shoes is the most colorful.*).

**EXERCISE 5** page 261

🕐 Time: 5–10 min.

**Answers: 1.** the largest; **2.** The biggest; **3.** The longest; **4.** The highest; **5.** the most popular; **6.** the most expensive; **7.** the most beautiful; **8.** the best; **9.** the worst; **10.** the oldest; **11.** The most recent; **12.** the farthest

---

**PRACTICE IDEA: SPEAKING**

Have students discuss in pairs which statements from Exercise 5 they already knew and which facts are new for them.

---

**EXERCISE 6** pages 261–262

🕐 Time: 5–10 min.

**Answers will vary.**

---

**PRESENTATION IDEA**

Have students work in pairs to create a tourist brochure or poster for the community or city they currently live in. Have them include items 1, 2, 3, and 8 from Exercise 6. Give them time to research additional facts about the city. Remind them the brochure must use superlatives and be as attractive as possible. Have each pair present their brochures or posters to the class.

---

# 11.5 Word Order with Superlatives, page 262 ⭐

🕐 Time: 10–15 min.

1. Copy the sentences from the chart on the board. Have students look at grammar chart **11.5**. Have students read examples aloud.

2. As you review the explanations, label the parts of speech above the words and take notes on the board (e.g., circle the adjectives, draw an arrow to the noun it describes, underline different phrases).

**EXERCISE 7** page 262

🕐 Time: 5–10 min.

**Answers: 1.** the smallest state; **2.** The biggest lake; **3.** The largest population; **4.** the most diverse population; **5.** is increasing the fastest; **6.** the youngest minority group; **7.** the longest coastline; **8.** walk the most; **9.** The oldest trees; **10.** is growing the fastest

---

**PRACTICE IDEA: READING**

Have students go back to the reading on page 266. Have them underline all the superlative phrases in the reading and circle the nouns they describe. Have students compare notes in pairs.

---

**READING**

# An Unusual Trip, page 263

## PRE-READING

🕐 Time: 5–10 min.

1. Have students look at the photo and read the caption. Ask: *What do you see in the picture?* (mountains, roads, sky) *Where do you think this photo was taken?* (Arizona)

2. Have students read the title and then skim the reading. Ask: *What is the reading about? How do you know?* Have students make predictions.

3. Pre-teach any vocabulary words your students may not know, such as *to feel connected, boots,* and *to cross.*

4. Ask: *What is the longest trip you have taken? Did you enjoy it? Why or why not?* Have volunteers share their knowledge and personal experiences.

## READING GLOSSARY

**to feel connected:** to feel joined or linked together

**boots:** a shoe for the entire foot and the lower part of the leg

**to cross:** to go from one side to the other

## READING

🕐 Time: 10–15 min.

Go over the answers to the Comprehension Check on page 274: **1.** F; **2.** T; **3.** F.

## ADDITIONAL COMPREHENSION QUESTIONS

*How long did Nate Damm's trip take?* (over 7 months) *How many miles did he walk?* (more than 3,000 miles) *How many states did he cross?* (fourteen) *How fast was he traveling?* (3 miles per hour) *Where did Damm grow up?* (Maine) *Why did he choose to wear shoes instead of boots?* (They were more comfortable, lighter, and dried faster) *How many cross the United States on foot each year?* (about ten to twenty)

**PRACTICE IDEA: LISTENING**

Have students first listen to the audio alone. Ask a few comprehension questions, such as: *How did Nate Damm cross the United States?* (He walked) *When did he take this trip?* (in 2011) *Why did he choose to walk?* (He felt more connected to the people and the land) Repeat the audio if necessary. Then have students open their books and read along as they listen to the audio.

**PRACTICE IDEA: SPEAKING**

Put students in teams and quiz them on their knowledge of some U.S. regions. Display a map (without labels), and ask: *Do you know which states form New England?* (CT, RI, MA, VT, NH, and ME) *Which states are considered the Northeast?* (New England plus NY, NJ, and PA) *Which states are considered the South?* (FL, GE, SC, NC, MD, WV, VA, KY, TN, AK, LA, MS, AL, OK, and TX) *The Midwest and the Great Plains?* (OH, MI, IN, WI, IL, MN, IA, MO, ND, SD, NE, and KS) *The Rocky Mountain States?* (MT, ID, WY, NV, UT, CO, AZ, and NM) *The Southwest?* (CO, NM, UT, AZ, NV, and CA) *The Pacific States?* (CA, OR, and WA)

# 11.6 Using Comparatives,
page 264

🕐 Time: 10–15 min.

1. Have students look at grammar chart **11.6**. Have volunteers read examples aloud. Review the explanations. Review noncount and count nouns and auxiliary verbs if necessary. Provide additional examples of formal and informal use illustrated in the final row.

2. Have students work in pairs to change the example statements into questions. Review the questions as a class.

## ADDITIONAL PRACTICE

1. Do a class brainstorm of descriptive adjectives (e.g., *fast, comfortable, tall, big, hot, cold*). Write them on the board. Then, write the following sentence structure on the board: _____ *is/are* _____ *than* _____. Have students use the adjectives on the board to compare things relevant in their daily lives. Provide an example first (e.g., *My new house is bigger than my old apartment.*). Have volunteers share their experiences with the class.

2. Have students collect and bring in store advertisements or coupon books. Have them make comparative statements about the products and share in pairs (e.g., *This Nike pair of shoes is cheaper than the New Balances. I like the blue earbuds more than the red ones.*).

3. Have students bring in or pull up photos of their family on their phones. Have them make comparative statements about their family members and share these comparisons in pairs (e.g., *My sister is 4 years older. She has a job that makes a higher salary than my brother's job, but my brother likes his job more than my sister.*).

4. Do a class brainstorm of different jobs (e.g., engineer, businessperson, computer programmer, bartender, musician, salesperson, flight attendant). Write students' ideas on the board and add to the list as necessary. Have students compare the jobs in small groups, talking about which jobs are better and why (e.g. *I would rather be a mathematician. Salespeople have to talk more than mathematicians, and I am a shy person.*). Take a class survey to see how many people like the same jobs.

**EXERCISE 8** page 264
🕐 Time: 5–10 min.
**Answers: 1.** farther than; **2.** more difficult than; **3.** older than; **4.** thinner than; **5.** more connected than; **6.** easier than; **7.** better than; **8.** more slowly than; **9.** more dangerous than

**EXERCISE 9** page 265
🕐 Time: 5–10 min.
**Answers: 1.** larger than; **2.** bigger than; **3.** wealthier than; **4.** more expensive than; **5.** cheaper than / less expensive

than; **6.** cooler than; **7.** worse than; **8.** more pleasant than; **9.** older than

---

**PRACTICE IDEA: SPEAKING**

Have students close their books. Display photos of Chicago and San Francisco side by side. Have students recall information from Exercise 9 and make comparative statements about the two cities in pairs. Have volunteers share what they remember with the class.

---

**EXERCISE 10** page 266

🕐 Time: 10–15 min.

**Answers will vary.**

---

**PRACTICE IDEA: WRITING**

Have students write a paragraph comparing two cities in pairs. If possible, have students from the same country or region (South America, for example) compare towns and cities.

---

## 11.7 Word Order with Comparatives, page 266

🕐 Time: 10–15 min.

1.  Have students close their books. Make a matching exercise on the board:

    1.  *Houses in San Francisco are more expensive than houses in Chicago.*
    2.  *It rains less in San Francisco than in Chicago.*
    3.  *The Asian population is growing more quickly than the Latino population.*
    4.  *San Francisco has more sunshine than Chicago.*
    a.  *Put* more, less, better, *and* worse *after a verb.*
    b.  *Put comparative adjectives after the verb* be.
    c.  *Put* more, less, fewer, better, *and* worse *before a noun.*
    d.  *Put comparative adverbs after the verb.*

    Have volunteers match the examples with the explanations on the board.

2.  Have students look at grammar chart **11.7** and compare their answers. (**Answers: 1.** b; **2.** a; **3.** d; **4.** c) Review explanations.

---

**PRACTICE IDEA: READING**

Have students go back to the reading on page 273. Have them underline all the comparative phrases in the reading. Have students compare notes in pairs and point out the two things being compared.

---

**EXERCISE 11** page 267

🕐 Time: 5–10 min.

**Answers: 1.** more people; **2.** younger population; **3.** fewer people; **4.** travel longer / farther; **5.** more educated people; **6.** more children; **7.** more foreign-born people; **8.** increasing faster / more quickly

---

**EXERCISE 12** pages 267–268

🕐 Time: 5–10 min.

**Answers will vary.**

---

**EXERCISE 13** page 268

🕐 Time: 10–15 min.

**Answers: 1.** much bigger than; **2.** easier; **3.** less traffic; **4.** less time; **5.** more expensive; **6.** much farther; **7.** more exercise; **8.** better public transportation than; **9.** friendlier than; **10.** safer than; **11.** more activities; **12.** more money than; **13.** more quickly; **14.** less equipment; **15.** fewer workers; **16.** much more comfortable; **17.** much more relaxed; **18.** quieter / more quiet than

---

**EXERCISE 14** page 269

🕐 Time: 5–10 min.

**Answers: 1.** hotter than; **2.** the coldest month; **3.** warmer than; **4.** the biggest; **5.** is farthest; **6.** more crowded than; **7.** the most popular; **8.** the most beautiful; **9.** The tallest; **10.** The most expensive

---

**EXERCISE 15** page 269

🕐 Time: 5–10 min.

**Answers will vary.**

---

**PRACTICE IDEA: SPEAKING**

Do a class survey about life in the United States. Do students in the class have similar or different experiences about living in the United States? Have students share their experiences. Write their results on the board.

---

⏱ Time: 20–30 min.

## PART A  ADJECTIVES

Have students close their books. Say: *Write three sentences with* big *and three sentences with* populated. *Write a sentence with* big *as a simple adjective, as a comparative, and as a superlative. Do the same with* populated. Then have students compare their sentences with those in the summary. If necessary, have students review:

**11.2** Comparatives and Superlatives––Adjective and Adverb Forms (page 268)

**11.3** Short Adjectives and Adverbs––Spelling of Comparatives and Superlatives (page 269)

## PART B  ADVERBS

Have students close their books. Say: *Write three sentences with* fast *and three sentences with* rapid. *Write a sentence with* fast *as a simple adverb, as a comparative, and as a superlative. Do the same with* rapid. Then have students compare their sentences with those in the summary. If necessary, have students review:

**11.2** Comparatives and Superlatives––Adjective and Adverb Forms (page 268)

**11.3** Short Adjectives and Adverbs––Spelling of Comparatives and Superlatives (page 269)

## PART C  COMPARISONS WITH *LESS* AND *FEWER*

Display images of Los Angeles and Seattle. Have students discuss in pairs what they know about the two cities. Write students' ideas on the board. If necessary, give students time to conduct online research. Then, have students use *less* and *fewer* and write at least five sentences comparing the two cities. Have students share in pairs then compare their sentences with those in the summary. If necessary, have students review:

**11.6** Using Comparatives (page 264)

**11.7** Word Order with Comparatives (page 266)

## PART D  WORD ORDER

Have students close their books. Scramble the example sentences in the Word Order chart, and write them on the board. Have students unscramble the sentences and compare their answers with the summary. If necessary, have students review:

**11.5** Word Order with Superlatives (page 262)

**11.7** Word Order with Comparatives (page 266)

⏱ Time: 15 min.

Have students do the exercise on page 281. For additional practice, use the Assessment CD-ROM with Exam*View*® and the Online Workbook.

**Answers: 1.** the most beautiful cities; **2.** bigger than; **3.** the tallest buildings; **4.** much farther; **5.** better weather than; **6.** the worst month; **7.** much bigger than; **8.** the largest lakes; **9.** much sunnier; **10.** best architects; **11.** much more expensive than; **12.** safer; **13.** more crime than; **14.** the most interesting cities

## WRITING

## PART 1  EDITING ADVICE

⏱ Time: 10–15 min.

1. Have students close their books. Write the first few sentences without editing marks or corrections on the board. For example:

   *The weather in May is more better than the weather in January.*

   *Mount Everest is higher that Denali.*

2. Ask students to correct each sentence and provide a rule or an explanation for each correction. This activity can be done individually, in pairs, or as a class.

3. After students have corrected each sentence, tell them to turn to page 282. Say: *Now compare your work with the Editing Advice in the book.* Have students read through all the advice.

## PART 2  EDITING PRACTICE

⏱ Time: 10–15 min.

1. Tell students they are going to put the Editing Advice into practice. Ask: *Do all the shaded words and phrases have mistakes?* (no) Go over the examples with the class. Then do #1 together.

2. Have students complete the practice individually. Then have them compare answers with a partner before checking answers as a class.

3. For the items students had difficulties with, have them go back and find the relevant grammar chart and review it. Monitor and give help as necessary.

**Answers: 1.** C; **2.** bigger; **3.** one of the biggest cities; **4.** the largest; **5.** C; **6.** prettier; **7.** than; **8.** more interesting than; **9.** more pollution than; **10.** My oldest; **11.** C; **12.** the most crowded subway; **13.** C

## PART 3 WRITE ABOUT IT

⏱ Time: 30–40 min.

1. Review the topic with students. With the class, brainstorm different cities in the world and have students suggest ideas for comparing. Write them on the board. Begin a paragraph on the board following the model in the book. Then have students write their own comparisons individually. Remind them to include any useful and relevant vocabulary from this lesson on American experiences and to double-check their use of comparatives and superlatives. Have them exchange their comparisons for peer feedback.

2. Do a class brainstorm of important things to consider when choosing where to live. Write class ideas on the board. Have students tell a partner about the most important things for them. Encourage students to organize their ideas before writing. Then have them write their paragraphs individually. Collect for assessment and/or have students present their paragraphs to a group.

## PART 4 EDIT YOUR WRITING

⏱ Time: 15–20 min.

Have students edit their writing by reviewing the Lesson Summary on page 280 and the Editing Advice on page 282. Collect for assessment and/or have students share their essays in small groups.

## EXPANSION ACTIVITIES

1. Do a class brainstorm of basic questions the students can ask each other (e.g., *How old are you? How tall are you? Where do you live? Where have you traveled?*). Write these questions on the board. Have students mingle and ask each other these questions. As they do, they should record the information on a sheet of paper. Then, have students make comparative statements about their classmates (e.g., *Marta is older than Harry. Ahmed lives further away from school than Vincent does.*).

2. Have students work in pairs to compare and contrast the lives of women and men in different countries. If possible, have students partner with a classmate from a different country or culture. Have students write at least five sentences (e.g., *Women in the United States have less time off work when they have a baby. Men in Turkey hug and kiss more than men in the United States.*).

3. Write on the board: *problems in the United States* and *living in big cities/small towns*. Elicit ideas for these two topics and write them on the board. Then have students discuss each question in groups. Then have them report back to the class.

4. Have students interview somebody who has been living in the United States for their whole lives. Remind students they will share their results with the class. Have students create questions and follow-up questions around relevant topics, such as:

   a. good cars (e.g., *Which cars are better than others? Why?*)
   b. beautiful actors and actresses
   c. good presidents in the last 25 years
   d. beautiful U.S. cities
   e. popular singers in the United States
   f. the best U.S. university (e.g., *What do you think is the best university in the United States? Why?*)
   g. the best movie of all time
   h. the worst tragedy in American history
   i. the biggest problem in the United States today
   j. the best athletes in the United States

   Have students take notes as they interview, compile their results, and make a short presentation to the class. As a follow-up activity, have students present on these same topics using their own countries.

5. Have students use the Internet to find a site that compares cities. Tell them to compare any two cities in the world that interest them. Ask them to print out the information and photos they find on the Internet and to bring it to class to present.

6. Have students use the Internet to find out about the city where you grew up. Have them find out:

   a. the name of the mayor
   b. the population
   c. the annual rainfall
   d. the coldest month
   e. interesting places to visit

   Have them prepare a brochure for your hometown with the information they find online. As a follow-up activity, have students do the same for their hometown.

# 12 PEOPLE ON THE MOVE

## GRAMMAR CHARTS

**12.1** Verb Review (pages 277–278)

**12.2** Statements, Questions, and Short Answers (pages 281–282)

**12.3** Auxiliary Verbs with *Too* and *Either* (page 288)

**12.4** Auxiliary Verbs in Tag Questions (page 290)

## LESSON OPENER

Have students look at the photo and read the caption. Ask: *What is the man in the photo doing?* (leading camels) *Where is he?* (in the desert) Have students read the quotation. Ask: *Are you comfortable taking risks and doing new things? What helps people move forward in their lives?*

**Background:** Americans are known for being on the move, both domestically and internationally. Since the early twentieth century, automobiles and road travel have allowed Americans to explore and expand their nation, expanding the country to the west and south as Americans settled the land. During the mid-1900s, air travel further contributed to exploration within the vast United States, not only for Americans but also for international visitors. Today, travel and tourism is one of the top industries contributing to American revenue. Americans travel abroad, as well, for both tourism and business. There are more opportunities overseas for businesspeople, journalists, and teachers than ever before. Finally, there are somewhere between 3 and 6 million American who relocate, either temporarily or permanently, to foreign countries. Immigration into the United States is another mobility phenomenon that not only lends to population growth but also continues to shape cultural change in the United States. When strict bans were lifted in the 1960s, immigration quadrupled; there were about 38 million first-generation immigrants living in the United States in 2007. International visitors also come for tourism and to study at world-renowned American universities. The United States enrolled 819,644 international students for the 2012–2013 academic year in colleges and universities throughout the country.

Walt Disney was an American animator, film producer, and entrepreneur. He is regarded as an American cultural icon for his work in the animation industry during the twentieth century. He founded the Walt Disney Company and created characters, such as Mickey Mouse, Donald Duck, and Goofy, which are famous worldwide. He died in 1966 from lung cancer.

## CONTEXT

This unit is about People on the Move. Students will read about the pilot Barrington Irving, the journalist Paul Salopek, and the international student Chimene Ntakarutimana.

1. Give students a few minutes to look through the lesson. Have them look at the photos and titles. Ask: *How do they relate to the context?*

2. Elicit the topics that will be discussed.

3. Have students discuss what they know about people and mobility in pairs or small groups.

## GRAMMAR

Students will review verbs and learn more about auxiliary verbs with *too* and *either* and in tag questions.

1. To activate students' prior knowledge, ask what students know about auxiliary verbs and tag questions.

2. Give several examples of the auxiliary verbs and tag questions (e.g., auxiliary verbs: *do, does, did*; tag questions: *did he?*).

3. Have volunteers give examples and write them on the board.

### EXPANDING ON THE CONTEXT

The context for this lesson can be enhanced with the following items:

1. Biographies of famous explorers
2. Maps of human migration patterns

# Barrington Irving: Flying to Inspire, page 276

## PRE-READING

🕐 Time: 5–10 min.

1. Have students look at the photo and read the caption. Ask: *Who is this man?* (Barrington Irving) *What is his job?* (pilot)

2. Have students read the title and then skim the reading. Ask: *What is the reading about? How do you know?* Have students make predictions.

3. Pre-teach any vocabulary words your students may not know, such as *poor, smart, dream, generation,* and *confidence.*

4. Ask: *Have you ever dreamed of being a pilot? What is your dream job?* Have volunteers share their knowledge and personal experiences.

## READING GLOSSARY

**poor:** having little money or few possessions

**smart:** very good at learning or thinking about things

**dream:** something you've wanted to do, be, or have for a long time

**generation:** a group of people born and living during the same time

**confidence:** the feeling that you can succeed at something

## READING  

🕐 Time: 10–15 min.

Go over the answers to the Comprehension Check on page 287: **1.** T; **2.** T; **3.** T.

## ADDITIONAL COMPREHENSION QUESTIONS

*Where is Barrington Irving from?* (Miami, Florida) *What was his first job when he was 15?* (working in his parents' bookstore) *How did he earn money for flight school?* (washing airplanes) *What did he study in college?* (aeronautical science) *At what age did he become the youngest person to fly around the world?* (23 years old) *How many days did it take him to fly around the world?* (97 days) *Why did Barrington Irving start Experience Aviation in 2005?* (to inspire students to learn about STEM fields)

## EXPANDING ON THE READING

The topic for this reading can be enhanced with the following items:

1. Photos of Barrington Irving and his planes

2. Clips of Barrington Irving's interview with *National Geographic Live!*

3. Experience Aviation YouTube channel

4. Short video of the super car from Build and Soar 2013

5. Interactive flight tracker map from The Flying Classroom

## PRACTICE IDEA: LISTENING

Have students first listen to the audio alone. Have students listen for verbs and write as many verbs as they can. Repeat the audio if necessary. Have students work in pairs to determine the verb tense and form of the verbs they wrote. Then have students open their books and read along as they listen to the audio.

## 12.1 Verb Review, pages 277–278

🕐 Time: 20–25 min.

1. Have students close their books. Ask: *What different verb tenses have we learned?* Write students' ideas on the board and add missing tenses as necessary. (should have *simple present tense, present continuous tense, future tense, simple past tense,* be *modals, infinitives*)

2. *Have students work in pairs and go back to the reading on page 276 and find two examples for each verb tense in the reading.* Have volunteers share their findings with the class.

3. Have students open their books to grammar chart **12.1**. Divide the class into six pairs or small groups. Assign each pair or small group one of the verb tenses in the chart. Give them 5 minutes to review the information in their specific chart. Then have each group present their verb tense to the class, reading the examples aloud and reviewing the explanations. Remind students they are responsible for knowing the answer if a question comes up.

🕐 Time: 5–10 min.

**Answers: 1.** wanted, past; **2.** believed, past; **3.** likes, present; **4.** to inspire, infinitive; **5.** going to grow, future; **6.** are learning, present continuous; **7.** built, past; **8.** will continue, future; **9.** are building, present continuous; **10.** should, modal; **11.** to learn, infinitive

---

### PRESENTATION IDEA

Have students choose their favorite reading from past lessons. Based on this information, have them write six statements about the reading. Each of these sentences must use a different verb tense. Have volunteers read their sentences aloud to the class. As they read, have the rest of the class write the verb tense used in each sentence.

---

**EXERCISE 2** page 279

🕐 Time: 10–15 min.

**Answers: 1.** to graduate; **2.** go; **3.** told; **4.** should; **5.** had to; **6.** received; **7.** moving; **8.** am taking; **9.** I'm gaining; **10.** know; **11.** go; **12.** I'll have; **13.** I have; **14.** graduated; **15.** She's planning; **16.** become; **17.** she finished; **18.** It'll be / It's going to be; **19.** to find; **20.** there; **21.** like; **22.** have; **23.** went; **24.** go; **25.** have; **26.** Theirs is; **27.** wear; **28.** to look; **29.** think; **30.** do

---

### PRACTICE IDEA: READING

Have students compare answers in Exercise 2 as they take turns reading the paragraphs aloud. If any of the answers are different, have each student justify their answer choice.

---

### PRACTICE IDEA: WRITING

Have students write two paragraphs about their experience as a student. Have them include what it was like when they arrived, how it is now, and what their plans are when they finish. Have students read their paragraphs aloud in pairs and share their experiences.

---

**READING**

# One Man, 7 Years, 21,000 Miles, page 280

## PRE-READING

🕐 Time: 5–10 min.

1. Have students look at the photo and read the caption. Ask: *Who is this man?* (Paul Salopek) *Where does his trip on the map start and end?* (It started in Ethiopia and ended in Tierra del Fuego)

2. Have students read the title and then skim the reading. Ask: *What is the reading about? How do you know?* Have students make predictions.

3. Pre-teach any vocabulary words your students may not know, such as *journalist, ancestor, to record, to interview,* and *dangerous.*

4. Ask: *How many times have you moved to another city or country? What's the best journey or trip you've ever been on? Why?* Have volunteers share their knowledge and personal experiences.

## READING GLOSSARY

**journalist:** the job of writing and editing news stories for media

**ancestor:** a person who was in someone's family in past times

**to record:** to store or save something so that it can be heard or seen later

**to interview:** to talk with someone in order to learn about that person

**dangerous:** involving possible injury, harm, or death

## READING

🕐 Time: 10–15 min.

Go over the answers to the Comprehension Check on page 291: **1.** T; **2.** T; **3.** F.

## ADDITIONAL COMPREHENSION QUESTIONS

*For how many years will Paul be walking?* (7 years) *About how many footsteps will it take for Paul to reach his destination?* (30 million) *How many miles will he walk?* (21,000 miles) *How often does he record his journey?* (about every 100 miles)

## EXPANDING ON THE READING

The topic for this reading can be enhanced with the following items:

1. Out of Eden Instagram photos and videos
2. Facts, data, and photos from the Milestones on the Out of Eden Walk Web site
3. Map of the Out of Eden Walk
4. Excerpts from Paul's Google Hangout discussing his trip, early 2014

---

### PRACTICE IDEA: LISTENING

Have students first listen to the audio alone. Ask a few comprehension questions, such as: *Why is Paul Salopek walking across the world?* (to understand human migration) *How many people are moving across the planet today?* (nearly a billion people) *How does he record his journey?* (he interviews local people, shares his journey in real time) Repeat the audio if necessary. Then have students open their books and read along as they listen to the audio.

---

### PRESENTATION IDEA

Have students work in pairs to make a short time line of important dates from the Out of Eden walk. They should reference the Out of Eden Web site and Milestones to pick events to include. Encourage them to write complete sentences in the simple past tense when describing the events. Hang time lines on the wall and have volunteers present their work.

## 12.2 Statements, Questions, and Short Answers,
pages 281–282

 Time: 20–25 min.

1. Have students look at grammar chart **12.2**. Give them 10 minutes to read the examples aloud in pairs.
2. Have students share in pairs one thing they are good at (e.g., *dancing, cooking, English, parenting, playing video games*). Then have students choose one verb tense and write seven sentences about this topic following the models in the chart (e.g., simple present:

1. *I cook dinner every night.* 2. *My wife doesn't cook dinner for the family. I do.* 3. *Do you cook dinner every night?* 4. *Yes, I do.* 5. *What do you cook for dinner?* 6. *What ingredients don't you like to use when you cook?* 7. *Who cooks dinner for your family?*). Have students share their sentences in pairs.

### EXERCISE 3  pages 282–283

Time: 5–10 min.

(Note: spelled-out forms [*did not, will not,* etc.] are also acceptable.)

**Answers: 1.** isn't; **2.** didn't start; **3.** won't finish; **4.** isn't walking; **5.** isn't going to walk; **6.** didn't ride; **7.** doesn't send; **8.** isn't; **9.** shouldn't

---

### PRACTICE IDEA: WRITING

Have students choose one important person in their lives to write about. Have them write three affirmative and negatives statements (six sentences total) about this person using Exercise 3 as a model. Have students share their sentences in pairs.

---

### EXERCISE 4  pages 283–284

Time: 5–10 min.

**Answers:**

1. Is Irving brave? Yes, he is.
2. Does Irving like to teach children? Yes, he does.
3. Is Irving walking around the world? No, he isn't.
4. Did Irving begin his journey in Africa? No, he didn't.
5. Did Salopek fly solo around the world? No, he didn't.
6. Is Irving sharing his knowledge with schoolchildren? Yes, he is.
7. Does Salopek know a lot about the world? Yes, he does.
8. Can Salopek teach children about the world? Yes, he can.
9. Will Irving finish his project at the end of 7 years? No, he won't.

### EXERCISE 5  page 284

Time: 5–10 min.

**Answers:**

1. What kind of learning experiences do kids need?
2. What kind of project are they working on?

3. Why did Irving / he wash airplanes when he was young?

4. Who created the organization Experience Aviation?

5. How can teachers inspire students?

6. Why didn't Irving / he believe in himself at first?

7. Why is Salopek / he going to walk to Tierra del Fuego?

8. How many years is Salopek's / his trip going to take?

9. When will Salopek / he finish his walk?

---

**PRACTICE IDEA: WRITING AND SPEAKING**

Have students get in pairs with somebody from a different country. Have them write five to ten *Yes/No* and *Wh-* questions they have about their partner's home country (e.g., *Is it cold in the winter? How many people live there? What kinds of food are common to eat for breakfast?*). Then, have students interview each other in pairs. Encourage them to ask follow-up questions.

---

## EXERCISE 6 page 285

⏱ Time: 10–15 min.

**Answers: 1.** 'm; **2.** hear; **3.** never call; **4.** don't have; **5.** don't you have; **6.** went; **7.** drove; **8.** used; **9.** Are you getting; **10.** cooks; **11.** 'm learning; **12.** Are you; **13.** cooked; **14.** cook; **15.** invite; **16.** is / 's; **17.** tell; **18.** comes; **19.** remember; **20.** is / 's your job; **21.** Do you like; **22.** 'm learning; **23.** Do you have; **24.** spent; **25.** needed to buy; **26.** Can you come; **27.** will / 'll; **28.** pay; **29.** have; **30.** Will you call; **31.** have; **32.** 'll call

---

**PRACTICE IDEA: SPEAKING**

Have students read the conversation from Exercise 6 aloud in pairs. Have volunteers role-play the conversation in front of the class.

---

## EXERCISE 7 page 286

⏱ Time: 10–15 min.

**Answers will vary.**

---

**PRACTICE IDEA: SPEAKING**

Have volunteers share their opinions about school, jobs, and family from Exercise 7 with the class. Take a class survey to learn which students share similar experiences and opinions.

---

## EXERCISE 8 page 286

⏱ Time: 5–10 min.

**Answers will vary.**

---

# Chimene Ntakarutimana: From Africa to America, page 287

## PRE-READING

⏱ Time: 5–10 min.

1. Have students look at the photo. Ask: *Who is the young woman in the photo?* (Chimene Ntakarutimana) *What does she do?* (She's a student) *Where is she?* (a library or bookstore)

2. Have students read the title and then skim the reading. Ask: *What is the reading about? How do you know?* Have students make predictions.

3. Pre-teach any vocabulary words your students may not know, such as *danger, vacation, agency,* and *optimist.*

4. Ask: *Have you ever immigrated to another country? Why? What was the experience like? Who were some people who helped you when you moved?* Have volunteers share their knowledge and personal experiences.

## READING GLOSSARY

**danger:** the possibility you will be hurt or killed

**vacation:** period of time a person spends away from home

**agency:** a business that provides a particular service

**optimist:** a person who expects good things to happen

## READING 🎧 CD 2 TR 23

⏱ Time: 10–15 min.

Go over the answers to the Comprehension Check on page 298: **1.** F; **2.** F; **3.** T.

## ADDITIONAL COMPREHENSION QUESTIONS

*How many children were in Chimene's family?* (four) *How did Chimene and her siblings feel while living in Africa?* (in fear, in danger) *Where was the first place they lived in America?* (in a small apartment in Chicago) *Who helped her family when they first arrived?* (refugee agency, an American woman) *What is Chimene's favorite subject in school?* (history)

## PRACTICE IDEA: LISTENING

Have students first listen to the audio alone. Ask a few comprehension questions, such as: *Where was Chimene Ntakarutimana born*? (Burundi) *Why did her family leave Africa?* (They were in great danger) *What is Chimene preparing for now?* (college applications) Repeat the audio if necessary. Then have students open their books and read along as they listen to the audio.

## PRESENTATION IDEA

Display a diagram of the refugee resettlement process. Have students describe the process while looking at the diagram in pairs. Answer any questions about vocabulary as needed. Then, have students switch pairs and talk through the resettlement process without looking at the diagram. Encourage students to use the simple present tense (e.g., *When they arrive in the United States, they get permanent status after 1 year. After 5 years, they become a citizen.*).

# 12.3 Auxiliary Verbs with *Too* and *Either*, page 288

🕐 Time: 10–15 min.

1. Write on the board: *be, do, does, did, modals (can, could, will,* etc.). Say: *These verbs are all auxiliary verbs.* Ask: *What does an auxiliary verb do?* (help the main verb) Elicit examples of sentences with auxiliary verbs. Write students' ideas on the board.

2. Have students go back to the reading on page 297 and circle the words *too* and *either*. Have students analyze the sentences from the reading using *too* and *either*. Ask: What is the word order when we use *too* or *either* with auxiliary verbs? Write students' ideas on the board.

3. Have students look at grammar chart **12.3**. Explain that auxiliary verbs with *too* and *either* are used to show similarity and avoid repetition. Have volunteers read examples aloud. Review the explanations. Point out that opposite statements are often connected with the word *but*. Provide additional examples (e.g., *I got 100 percent on the test, but my friend didn't. Next time I will study with him more.*).

## PRESENTATION IDEA

If possible, bring in or show the read-aloud video of the Little Critter children's audio book *Me Too!* Have students work in small groups to create a short children's book using *Me Too!* as a model. Have each group present their children's book, reading it aloud to the class.

**EXERCISE 9** page 288

🕐 Time: 5–10 min.

**Answers: 1.** was too; **2.** does too; **3.** did too; **4.** can too; **5.** are too; **6.** were too

**EXERCISE 10** page 289

🕐 Time: 5–10 min.

**Answers: 1.** can't either; **2.** isn't either; **3.** weren't either; **4.** didn't either; **5.** doesn't either; **6.** don't either

**EXERCISE 11** page 289

🕐 Time: 5–10 min.

**Answers: 1.** don't; **2.** does; **3.** isn't; **4.** doesn't; **5.** isn't; **6.** weren't

## PRACTICE IDEA: SPEAKING AND WRITING

Do a class brainstorm of basic questions the students can ask each other (e.g., *How old are you? What languages do you speak? Where do you live? Where have you traveled?*). Write these questions on the board. Have students mingle and ask each other these questions. As they do, they should record the information on a sheet of paper. Then, have students make comparative statements about their classmates using auxiliary verbs and *too* and *either* (e.g., *Marta is 19 years old, and Harry is too. Ahmed speaks Arabic and French, but Vincent doesn't. Vincent speaks Spanish.*).

### EXERCISE 12 pages 289–290

🕐 Time: 5–10 min.

**Answers: 1.** 'm not; **2.** does; **3.** doesn't; **4.** does too; **5.** do too; **6.** either; **7.** does; **8.** either

---

### PRACTICE IDEA: SPEAKING

Have students read the conversation from Exercise 12 aloud in pairs. Have volunteers role-play the conversation in front of the class.

---

## 12.4 Auxiliary Verbs in Tag Questions, page 290

🕐 Time: 10–15 min.

1. Have students take out a blank sheet of paper. Do a short dictation. Read the following questions aloud. As you do, have students write the sentences exactly as you say them.

   1. *It's hot outside, isn't it?*
   2. *You weren't born in the United States, were you?*
   3. *I'm speaking English well, aren't I?*

   Have volunteers write the sentences from the dictation on the board. Correct any spelling mistakes. Then, have students ask and answer the questions in pairs.

2. Circle the tag questions in the sentences on the board. Have students analyze the sentences in pairs. Ask: *What is the purpose of these short questions at the end of the sentence? What are they called?* Have volunteers share their ideas.

3. Have students look at grammar chart **12.4** and compare their ideas. Have volunteers read the examples aloud. Carefully review the explanations. Provide a short review of subject pronouns if necessary.

4. Direct students' attention to the Language Notes. Provide additional examples of formal versus informal use of tag questions with auxiliary verbs.

### EXERCISE 13 page 291

🕐 Time: 5–10 min.

**Answers: 1.** do you; **2.** weren't we; **3.** didn't we; **4.** didn't she; **5.** isn't it; **6.** didn't you; **7.** is she; **8.** didn't she; **9.** didn't you

---

### PRACTICE IDEA: SPEAKING AND WRITING

Have students read the conversation from Exercise 13 aloud in pairs. Then have students write their own conversation between two people at a party. Have volunteers role-play their conversations in front of the class.

---

## SUMMARY OF LESSON 12

🕐 Time: 20–30 min.

### PART A VERB REVIEW

Copy the chart from the summary on the board, but leave blanks for students to fill in the correct verb. Have students work in pairs. Then, have them compare their answers with the summary. Review the explanations and address any questions. If necessary, have students review:

**12.1** Verb Review (pages 277–278)

**12.2** Statements, Questions, and Short Answers (pages 281–282)

### PART B AUXILIARY VERBS

Have students close their books. On the board, create an exercise from the Summary chart. Have students fill in the blanks.

   *Affirmative* + too
   1. *Irving likes adventures. Salopek* _____.
   *Negative* + either
   2. *I wasn't born here. You* _____.
   *Avoid repetition.*
   3. *Chimene can't remember her native language, but her older sister* _____.

Review as a class. Then, write the following exercises on the board.

As a class, complete the following Negative and Affirmative Tags. Have students compare their answers with the summary.

1. *Irving helps kids, _____?*
2. *Salopek won't stop in France, _____?*

Then, have them complete the following and ask: *Which kind of tag is it? Complete the sentences.*

1. *There are a lot of things to do, _____?*
2. *You don't like fishing, _____?*
3. *We never have time together, _____?*

Have students compare their answers in pairs. If necessary, have students review:

**12.3** Auxiliary Verbs with *Too* and *Either* (page 288)

**12.4** Auxiliary Verbs in Tag Questions (page 290)

## TEST/REVIEW

⏱ Time: 15 min.

Have students do the exercise on page 303. For additional practice, use the Assessment CD-ROM with Exam*View®* and the Online Workbook.

**Answers:**

**Part 1**

**1.** was born; **2. a.** was, **b.** met; **3.** became; **4.** loves; **5.** flew; **6. a.** wants, **b.** to inspire; **7.** are working; **8.** are gaining; **9.** to fly; **10. a.** he flies, **b.** he'll share

**Part 2**

**1.** wasn't; **2.** isn't; **3.** didn't speak; **4.** didn't have; **5.** doesn't live; **6.** can't imagine; **7.** isn't preparing; **8.** doesn't know; **9.** doesn't have to; **10.** won't start

**Part 3**

**1. B:** is he; **2. B:** Will he / Salopek travel, **A:** won't; **3. B:** did he work; **4. B:** is he writing; **5. B:** Is he going to walk, **A:** isn't; **6. B:** won't he walk; **7. A:** will be, **B:** will he be; **8. B:** did it / human migration start?; **9. B:** Is he sharing, **A:** is; **10. B:** can he learn

**Part 4**

(Note: commas before *too/either* are acceptable.)

**1.** does too; **2.** is too; **3.** will too; **4.** isn't; **5.** weren't; **6.** didn't either; **7.** doesn't either; **8.** does; **9.** doesn't; **10.** should too

**Part 5**

**1.** isn't he; **2.** didn't he; **3.** is he; **4.** will he; **5.** isn't there; **6.** doesn't he; **7.** didn't they; **8.** did they; **9.** wasn't it; **10.** shouldn't we

## WRITING

### PART 1  EDITING ADVICE

⏱ Time: 10–15 min.

1. Have students close their books. Write the first few sentences without editing marks or corrections on the board. For example:

   *Where does Chimene goes to school?*
   *Children are need confidence.*

2. Ask students to correct each sentence and provide a rule or an explanation for each correction. This activity can be done individually, in pairs, or as a class.

3. After students have corrected each sentence, tell them to turn to pages 296–297. Say: *Now compare your work with the Editing Advice in the book.* Have students read through all the advice.

### PART 2  EDITING PRACTICE

⏱ Time: 10–15 min.

1. Tell students they are going to put the Editing Advice into practice. Ask: *Do all the shaded words and phrases have mistakes?* (no) Go over the examples with the class. Then do #1 together.

2. Have students complete the practice individually. Then have them compare answers with a partner before checking answers as a class.

3. For the items students had difficulties with, have them go back and find the relevant grammar chart and review it. Monitor and give help as necessary.

**Answers: 1.** C; **2.** live; **3.** don't live; **4.** don't you live; **5.** C; **6.** found; **7.** moved; **8.** did you move; **9.** C; **10.** C; **11.** didn't realize; **12.** I'm lonely / I am lonely; **13.** calls; **14.** C; **15.** I know; **16.** C; **17.** C; **18.** to be; **19.** does your family live; **20.** C; **21.** want to visit; **22.** save; **23.** C; **24.** have; **25.** I'll have; **26.** will they stay; **27.** can stay; **28.** C; **29.** C; **30.** C; **31.** to talk; **32.** C; **33.** does a phone card cost; **34.** costs

### PART 3  WRITE ABOUT IT

⏱ Time: 30–40 min.

1. Review the topic with students. Give students a personal example of when your life was on the move and how it affected your life trajectory. Write specific before and after example sentences on the board. Have students discuss their own experiences in pairs. Encourage them to organize their ideas before writing, then have students write their own

paragraph. Remind them to include any useful and relevant vocabulary from this lesson on migration and mobility. Address any verb questions as students write. Have them exchange the paragraphs for peer feedback.

2. Have students think of the most unusual person they have ever met. Have them describe this person to a partner. If students can't think of anyone, allow them time to research online for more ideas. Then have them write their paragraphs individually. Collect for assessment and/or have students present their paragraphs to a group.

## PART 4 EDIT YOUR WRITING

Time: 15–20 min.

Have students edit their writing by reviewing the Lesson Summary on page 292 and the Editing Advice on pages 296–297. Collect for assessment and/or have students share their essays in small groups.

## EXPANSION ACTIVITIES

1. Have students work with a partner to write six to ten statements with tag questions on what they think they know about the United States and Americans. Have them respond to the questions in front of the class.

2. Have students meet three new people and interview them about somewhere they moved and how it changed their lives. Have them come up with questions during class with a small group. Remind them they will report their results to the class.

3. Ask students to get in touch with a family member and ask them about a time when they moved. Students can conduct the interview in any language, but they must share the stories with the class in English.

4. Have students interview each other about the steps taken after arrival in the United States (or current country of study). Students should first make a time line of the events, including details about who helped them and where each event took place. Then, have students create a brochure to help newcomers to the United States (or current country of study) based on their steps.

5. If applicable, set up a visit to a local immigrant or refugee organization. Have students prepare questions about immigration and refugee resettlement before going. Be sure each student asks at least one question while at the site.